Spanish Vocabulary

by

Julianne Dueber

University of Missouri-St. Louis

BARRON'S

New York • London • Toronto • Sydney

To my father, Clarence E. Dueber

© Copyright 1990 by Barron's Educational Series, Inc.

All inquiries should be addressed to:
Barron's Educational Series, Inc.
250 Wireless Boulevard
Hauppauge, NY 11788

International Standard Book No. 0-8120-4498-3

Library of Congress Catalog Card No. 90-40644

Library of Congress Cataloging-in-Publication Data

Dueber, Julianne.
    Spanish vocabulary / by Julianne Dueber.
        p. cm.
    Includes index.
    ISBN 0-8120-4498-3
    1. Spanish language—Glossaries, vocabularies, etc. I. Title.
PC4680.D8   1990
468.1—dc20   90-40644
                                                                        CIP

PRINTED IN THE UNITED STATES OF AMERICA
    1 2 3 5 5 0 0 9 8 7 6 5 4 3 2

CONTENTS

HOW TO USE THIS BOOK

THIS IS NOT JUST ANOTHER DICTIONARY!

This book will help you to study vocabulary systematically on those topics of special interest to you. It is a programmed study guide to almost 6,000 Spanish words you will need to talk about any subject, and in situations such as buying supplies at the hardware store, discussing environmental problems, and reporting an emergency.

OVERALL DESIGN

Spanish Vocabulary consists of a pronunciation guide, nine chapters, an appendix, and an English-Spanish vocabulary list.

Each chapter is divided into main themes. For example, the chapter entitled People is divided into: (a) family and friends, (b) describing people, and (c) the body. The vocabulary presented in this chapter deals with such diverse topics as family relationships, physical appearance, marital status, religion, personality traits, parts of the body, etc.

USING THIS BOOK FOR DIFFERENT LEARNING GOALS

If you are attempting to learn Spanish by yourself, you will find that *Spanish Vocabulary* provides you with an easy system for acquiring the most important basic vocabulary for dealing with a wide variety of topics. If you already have some knowledge of Spanish, you will easily expand your vocabulary and quickly increase your speaking ability. If you are currently a Spanish student, you will find this guide useful in preparing oral and written reports on specific topics.

FEATURES

Each chapter lists the English word first, followed by its Spanish equivalent or equivalents, and its phonetic pronunciation. Please note that *Spanish Vocabulary* stresses the Latin American pronunciation. If you are visiting or living in Spain, remember to make allowances for the pronunciation of words with *ce, ci,* and *z.*

The English words are arranged in alphabetical order, unless the nature of the theme requires some other logical system of organization (e.g., numbers). Related items, concepts, or specific uses are indented.

GENDER AND PLURALIZATION OF NOUNS

A regular masculine noun in Spanish ends in *-o.* A regular feminine noun in Spanish ends in *-a.* Any noun that does not fall into these categories is marked as masculine (*m*) or feminine (*f*). (See Abbreviations section for all other grammar symbols that are used throughout this book.) Most professions are given in the masculine form only. For the feminine, replace the **o** ending with an **a**. The designation (*m/f*) indicates that the form given is both masculine and feminine.

Nouns ending in a vowel usually add -*s* to form the plural; those ending in a consonant add -*es*. Nouns that do not follow these rules are noted as they occur in the text.

OTHER PARTS OF SPEECH

Other parts of speech are identified as they arise. Spanish has three verb conjugations, each according to the verb endings: *ar, -er,* and *-ir*. Spanish verbs that are irregular in some way are followed by an asterisk (*). (Check the Appendix for the conjugation of irregular verbs.)

Adjectives are given in their masculine singular forms only (*diario, alto*). Some adjectives have the same form for both masculine and feminine (*e.g., verde, importante*).

ABBREVIATIONS

FOR NOUNS:

m   masculine noun
f   feminine noun

s   singular form
pl plural form

FOR VERBS:

v   verb
pp past participle
*   A verb with some irregularity. Look for its conjugation in the verb appendix.

GENERAL ABBREVIATIONS

fam	familiar *you* form	*n*	noun
pol	polite *you* form	*prep*	preposition
adj	adjective	*pron*	pronoun
adv	adverb		
conj	conjunction		

PRONUNCIATION GUIDE

The pronunciation of Spanish is easy when compared to other languages. The following charts will help you pronounce the vowels and consonants. Note the Symbols Used column, which indicates how pronunciation of the Spanish words is given throughout the book.

VOWELS

Spanish vowels	English equivalents	Approximate pronunciation	Symbol used
a _casa_	father	ah	_ah_
e _Pepe_	they	eh	_eh_
i _tipo_	machine	ee	_ee_
o _nota_	cone	oh	_oh_
u _uno_	soon	oo	_oo_

DIPHTHONGS

The combination of strong (_a_, _e_, and _o_) and weak vowels (_u_ and _i_) or two weak ones, forms a diphthong, which may not be separated into a syllable unless the weak one carries a written accent: _fiesta, familia, alegría, Raúl._

Spanish	English equivalent	Symbols used
ai (ay) _aire, hay_	I	_ah·ee_
au _causa_	out	_ow_

Spanish	English equivalent	Symbols used
ei *seis*	p<u>ay</u>	*eh·ee*
eu *deuda*	ay-oo	*eh·oo*
ia *diablo*	ee-ah	*ee·ah*
io *serio*	ee-o	*ee·oh*
ie *fiesta*	ee-eh	*ee·eh*
iu *ciudad*	you	*ee·oo*
oi, oy *hoy, soy*	f<u>oi</u>l, t<u>oy</u>	*oy*
ua *agua*	oo-ah	*wah*
uo *cuota*	whoa	*woh*
ue *bueno*	oo-eh	*weh*
ui *cuidado*	oo-ee	*wee*
uy *muy*	oo-ee	*wee*

CONSONANTS

Most consonants are pronounced like their English equivalents. However, the following consonants and consonant-vowel combinations have special pronunciations.

Spanish	English equivalent	Symbols used
ce	<u>th</u>ink	*th* (Spain)
ce	say	*seh* (Hispanic America)
ci	<u>th</u>ink	*th* (Spain)
ci	see	*see* (Hispanic America)
ge	hay	*heh*
gi	<u>h</u>eep	*hee*
h	is never pronounced	
j	<u>h</u>ope	*h*
ll	<u>y</u>es mi<u>ll</u>ion	*y* (the majority use)
ñ	can<u>y</u>on	*ny*
qui	mos<u>qui</u>to	*kee*
que	Kay	*keh*
r	<u>R</u>oy	*r* (slightly rolled in the middle of a word [*señorita*]) and trilled at the beginning of a word (*Raúl*)
rr	no English equivalent	*rr* (strongly trilled)
v	<u>b</u>oy	*b* (a soft sound)
x	e<u>x</u>ert	*ks* or *s* (has the sound of *ks* between vowels)
z	<u>s</u>uit	*s* NOTE: In Spain, *z* is pronounced as in <u>th</u>ink

BASIC INFORMATION

1. ARITHMETIC

a. CARDINAL NUMBERS

zero	cero	*'seh-roh*
one	uno	*'oo-noh*
two	dos	*dohs*
three	tres	*trehs*
four	cuatro	*'kwah-troh*
five	cinco	*'seen-koh*
six	seis	*'seh·ees*
seven	siete	*'see·eh-teh*
eight	ocho	*'oh-choh*
nine	nueve	*'nweh-beh*
ten	diez	*dee·'ehs*
eleven	once	*'ohn-seh*
twelve	doce	*'doh-seh*
thirteen	trece	*'treh-seh*
fourteen	catorce	*kah-'tohr-seh*
fifteen	quince	*'keen-seh*
sixteen	dieciséis	*dee·eh-see-'seh·ees*
seventeen	diecisiete	*dee·eh-see-'see·eh-teh*
eighteen	dieciocho	*dee·eh-see-'oh-choh*
nineteen	diecinueve	*dee·eh-see-'nweh-beh*
twenty	veinte	*'veh·een-teh*
twenty-one	veintiuno	*veh·een-tee-'oo-noh*
twenty-two	veintidós	*veh·een-tee-'dohs*
twenty-three	veintitrés	*veh·een-tee-'trehs*
twenty-four	veinticuatro	*veh·een-tee-'kwah-troh*
twenty-five	veinticinco	*veh·een-tee-'seen-koh*
twenty-six	veintiséis	*veh·een-tee-'seh·ees*
twenty-seven	veintisiete	*veh·een-tee-see-'eh-teh*
twenty-eight	veintiocho	*veh·een-tee-'oh-choh*
twenty-nine	veintinueve	*veh·een-tee-'nweh-beh*
thirty	treinta	*'treh·een-tah*
thirty-one	treinta y uno	*'treh·een-tah ee 'oo-noh*
thirty-two	treinta y dos	*'treh·een-tah ee dohs*
forty	cuarenta	*kwah-'rehn-tah*
forty-one	cuarenta y uno	*kwah-'rehn-tah ee 'oo-noh*
forty-two	cuarenta y dos	*kwah-'rehn-tah ee dohs*
fifty	cincuenta	*seen-'kwehn-tah*
fifty-one	cincuenta y uno	*seen-'kwehn-tah ee 'oo-noh*

sixty	sesenta	*seh-'sehn-tah*
sixty-one	sesenta y uno	*seh-'sehn-tah ee 'oo-noh*
seventy	setenta	*seh-'tehn-tah*
eighty	ochenta	*oh-'chehn-tah*
ninety	noventa	*noh-'behn-tah*
one hundred	cien	*see-ehn*
one hundred and one	ciento uno	*see-'ehn-toh 'oo-noh*
one hundred and two	ciento dos	*see-'ehn-toh dohs*
one hundred and twenty	ciento veinte	*see-'ehn-toh 'veh-een-teh*
two hundred	doscientos	*dohs-see-'ehn-tohs*
two hundred and one	doscientos uno	*dohs-see-'ehn-tohs 'oo-noh*
three hundred	trescientos	*trehs-see-'ehn-tohs*
four hundred	cuatrocientos	*kwah-troh-see-'ehn-tohs*
five hundred	quinientos	*kee-nee-'ehn-tohs*
six hundred	seiscientos	*seh-ees-see-'ehn-tohs*
seven hundred	setecientos	*seh-teh-see-'ehn-tohs*
eight hundred	ochocientos	*oh-choh-see-'ehn-tohs*
nine hundred	novecientos	*noh-beh-see-'ehn-tohs*
one thousand	mil	*meel*
one thousand and one	mil y uno	*meel ee 'oo-noh*
one thousand forty	mil cuarenta	*meel kwah-'rehn-tah*
one thousand three hundred	mil trescientos	*meel trehs-see-'ehn-tohs*
1990	mil novecientos noventa	*mil noh-beh-see-'ehn-tohs noh-'behn-tah*
two thousand	dos mil	*dohs meel*
two thousand and one	dos mil y uno	*dohs meel ee 'oo-noh*
two thousand four hundred	dos mil cuatrocientos	*dohs meel kwah-troh-see-'ehn-tohs*
one hundred thousand	cien mil	*see-ehn meel*
two hundred thousand	doscientos mil	*dohs-see-'ehn-tohs meel*
one million	un millón	*oon mee-'yohn*
two million	dos millones	*dohs mee-'yoh-nehs*
one hundred million	cien millones	*see-ehn mee-'yoh-nehs*
one billion	un billón	*oon bee-'yohn*
two billion	dos billones	*dohs bee-'yoh-nehs*

b. ORDINAL NUMBERS

first	primero	*pree-'meh-roh*
second	segundo	*seh-'goon-doh*

third	tercero	*tehr-'seh-roh*
fourth	cuarto	*'kwahr-toh*
fifth	quinto	*'keen-toh*
sixth	sexto	*'sehks-toh*
seventh	séptimo	*'sehp-tee-moh*
eighth	octavo	*ohk-'tah-boh*
ninth	noveno	*noh-'behn-oh*
tenth	décimo	*'deh-see-moh*
eleventh	undécimo	*oon-'deh-see-moh*
twelfth	duodécimo	*dwoh-'deh-see-moh*
thirteenth	decimotercero	*deh-see-moh-tehr-'seh-roh*
fourteenth	decimocuarto	*deh-see-moh-'kwahr-toh*
fifteenth	decimoquinto	*deh-see-moh-'keen-toh*
sixteenth	decimosexto	*deh-see-moh-'sehks-toh*
seventeenth	decimoséptimo	*deh-see-moh-'sehp-tee-moh*
eighteenth	decimoctavo	*deh-see-moh-ohk-'tah-boh*
nineteenth	decimonoveno	*deh-see-moh-noh-'behn-noh*
twentieth	vigésimo	*bee-'heh-see-moh*
twenty-first	vigésimo primero	*bee-'heh-see-moh pree-'meh-roh*
twenty-second	vigésimo segundo	*bee-'heh-see-moh seh-'goon-doh*
thirtieth	trigésimo	*tree-'heh-see-moh*
fortieth	cuadragésimo	*kwah-drah-'heh-see-moh*
fiftieth	quincuagésimo	*keen-kwah-'heh-see-moh*
sixtieth	sexagésimo	*sehks-ah-'heh-see-moh*
seventieth	septuagésimo	*sehp-twah-'heh-see-moh*
eightieth	octogésimo	*ohk-toh-'heh-see-moh*
ninetieth	nonagésimo	*noh-nah-'heh-see-moh*
hundredth	centésimo	*sehn-'teh-see-moh*
two hundredth	ducentésimo	*doo-sehn-'teh-see-moh*
three hundredth	tricentésimo	*tree-sehn-'teh-see-moh*
four hundredth	cuadringentésimo	*kwah-dreen-hehn-'teh-see-moh*
five hundredth	quingentésimo	*keen-hehn-'teh-see-moh*
six hundredth	sexcentésimo	*sehks-sehn-'teh-see-moh*
seven hundredth	septingésimo	*sehp-teen-'heh-see-moh*
eight hundredth	octingentésimo	*ohk-teen-hehn-'teh-see-moh*
nine hundredth	noningentésimo	*noh-neen-hehn-'teh-see-moh*
thousandth	milésimo	*mee-'leh-see-moh*
two thousandth	dos milésimo	*dohs mee-'leh-see-moh*
two hundred thousandth	doscientos milésimo	*dohs-see·'ehn-tohs mee-'leh-see-moh*

millionth	millonésimo	*mee-yoh-'neh-see-moh*
billionth	billonésimo	*bee-yoh-'neh-see-moh*

c. FRACTIONS

one-half	un medio	*oon 'meh-dee·oh*
one-third	un tercio	*oon 'tehr-see·oh*
one-fourth	un cuarto	*oon 'kwahr-toh*
two-thirds	dos tercios	*dohs 'tehr-see·ohs*
three-fourths	tres cuartos	*trehs 'kwahr-tohs*
four-sevenths	cuatro séptimos	*'kwah-troh 'sehp-tee-mohs*
eight-tenths	ocho décimos	*'oh-choh 'deh-see-mohs*

d. TYPES OF NUMBERS

number	número	*'noo-meh-roh*
• **number**	numerar (*v*)	*noo-meh-'rahr*
• **numeral**	número	*'noo-meh-roh*
• **numerical**	numérico (*adj*)	*noo-'meh-ree-koh*
Arabic numerals	numeración (*f*) arábica	*noo-meh-rah-see-'ohn ah-'rah-bee-kah*
cardinal number	número cardinal	*'noo-meh-roh kar-dee-'nahl*
complex number	número complejo	*'noo-meh-roh kohm-'pleh-hoh*
digit	dígito	*'dee-hee-toh*
even	par (*adj*)	*pahr*
fractional	fraccionario (*adj*)	*frahk-see·oh-'nah-ree-oh*
• **fraction**	fracción (*f*)	*frahk-see-'ohn*
imaginary	imaginario (*adj*)	*ee-mah-hee-'nah-ree-oh*
integer	entero	*ehn-'teh-roh*
irrational number	número irracional	*'noo-meh-roh ee-rrah-see-oh-'nahl*
natural	natural (*adj*)	*nah-too-'rahl*
negative	negativo (*adj*)	*neh-gah-'tee-boh*
odd	impar (*adj*)	*eem-'pahr*
ordinal	ordinal (*adj*)	*ohr-dee-'nahl*
positive	positivo (*adj*)	*poh-see-'tee-boh*
prime	primo (*adj*)	*'pree-moh*
rational	racional (*adj*)	*rah-see·oh-'nahl*
real	real (*adj*)	*reh-'ahl*
reciprocal	recíproco (*adj*)	*reh-'see-proh-koh*
Roman numeral	número romano	*'noo-meh-roh roh-'mah-noh*

e. BASIC OPERATIONS

arithmetical operations	operaciones aritméticas (f, pl)	oh-peh-rah-see-'oh-nehs ah-reet-'meh-tee-kahs
add up	sumar (v)	soo-'mahr
• addition	suma (f)	'soo-mah
• plus	más	mahs
• Two plus two equals four	Dos más dos son cuatro.	Dohs mahs dohs sohn 'kwah-troh
subtract	restar (v)	rehs-'tahr
• subtraction	resta (f)	'rehs-tah
• minus	menos	'meh-nohs
• Three minus two are one.	Tres menos dos son uno.	Trehs 'meh-nohs dohs sohn 'oo-noh
multiply	multiplicar (v)	mool-tee-plee-'kahr
• multiplication	multiplicación (f)	mool-tee-plee-kah-see-'ohn
• multiplication table	tabla de multiplicación	'tah-blah deh mool-tee-plee-kah-see-'ohn
• multiplied by	multiplicado por	mool-tee-plee-'kah-doh pohr
• Three times two equals six.	Tres por dos son seis.	Trehs pohr dohs sohn 'seh·ees
divide	dividir (v)	dee-bee-'deer
• divided by	dividido por	dee-bee-'dee-doh pohr
• division	división (f)	dee-bee-see-'ohn
• Six divided by two equals three.	Seis dividido por dos son tres.	'Seh·ees dee-bee-'dee-doh pohr dohs sohn trehs.
raise to the . . . power	elevar a la . . . potencia	eh-leh-'bahr ah lah poh-'tehn-see·ah
• to the fourth power	a la cuarta potencia	ah lah 'kwar-tah poh-'tehn-see·ah
• to the nth power	a la enésima potencia	ah lah eh-'neh-see-mah poh-'tehn-see·ah
• squared	al cuadrado	ahl kwah-'drah-doh
• cubed	al cubo	ahl 'koo-boh
• Two squared equals four.	Dos al cuadrado son cuatro.	Dohs ahl kwah-'drah-doh sohn 'kwah-troh
extract a root	extraer* una raíz	ehks-trah-'ehr 'oo-nah rah·'ees
• square root	raíz cuadrada	rah·'ees kwah-'drah-dah
• cube root	raíz cúbica	rah·'ees 'koo-bee-kah
• nth root	enésima raíz	eh-'neh-see-mah rah·'ees
• The square root of nine is three.	La raíz cuadrada de nueve es tres.	lah rah·'ees kwah-'drah-dah deh 'nweh-beh ehs trehs
ratio	proporción (f)	proh-pohr-see·'ohn

FOCUS: Arithmetical Operations

Addition—Adición
$2 + 3 = 5$ two plus three equals five   dos más tres son cinco

Subtraction—Substracción
$9 - 3 = 6$ nine minus three equals six   nueve menos tres son seis

Multiplication—Multiplicación
$4 \times 2 = 8$
$4 \cdot 2 = 8$ four times two equals eight   cuatro por dos son ocho

Division—División
$10 : 2 = 5$ ten divided by two equals five   diez dividido por dos son cinco

Raising to a power—Elevación a una potencia
$3^2 = 9$ three squared equals nine   tres al cuadrado son nueve

$2^3 = 8$ two cubed equals eight   dos al cubo son ocho

$2^4 = 16$ two to the fourth power equals sixteen   dos a la cuarta potencia son dieciséis

x^n x to the nth power   x a la enésima potencia

Extraction of root—Extracción de raíz
$\sqrt{4} = 3$ the square root of four is two   la raíz cuadrada de cuatro es dos

$\sqrt[3]{27} = 3$ the cube root of twenty-seven is three   la raíz cúbica de veintisiete es tres

$\sqrt[n]{x}$ the nth root of x   la enésima raíz de x

---

f. ADDITIONAL MATHEMATICAL CONCEPTS

algebra	álgebra (*m*)	*'ahl-heh-brah*
• **algebraic**	algebraico (*adj*)	*ahl-heh-'brah·ee-koh*
arithmetic	aritmética	*ah-reet-'meh-tee-kah*
• **arithmetic**	aritmético (*adj*)	*ah-reet-'meh-tee-koh*
average	promedio	*proh-'meh-dee·oh*

calculate	calcular (v)	*kahl-koo-'lahr*
• calculation	cálculo	*'kahl-koo-loh*
decimal	decimal (adj)	*deh-see-'mahl*
difference	diferencia	*dee-feh-'rehn-see·ah*
equality	igualdad (f)	*ee-gwal-'dahd*
• equals	es igual a	*ehs ee-'gwal ah*
• is not equal to	no es igual a	*noh ehs ee-'gwal ah*
• is equivalent to	equivale a	*eh-kee-'bah-leh ah*
• is greater than	es mayor que	*ehs mah-'yohr keh*
• is less than	es menor que	*ehs meh-'nohr keh*
• is similar to	es semejante a	*ehs seh-meh-'hahn-teh ah*
equation	ecuación (f)	*eh-kwah-see-'ohn*
• quadratic equation	ecuación de segundo grado	*eh-kwah-see-'ohn deh seh-'goon-doh 'grah-doh*
factor	factor (m)	*fahk-'tohr*
logarithm	logaritmo	*loh-gah-'reet-moh*
• logarithmic	logarítmico	*loh-gah-'reet-mee-koh*
multiple	múltiple (adj)	*'mool-tee-pleh*
percent	por ciento	*pohr see-'ehn-toh*
• percentage	porcentaje (m)	*pohr-sehn-'tah-heh*
problem	problema (m)	*proh-'bleh-mah*
• problem to solve	problema para resolver	*proh-'bleh-mah 'pah-rah reh-sohl-'behr*
product	producto	*proh-'dook-toh*
quotient	cociente (m)	*koh-see-'ehn-teh*
set	conjunto	*kohn-'hoon-toh*
solution	solución (f)	*soh-loo-see-'ohn*
• solve	resolver (v)	*reh-sohl-'behr*
statistical	estadístico (adj)	*ehs-tah-'dees-tee-koh*
• statistics	estadística (f)	*ehs-tah-'dees-tee-kah*
sum	suma	*'soo-mah*
• sum up	sumar (v)	*soo-'mahr*
symbol	símbolo	*'seem-boh-loh*
variable	variable	*bah-ree-'ah-bleh*

2. GEOMETRY

a. FIGURES

plane figures	figuras planas	*fee-'goo-rahs 'plah-nahs*
triangle	triángulo	*tree-'ahn-goo-loh*
• acute-angled	ángulo agudo	*'ahn-goo-loh ah-'goo-doh*
• equilateral	equilátero (adj)	*eh-kee-'lah-teh-roh*
• isosceles	isósceles	*ee-'sohs-seh-lehs*

• obtuse-angled	obtuso (*adj*)	*ohb-'too-soh*
• right-angled	recto (*adj*)	*'rehk-toh*
• scalene	escaleno (*adj*)	*ehs-kah-'leh-noh*
four-sided figures	figuras cuadriláteras	*fee-'goo-rahs kwah-dree-'lah-teh-rahs*
• parallelogram	paralelogramo	*pah-rah-leh-loh-'grah-moh*
• rectangle	rectángulo	*rehk-'tahn-goo-loh*
• rhombus	rombo	*'rohm-boh*
• square	cuadrado	*kwah-'drah-doh*
• trapezium (trapezoid)	trapecio	*trah-'peh-see·oh*
n-sided figures	polígonos	*poh-'lee-goh-nohs*
• decagon	decágono	*deh-'kah-goh-noh*
• heptagon	heptágono	*ehp-'tah-goh-noh*
• hexagon	hexágono	*ekhs-'ah-goh-noh*
• octagon	octógono (octágono)	*ohk-'toh-goh-noh (ohk-'tah-goh-noh)*
• pentagon	pentágono	*pehn-'tah-goh-noh*
circle	círculo	*'seer-koo-loh*
• center	centro	*'sehn-troh*
• circumference	circunferencia	*seer-koon-feh-'rehn-see·ah*
• diameter	diámetro	*dee-'ah-meh-troh*
• radius	radio	*'rah-dee·oh*
• tangent	tangente (*f*)	*tahn-'hehn-teh*
solid figures	figuras sólidas	*fee-'goo-rahs 'soh-lee-dahs*
cone	cono	*'koh-noh*
cube	cubo	*'koo-boh*
cylinder	cilindro	*see-'leen-droh*
parallelepiped	paralelopípedo	*pah-rah-leh-loh-'pee-peh-doh*
polyhedron	poliedro	*poh-lee-'eh-droh*
• dodecahedron	dodecaedro	*doh-deh-kah-'eh-droh*
• icosahedron	icosaedro	*ee-koh-sah-'eh-droh*
• octahedron	octaedro	*ohk-tah-'eh-droh*
• tetrahedron	tetraedro	*teh-trah-'eh-droh*
prism	prisma (*m*)	*'prees-mah*
pyramid	pirámide (*f*)	*pee-'rah-mee-deh*
sphere	esfera	*ehs-'feh-rah*

b. CONCEPTS

angle	ángulo (*adj*)	*'ahn-goo-loh*
• acute	agudo (*adj*)	*ah-'goo-doh*

FOCUS: Geometrical Figures

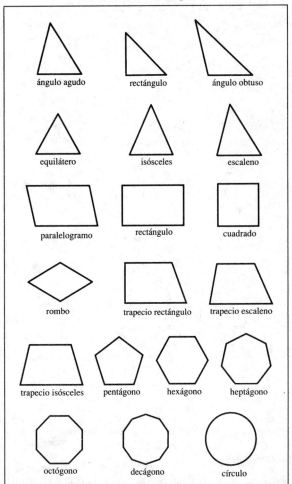

ángulo agudo

rectángulo

ángulo obtuso

equilátero

isósceles

escaleno

paralelogramo

rectángulo

cuadrado

rombo

trapecio rectángulo

trapecio escaleno

trapecio isósceles

pentágono

hexágono

heptágono

octógono

decágono

círculo

FOCUS: Geometrical Solids

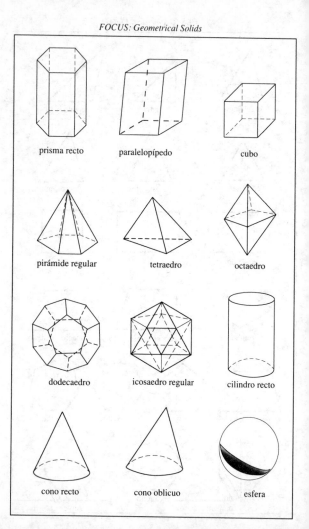

prisma recto   paralelopípedo   cubo

pirámide regular   tetraedro   octaedro

dodecaedro   icosaedro regular   cilindro recto

cono recto   cono oblicuo   esfera

FOCUS: Angles

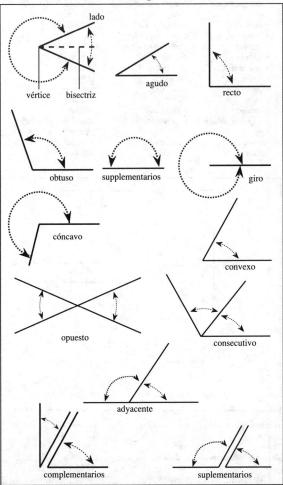

lado

vértice   bisectriz

agudo

recto

obtuso   supplementarios   giro

cóncavo

convexo

opuesto

consecutivo

adyacente

complementarios   suplementarios

• adjacent	adyacente (*adj*)	*ahd-yah-'sehn-teh*
• bisector	bisectriz (*f*)	*bee-sehk-'trees*
• complementary	complementario (*adj*)	*kohm-pleh-mehn-'tah-ree·oh*
• concave	cóncavo (*adj*)	*'kohn-kah-boh*
• consecutive	consecutivo (*adj*)	*kohn-seh-koo-'tee-boh*
• convex	convexo (*adj*)	*kohn-'behk-soh*
• obtuse	obtuso (*adj*)	*ohb-'too-soh*
• one turn (360°)	giro (*m*)	*'hee-roh*
• opposite	opuesto (*adj*)	*oh-'pwehs-toh*
• right	recto (*adj*)	*'rehk-toh*
• side	lado	*'lah-doh*
• straight	plano (*adj*)	*'plah-noh*
• supplementary	suplementario	*soo-pleh-mehn-'tah-ree·oh*
• vertex	vértice (*m*)	*'behr-tee-seh*
• axis	axis (*m*)	*'ahks-ees*

FOCUS: Lines

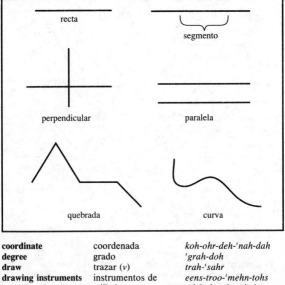

recta

segmento

perpendicular

paralela

quebrada

curva

coordinate	coordenada	*koh-ohr-deh-'nah-dah*
degree	grado	*'grah-doh*
draw	trazar (*v*)	*trah-'sahr*
drawing instruments	instrumentos de dibujo	*eens-troo-'mehn-tohs deh dee-'boo-hoh*
• compass	compás (*m*)	*kohm-'pahs*

• eraser	goma de borrar	'goh-mah deh boh-'rrahr
• pen	pluma	'ploo-mah
• pencil	lápiz (m)	'lah-pees
• protractor	transportador (m)	trahns-pohr-tah-'dohr
• ruler	regla	'reh-glah
geometrical	geométrico	heh-oh-'meh-tree-koh
• geometry	geometría	heh-oh-meh-'tree-ah
line	línea	'lee-neh-ah
• broken	quebrada (adj)	keh-'brah-dah
• curved	curva (adj)	'koor-bah
• parallel	paralela (adj)	pah-rah-'leh-lah
• perpendicular	perpendicular (adj)	pehr-pehn-dee-koo-'lahr
• segment	segmento	sehg-'mehn-toh
• straight	recta (adj)	'rehk-tah
point	punto	'poon-toh
space	espacio	ehs-'pah-see·oh
trigonometry	trigonometría	tree-goh-noh-meh-'tree-ah
• trigonometric	trigonométrico	tree-goh-noh-'meh-tree-koh
• cosecant	cosecante (f)	koh-seh-'kahn-teh
• cosine	coseno	koh-'seh-noh
• cotangent	cotangente (f)	koh-tahn-'hehn-teh
• secant	secante (f)	seh-'kahn-teh
• sine	seno	'seh-noh
• tangent	tangente (f)	tahn-'hehn-teh
vector	vector (m)	behk-'tohr

3. QUANTITY AND SPACE

a. WEIGHTS AND MEASURES

area	área (f)	'ah-reh·ah
• hectare	hectárea	ehk-'tah-reh·ah
• square centimeter	centímetro cuadrado	sehn-'tee-meh-troh kwah-'drah-doh
• square kilometer	kilómetro cuadrado	kee-'loh-meh-troh kwah-'drah-doh
• square meter	metro cuadrado	'meh-troh kwah-'drah-doh
• square millimeter	milímetro cuadrado	mee-'lee-meh-troh kwah-'drah-doh
length	longitud (f)	lohn-hee-'tood
• centimeter	centímetro	sehn-'tee-meh-troh
• kilometer	kilómetro	kee-'loh-meh-troh
• meter	metro	'meh-troh
• millimeter	milímetro	mee-'lee-meh-troh
volume	volumen (m)	boh-'loo-mehn

• **cubic centimeter**	centímetro cúbico	*sehn-'tee-meh-troh 'koo-bee-koh*
• **cubic kilometer**	kilómetro cúbico	*kee-'loh-meh-troh 'koo-bee-koh*
• **cubic meter**	metro cúbico	*'meh-troh 'koo-bee-koh*
• **cubic millimeter**	milímetro cúbico	*mee-'lee-meh-troh 'koo-bee-koh*
• **liter**	litro	*'lee-troh*
• **quart**	cuarto	*'kwahr-toh*
weight	peso	*'peh-soh*
• **gram**	gramo	*'grah-moh*
• **hectogram**	hectogramo	*ehk-toh-'grah-moh*
• **kilogram**	kilogramo	*kee-loh-'grah-moh*
	kilo	*'kee-loh*

b. WEIGHING AND MEASURING

dense	denso (*adj*)	*'dehn-soh*
• **density**	densidad (*f*)	*dehn-see-'dahd*
dimension	dimensión (*f*)	*dee-mehn-see-'ohn*
extension	extensión (*f*)	*ehks-tehn-see-'ohn*
heavy	pesado (*adj*)	*peh-'sah-doh*
heavy (*liquid*)	espeso (*adj*)	*ehs-'peh-soh*
light	ligero (*adj*)	*lee-'heh-roh*
long	largo (*adj*)	*'lahr-goh*
mass	masa	*'mah-sah*
maximum	máximo (*adj*)	*'mah-ksee-moh*
measure	medir*	*meh-'deer*
• **measuring tape**	cinta métrica	*'seen-tah 'meh-tree-kah*
• **medium**	mediano (*adj*)	*meh-dee-'ah-noh*
• **minimum**	mínimo (*adj*)	*'mee-nee-moh*
• **narrow**	estrecho (*adj*)	*ehs-'treh-choh*
• **short** (*thing*)	corto (*adj*)	*'kohr-toh*
• **size**	tamaño	*tah-'mah-nyoh*
speed	velocidad (*f*)	*beh-loh-see-'dahd*
• **per hour**	por hora	*pohr 'oh-rah*
• **per minute**	por minuto	*pohr mee-'noo-toh*
• **per second**	por segundo	*pohr seh-'goon-doh*
tall	alto (*adj*)	*'ahl-toh*
thick	espeso (*adj*)	*ehs-'peh-soh*
thin	delgado	*dehl-'gah-doh*
	fino (*adj*)	*'fee-noh*
weigh	pesar (*v*)	*peh-'sahr*
wide	ancho (*adj*)	*'ahn-choh*
• **width**	anchura	*ahn-'choo-rah*

c. CONCEPTS OF QUANTITY

a lot, much	mucho (*adj, adv*)	*'moo-choh*
all, everything	todo (*adj, pron*)	*'toh-doh*

• everyone	todos (*pron*)	'toh-dohs
	todo el mundo (*pron*)	'toh-doh ehl 'moon-doh
almost, nearly	casi (*adv*)	'kah-see
approximately	aproximadamente (*adv*)	ah-proh-ksee-mah-dah-'mehn-teh
as much as	tanto . . . como	'tahn-toh 'koh-moh
big, large	grande (*adj*)	'grahn-deh
both	ambos (*adj, pron*)	'ahm-bohs
capacity	capacidad (*f*)	kah-pah-see-'dahd
decrease	disminuir*	dees-mee-'nweer
• **decrease**	disminución (*f*)	dees-mee-noo-see·'ohn
double	doble (*adj*)	'doh-bleh
empty	vacío (*adj*)	bah-'see-oh
• **empty**	vaciar (*v*)	bah-see-'ahr
enough	bastante (*adj, adv*)	bahs-'tahn-teh
• **be enough**	bastar (*v*)	bahs-'tahr
	ser* bastante	sehr bahs-'tahn-teh
entire	entero (*adj*)	ehn-'teh-roh
every, each	cada (*adv*)	'kah-dah
fill	llenar (*v*)	yeh-'nahr
• **full**	lleno (*adj*)	'yeh-noh
grow	crecer (*v*)	kreh-'sehr
• **growth**	crecimiento	kreh-see-mee·'ehn-toh
half	mitad (*f*)	mee-'tahd
	medio (*adj*)	'meh-dee·oh
how much	¿cuánto? (*adj, pron*)	'kwahn-toh
increase	aumentar (*v*)	ow-mehn-'tahr
• **increase**	aumento	ow-'mehn-toh
less	menos	'meh-nohs
little	pequeño (*adj*)	peh-'keh-nyoh
• **a little**	un poco	oon 'poh-koh
more	más	mahs
no one	nadie (*pron*)	'nah-dee·eh
nothing	nada	'nah-dah
pair	par (*m*)	pahr
part	parte (*f*)	'pahr-teh
piece	pedazo	peh-'dah-soh
portion	porción (*f*)	pohr-see·'ohn
quantity	cantidad (*f*)	kahn-tee-'dahd
several	varios	'bah-ree·ohs
small	pequeño	peh-'keh-nyoh
some	algunos (-as), (*adj*)	ahl-'goo-nohs (-nahs)
suffice	bastar (*v*)	bahs-'tahr
	ser* suficiente	sehr soo-fee-see·'ehn-teh
• **sufficient**	suficiente (*adj*)	soo-fee-see·'ehn-teh

| too much | demasiado (*adj, adv*) | *deh-mah-see·'ah-doh* |
| triple | triple (*adj*) | *'tree-pleh* |

d. CONCEPTS OF LOCATION

above	arriba (*adv*)	*ah-'rree-bah*
	sobre (*prep*)	*'soh-breh*
across	a través de (*prep*)	*ah trah-'behs deh*
ahead	delante (*adj, adv*)	*deh-'lahn-teh*
	al frente (*adj, adv*)	*ahl 'frehn-teh*
among, between	entre (*prep*)	*'ehn-treh*
away	fuera (*adv*)	*'fweh-rah*
behind	detrás (*adv*)	*deh-'trahs*
beside, next to	junto a (*prep*)	*'hoon-toh ah*
	al lado de (*prep*)	*ahl 'lah-doh deh*
beyond	más allá	*mahs ah-'yah*
bottom	fondo	*'fohn-doh*
• at the bottom	en el fondo	*ehn ehl 'fohn-doh*
compass	brújula	*'broo-hoo-lah*
direction	dirección	*dee-reh-ksee-'ohn*
distance	distancia	*dees-'tahn-see·ah*
down below	abajo	*ah-'bah-hoh*
east	este (*m*)	*'ehs-teh*
• eastern	oriental (*adj*)	*oh-ree-ehn-'tahl*
	este (*adj*)	*'ehs-teh*
• to the east	al este	*ahl 'ehs-teh*
edge	borde	*'bohr-deh*
far	lejos (*adv*)	*'leh-hohs*
from	de (*prep*)	*deh*
here	aquí (*adv*)	*ah-'kee*
	acá (*adv*)	*ah-'kah*
horizontal	horizontal (*adj*)	*oh-ree-sohn-'tahl*
in	en (*prep*)	*ehn*
• inside of	dentro de (*prep*)	*'dehn-troh deh*
in front of	delante de (*prep*)	*deh-'lahn-teh deh*
in front of (*facing*)	en frente de (*prep*)	*ehn 'frehn-teh deh*
in the middle	en medio de (*prep*)	*ehn 'meh-dee-oh deh*
left	izquierdo (*adj*)	*ees-kee-'ehr-doh*
• to the left	a la izquierda	*ah lah ees-kee-'ehr-dah*
level	llano (*adj*)	*'yah-noh*
near	cerca (de) (*adv, prep*)	*'sehr-kah (deh)*
north	norte (*m*)	*'nohr-teh*
• northern	septentrional (*adj*)	*sehp-tehn-tree·oh-'nahl*
• to the north	al norte	*ahl 'nohr-teh*

nowhere	en ninguna parte (*adv*)	*ehn neen-'goo-nah 'pahr-teh*
on	encima (de) (*adv, prep*)	*ehn-'see-mah (deh)*
outside	fuera (de) (*adv, prep*)	*'fweh-rah (deh)*
place	lugar (*m*)	*loo-'gahr*
position	posición (*f*)	*poh-see-see·'ohn*
right	derecho (*adj*)	*deh-'reh-choh*
• **to the right**	a la derecha	*ah lah deh-'reh-chah*
somewhere	en alguna parte (*adv*)	*ehn ahl-'goo-nah 'pahr-teh*
south	sur (*m*)	*soor*
• **southern**	meridional	*meh-ree-dee·oh-'nahl*
• **to the south**	al sur	*ahl soor*
there	allí	*ah-'yee*
	allá	*ah-'yah*
through	a través de	*ah trah-'behs deh*
to, at	a (*prep*)	*ah*
• **at** (*someone's place*)	en (*prep*)	*ehn*
toward	hacia (*prep*)	*'ah-see·ah*
under	debajo (de) (*adv, prep*)	*deh-'bah-hoh deh*
up	arriba (*adv*)	*ah-'rree-bah*
vertical	vertical (*adj*)	*behr-tee-'kahl*
west	oeste (*m*)	*oh-'ehs-teh*

FOCUS: Compass Points

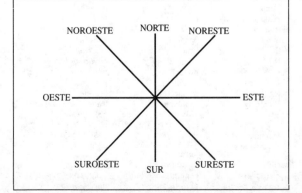

• western	occidental (*adj*)	*ohk-see-dehn-'tahl*
• to the west	al oeste	*ahl oh-'ehs-teh*
where	donde	*'dohn-deh*

e. MOVEMENT

arrive	llegar (*v*)	*yeh-'gahr*
come	venir*	*beh-'neer*
drive	manejar (*v*)	*mah-neh-'hahr*
	conducir*	*kohn-doo-'seer*
enter	entrar (*v*)	*ehn-'trahr*
fall	caer*	*kah-'ehr*
fast	rápido (*adj*)	*'rah-pee-doh*
follow	seguir*	*seh-'geer*
get up	levantarse (*v*)	*leh-bahn-'tahr-seh*
go	ir*	*eer*
• go away	irse*	*'eer-seh*
• go down	bajar (*v*)	*bah-'hahr*
• go on foot	ir* a pie	*eer ah pee·'eh*
• go out, exit	salir*	*sah-'leer*
• go up	subir (*v*)	*soo-'beer*
leave, depart	partir (*v*)	*pahr-'teer*
	irse*	*'eer-seh*
lie down	acostarse*	*ah-koh-'stahr-seh*
	tenderse*	*tehn-'dehr-seh*
lift	levantar (*v*)	*leh-bahn-'tahr*
	elevar (*v*)	*eh-leh-'bahr*
motion	movimiento	*moh-bee-mee·'ehn-toh*
• move	mover*	*moh-'behr*
• move oneself	moverse*	*moh-'behr-seh*
movement	movimiento	*moh-bee-mee·'ehn-toh*
pass by	pasar (*v*)	*pah-'sahr*
pull	tirar (*v*)	*tee-'rahr*
push	empujar (*v*)	*ehm-poo-'hahr*
put	poner*	*poh-'nehr*
	meter (*v*)	*meh-'tehr*
quick	rápido (*adj*)	*'rah-pee-doh*
• quickly	rápidamente (*adv*)	*'rah-pee-dah-mehn-teh*
return	volver*	*bohl-'behr*
	regresar (*v*)	*reh-greh-'sahr*
• return something	devolver*	*deh-bohl-'behr*
run	correr (*v*)	*koh-'rrehr*
send	mandar (*v*)	*mahn-'dahr*
sit down	sentarse*	*sehn-'tahr-seh*
slow	lento (*adj*)	*'lehn-toh*

• slowly	lentamente (adv)	lehn-tah-'mehn-teh
	despacio (adv)	dehs-'pah-see·oh
stop	parar (v)	pah-'rahr
	detener*	deh-teh-'nehr
• stop oneself	detenerse*	deh-teh-'nehr-seh
turn	volver*	bohl-'behr
	girar (v)	hee-'rahr
walk	andar (v)	ahn-'dahr
	caminar (v)	kah-mee-'nahr
• walk	caminata	kah-mee-'nah-tah

4. TIME

a. GENERAL EXPRESSIONS OF TIME

afternoon	tarde (f)	'tahr-deh
• in the afternoon	por la tarde	pohr lah 'tahr-deh
• this afternoon	esta tarde	'ehs-tah 'tahr-deh
• tomorrow afternoon	mañana por la tarde	mah-'nyah-nah pohr lah 'tahr-deh
dawn	amanecer (m)	ah-mah-neh-'sehr
day	día (m)	'dee-ah
• all day	todo el día	'toh-doh ehl 'dee-ah
evening	tarde (f)	'tahr-deh
	noche (f)	'noh-cheh
• in the evening	por la tarde	pohr lah 'tahr-deh
• this evening	esta tarde	'ehs-tah 'tahr-deh
• tomorrow evening	mañana por la tarde	mah-'nyah-nah pohr lah 'tahr-deh
midnight	medianoche (f)	meh-dee·ah-'noh-cheh
• at midnight	a la medianoche	ah lah meh-dee·ah-'noh-cheh
morning	mañana	mah-'nyah-nah
• in the morning	por la mañana	pohr lah mah-'nyah-nah
• this morning	esta mañana	'ehs-tah mah-'nyah-nah
• tomorrow morning	mañana por la mañana	mah-'nyah-nah pohr lah mah-'nyah-nah
night	noche (f)	'noh-cheh
• at night	de noche	deh 'noh-cheh
• last night	anoche	ah-'noh-cheh
• tomorrow night	mañana por la noche	mah-'nyah-nah pohr lah 'noh-cheh
• tonight	esta noche	'ehs-tah 'noh-cheh
noon	mediodía (m)	meh-dee·oh-'dee-ah
• at noon	al mediodía	ahl meh-dee·oh-'dee-ah
sunrise	salida del sol	sah-'lee-dah dehl sohl
sunset	puesta del sol	'poo·ehs-tah dehl sohl

time	tiempo	*'tee·ehm-poh*
• time (*hour*)	hora	*'oh-rah*
• time (*once, twice*)	vez (*f*)	*behs*
today	hoy (*adv*)	*oy*
tomorrow	mañana	*mah-'nyah-nah*
• day after tomorrow	pasado mañana	*pah-'sah-doh mah-'nyah-nah*
tonight	esta noche	*'ehs-tah 'noh-cheh*
yesterday	ayer	*ah-'yehr*
• day before yesterday	anteayer	*ahn-teh-ah-'yehr*
• yesterday morning	ayer por la mañana	*ah-'yehr pohr lah mah-'nyah-nah*

b. TELLING TIME

What time is it?	¿Qué hora es?	*keh 'oh-rah ehs*
• It's 1:00.	Es la una.	*ehs lah 'oo-nah*
• It's 2:00.	Son las dos.	*sohn lahs dohs*
• It's 3:00 sharp.	Son las tres en punto.	*sohn lahs trehs ehn 'poon-toh*
• It's 1:10.	Es la una y diez.	*ehs lah 'oo-nah ee dee·'ehs*
• It's 3:15.	Son las tres y cuarto.	*sohn lahs trehs ee kwahr-toh*
• It's 3:30.	Son las tres y media.	*sohn lahs trehs ee 'meh-dee·ah*
• It's 2:45.	Son las tres menos cuarto.	*sohn lahs trehs 'meh-nohs 'kwahr-toh*
• It's 5:50.	Son las seis menos diez.	*sohn lahs 'seh·ees 'meh-nohs dee·'ehs*
• It's 5:00 A.M.	Son las cinco de la mañana.	*sohn lahs 'seen-koh deh lah mah-'nyah-nah*
• It's 5:00 P.M.	Son las cinco de la tarde.	*sohn lahs 'seen-koh deh lah 'tahr-deh*
• It's 10:00 P.M.	Son las diez de la noche.	*sohn lahs dee·'ehs deh lah 'noh-cheh*
At what time?	¿a qué hora?	*ah keh 'oh-rah*
• at 1:00	a la una	*ah lah 'oo-nah*
• at 2:00	a las dos	*ah lahs dohs*
• at 3:00	a las tres	*ah lahs trehs*

c. UNITS OF TIME

century	siglo	*'see-gloh*
day	día (*m*)	*'dee-ah*

• daily	diario (*n, adj*)	*dee-'ah-ree-oh*
	cotidiano (*adj*)	*koh-tee-dee-'ah-noh*
decade	década	*'deh-kah-dah*
hour	hora	*'oh-rah*
• hourly (*per hour*)	por hora	*pohr 'oh-rah*
• hourly (*each hour*)	cada hora	*'kah-dah 'oh-rah*
instant	instante	*eens-'tahn-teh*
minute	minuto	*mee-'noo-toh*
moment	momento	*moh-'mehn-toh*
month	mes (*m*)	*mehs*
• monthly	mensual (*adj*)	*mehn-'swahl*
	mensualmente (*adv*)	*mehn-swahl-'mehn-teh*
second	segundo	*seh-'goon-doh*
week	semana	*seh-'mah-nah*
• weekly	semanal (*adj*)	*seh-mah-'nahl*
	por semana (*adv*)	*pohr seh-'mah-nah*
year	año	*'ah-nyoh*
• yearly	anual (*adj*)	*ah-'nwahl*
	anualmente (*adv*)	*ah-nwahl-'mehn-teh*

d. TIMEPIECES

alarm clock	despertador (*m*)	*dehs-pehr-tah-'dohr*
clock	reloj (*m*)	*reh-'loh*
dial	esfera	*ehs-'feh-rah*
grandfather clock	reloj de caja	*reh-'loh deh 'kah-hah*
hand (*of a clock*)	mano (*f*)	*'mah-noh*
watch	reloj (*m*)	*reh-'loh*
• The watch is fast.	El reloj anda adelantado.	*Ehl reh-'loh 'ahn-dah ah-deh-lahn-'tah-doh*
• The watch is slow.	El reloj anda atrasado.	*Ehl reh-'loh 'ahn-dah ah-trah-'sah-doh*
watchband	correa de reloj	*koh-'rreh-ah deh reh-'loh*
watch battery	pila	*'pee-lah*
wind	dar* cuerda a	*dahr 'kwehr-dah ah*
wristwatch	reloj de pulsera	*reh-'loh deh pool-'seh-rah*

e. CONCEPTS OF TIME

after	después (de) (*adv, prep*)	*dehs-'pwehs (deh)*
again	otra vez	*'oh-trah behs*
ago	hace	*'ah-seh*

almost never	casi nunca	*'kah-see 'noon-kah*
already	ya	*yah*
always	siempre	*see·'ehm-preh*
as soon as	así que	*as-'see keh*
	luego que	*'lweh-goh keh*
	tan pronto como	*tahn 'prohn-toh 'koh-moh*
at the same time	al mismo tiempo	*ahl 'mees-moh 'tee·ehm-poh*
be about to	estar para	*ehs-'tahr 'pah-rah*
be on time (*people*)	llegar a tiempo	*yeh-'gahr ah tee·'ehm-poh*
	ser puntual	*sehr poon-'twahl*
• **on time** (*e.g.,* trains)	a tiempo	*ah tee·'ehm-poh*

Time is money	= El tiempo es oro.
There is time for all things	= Cada cosa a su tiempo.
Time is up.	= Es la hora.

	a la hora	*ah lah 'oh-rah*
before	antes (de) (*adv, prep*)	*'ahn-tehs (deh)*
	antes (de) que (*conj*)	*'ahn-tehs (deh) keh*
begin	empezar*	*ehm-peh-'sahr*
	comenzar*	*koh-mehn-'sahr*
• **beginning**	principio	*preen-'see-pee-oh*
brief	breve (*adj*)	*'breh-beh*
• **briefly**	brevemente (*adv*)	*breh-beh-'mehn-teh*
by now	ya	*yah*
change	cambiar (*v*)	*kahm-bee-'ahr*
continue	continuar*	*kohn-tee-'nwahr*
• **continually**	continuamente	*kohn-tee-nwah-'mehn-teh*
during	durante	*doo-'rahn-teh*
early	temprano (*adv*)	*tehm-'prah-noh*
• **to be early**	llegar temprano	*yeh-'gahr tehm-'prah-noh*
end, finish	terminar (*v*)	*tehr-mee-'nahr*
• **end**	fin (*m*)	*feen*
frequent	frecuente (*adj*)	*freh-'kwehn-teh*
• **frequently**	frecuentemente (*adv*)	*freh-kwehn-teh-'mehn-teh*
	con frecuencia (*adv*)	*kohn freh-'kwehn-see·ah*
happen, occur	pasar (*v*)	*pah-'sahr*
	ocurrir (*v*)	*oh-koo-'reer*
	suceder (*v*)	*soo-seh-'dehr*

in an hour's time	dentro de una hora	'dehn-troh deh 'oo-nah 'oh-rah
• **in two minutes' time**	en dos minutos	ehn dohs mee-'noo-tohs
in the meantime	mientras tanto	mee·'ehn-trahs 'tahn-toh
in time	a tiempo	ah tee·'ehm-poh
just	justo (*adj, adv*)	'hoos-toh
last	durar (*v*)	doo-'rahr
• **last a long time**	durar mucho tiempo	doo-'rahr 'moo-choh tee·'ehm-poh
• **last a short time**	durar poco tiempo	doo-'rahr 'poh-koh tee·'ehm-poh
last	pasado (*adj*)	pah-'sah-doh
• **last month**	el mes pasado	ehl mehs pah-'sah-doh
• **last year**	el año pasado	ehl 'ah-nyoh pah-'sah-doh
late	tarde (*adj*)	'tahr-deh
• **to be late**	llegar tarde	yeh-'gahr 'tahr-deh
long-term	a largo plazo	ah 'lahr-goh 'plah-soh
look forward to	esperar con placer anticipado	ehs-peh-'rahr kohn plah-'sehr ahn-tee-see-'pah-doh
never	nunca	'noon-kah
• **almost never**	casi nunca	'kah-see 'noon-kah
now	ahora	ah-'oh-rah
• **for now**	por ahora	pohr ah-'oh-rah
• **from now on**	de ahora en adelante	deh ah-'oh-rah ehn ah-deh-'lahn-teh
nowadays	hoy día	oy 'dee-ah
occasionally	de vez en cuando	deh behs ehn 'kwahn-doh
often	con frecuencia	kohn freh-'koo·ehn-see·ah
once	una vez	'oo-nah behs
• **twice**	dos veces	dohs 'beh-sehs
• **once in a while**	de vez en cuando	deh behs ehn 'kwan-doh
• **once upon a time**	hace siglos	'ah-seh 'see-glohs
only	solo (*adj*)	'soh-loh
	sólo (*adv*)	'soh-loh
	solamente (*adv*)	soh-lah-'mehn-teh
past	pasado (*adj*)	pah-'sah-doh
present	presente (*m*)	preh-'sehn-teh
• **present**	actual (*adj*)	ahk-'twahl
• **presently**	actualmente (*adv*)	ahk-twahl-'mehn-teh
previous	anterior	ahn-teh-ree·'ohr
• **previously**	anteriormente (*adv*)	ahn-teh-ree·ohr-'mehn-teh
	antes (*adv*)	'ahn-tehs

rare	raro (*adj*)	*'rah-roh*
• rarely	raramente (*adv*)	*rah-rah-'mehn-teh*
	raras veces (*adv*)	*'rah-rahs 'beh-sehs*
recent	reciente (*adj*)	*reh-see-'ehn-teh*
• recently	recientemente (*adv*)	*reh-see·ehn-teh-'mehn-teh*
regular	regular (*adj*)	*reh-goo-'lahr*
	normal (*adj*)	*nohr-'mahl*
• regularly	regularmente (*adv*)	*reh-goo-lahr-'mehn-teh*
right away	ahora mismo	*ah-'oh-rah 'mees-moh*
short-term	a corto plazo	*ah 'kohr-toh 'plah-soh*
simultaneous	simultáneo (*adj*)	*see-mool-'tah-neh-oh*
• simultaneously	simultáneamente (*adv*)	*see-mool-tah-neh-ah-'mehn-teh*
since, for	desde (*prep*)	*'dehs-deh*
• since Monday	desde el lunes	*'dehs-deh ehl 'loo-nehs*
• since yesterday	desde ayer	*'dehs-deh ah-'yehr*
• for three days	desde hace tres días	*'dehs-deh 'ah-seh trehs 'dee-ahs*
slow	lento (*adj*)	*'lehn-toh*
• slowly	lentamente (*adv*)	*lehn-tah-'mehn-teh*
	despacio (*adv*)	*dehs-'pah-see-oh*
soon	pronto	*'prohn-toh*
• as soon as	así que	*ah-'see keh*
	tan pronto como	*tahn 'prohn-toh 'koh-moh*
• sooner or later	tarde o temprano	*'tahr-deh oh tehm-'prah-noh*
spend time	pasar (*v*)	*pah-'sahr*
sporadic	esporádico (*adj*)	*ehs-poh-'rah-dee-koh*
• sporadically	esporádicamente (*adv*)	*ehs-poh-'rah-dee-kah-'mehn-teh*
still	aún (*adv*)	*ah-'oon*
	todavía (*adv*)	*toh-dah-'bee-ah*
take place	tener* lugar	*teh-'nehr 'loo-gahr*
temporary	temporáneo (*adj*)	*tehm-poh-'rah-neh·oh*
• temporarily	temporáneamente (*adv*)	*tehn-poh'rah-neh-ah-mehn-teh*
then	entonces (*adv*)	*ehn-'tohn-sehs*

Better late than never. = Más vale tarde que nunca.

---

timetable, schedule	horario	*oh-'rah-ree·oh*
to this day	hasta la fecha	*'ahs-tah lah 'feh-chah*
until	hasta (*prep*)	*'ahs-tah*
	hasta que (*conj*)	*'ahs-tah keh*

usually	normalmente	*nohr-mahl-'mehn-teh*
wait for	esperar	*ehs-peh-'rahr*
when	cuando (*conj*)	*'kwahn-doh*
while	mientras	*mee·'ehn-trahs*
within	dentro de (*prep*)	*'dehn-troh deh*
yet	todavía (*adv*)	*toh-dah-'bee-ah*

5. DAYS, MONTHS, AND SEASONS

a. DAYS OF THE WEEK

day of the week	día de la semana	*'dee-ah deh lah seh-'mah-nah*
• Monday	el lunes	*ehl 'loo-nehs*
• Tuesday	el martes	*ehl 'mahr-tehs*
• Wednesday	el miércoles	*ehl mee·'ehr-koh-lehs*
• Thursday	el jueves	*ehl 'hweh-behs*
• Friday	el viernes	*ehl bee·'ehr-nehs*
• Saturday	el sábado	*ehl 'sah-bah-doh*
• Sunday	el domingo	*ehl doh-'meen-goh*
• on Mondays	los lunes	*lohs 'loo-nehs*
• on Saturdays	los sábados	*lohs 'sah-bah-dohs*
holiday	día de fiesta	*'dee-ah deh fee·'ehs-tah*
• Today is a holiday.	Hoy es fiesta.	*oy ehs fee·'ehs-tah*
weekend	fin de semana (*m*)	*feen deh seh-'mah-nah*
What day is it?	¿Qué día es hoy?	*keh 'dee-ah ehs oy*
workday	día laborable	*'dee-ah lah-boh-'rah-bleh*
	día de trabajo	*'dee-ah deh trah-'bah-hoh*

b. MONTHS OF THE YEAR

month of the year	mes (*m*) del año	*mehs dehl 'ah-nyoh*
• January	enero	*eh-'neh-roh*
• February	febrero	*feh-'breh-roh*
• March	marzo	*'mahr-soh*
• April	abril	*ah-'breel*
• May	mayo	*'mah-yoh*
• June	junio	*'hoo-nee·oh*
• July	julio	*'hoo-lee·oh*
• August	agosto	*ah-'gohs-toh*
• September	septiembre (*m*)	*sehp-tee·'ehm-breh*
• October	octubre (*m*)	*ohk-'too-breh*
• November	noviembre (*m*)	*noh-bee·'ehm-breh*
• December	diciembre (*m*)	*dee-see·'ehm-breh*

calendar	calendario	*kah-lehn-'dah-ree·oh*
leap year	año bisiesto	*'ah-nyoh bee-see-'ehs-toh*
monthly	mensual (*adj*)	*mehn-'swahl*
	mensualmente (*adv*)	*mehn-swahl-'mehn-teh*
school year	año escolar	*ah-'nyoh ehs-koh-'lahr*
What month is it?	¿En qué mes estamos?	*ehn keh mehs ehs-'tah-mohs*

c. SEASONS

season	estación (*f*)	*eh-stah-see-'ohn*
• spring	primavera	*pree-mah-'beh-rah*
• summer	verano	*beh-'rah-noh*
• fall	otoño	*oh-'toh-nyoh*
• winter	invierno	*een-vee-'ehr-noh*
equinox	equinoccio	*eh-kee-'nohk-see·oh*
moon	luna	*'loo-nah*
solstice	solsticio	*sohl-'stee-see·oh*
sun	sol (*m*)	*sohl*

FOCUS: The Seasons

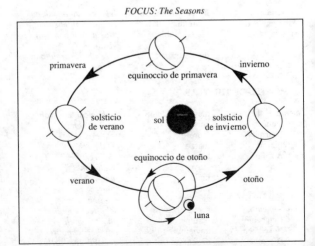

d. THE ZODIAC

> For the planets see Section 13.

horoscope	horóscopo	*oh-'rohs-koh-poh*
zodiac	Zodíaco (Zodiaco)	*soh-'dee-ah-koh (soh-dee-'ah-koh)*
signs of the zodiac	signos del Zodíaco	*'seeg-nohs dehl soh-'dee-ah-koh*
• Aries	Aries	*'ah-ree·ehs*
• Taurus	Tauro	*'tow-roh*
• Gemini	Géminis	*'heh-mee-nees*
• Cancer	Cáncer	*'kahn-sehr*
• Leo	Leo	*'leh-oh*
• Virgo	Virgo	*'veer-goh*
• Libra	Libra	*'lee-brah*
• Scorpio	Escorpión	*ehs-kohr-pee 'ohn*
• Sagittarius	Sagitario	*sah-hee-'tah-ree·oh*
• Capricorn	Capricornio	*kah-pree-'kohr-nee·oh*
• Aquarius	Acuario	*ah-'kwah-ree·oh*
• Pisces	Piscis	*'pees-sees*

e. EXPRESSING THE DATE

What's today's date?	¿Cuál es la fecha de hoy?	*'kwahl ehs lah 'feh-chah deh oy*
• October first	el primero de octubre	*ehl pree-'meh-roh deh ohk-'too-breh*
• February second	el dos de febrero	*ehl dohs deh feh-'breh-roh*
• June 3	el tres de junio	*ehl trehs deh 'hoo-nee·oh*
When were you born?	¿Cuándo nació Ud.? (*pol*)	*'kwahn-doh nah-see-'oh oos-'tehd*
	¿Cuándo naciste? (*fam*)	*kwahn-doh nah-'sees-teh*
I was born in 1972.	Nací en 1972.	*nah-'see ehn meel noh-beh-see-'ehn-tohs seh-'tehn-tah ee dohs*

f. IMPORTANT DATES

the New Year	el Año Nuevo	*ehl 'ah-nyoh 'nweh-boh*
New Year's Day	el Día de Año Nuevo	*ehl 'dee-ah deh 'ah-nyoh 'nweh-boh*

New Year's Eve	la Nochevieja	*lah noh-cheh-bee·'eh-hah*
	Víspera del Año Nuevo	*'bees-peh-rah dehl 'ah-nyoh 'nweh-boh*
Easter	Pascua Florida	*'pahs-kwah floh-'ree-dah*
Christmas	Navidad (*f*)	*nah-bee-'dahd*
Christmas Eve	la Nochebuena	*lah 'noh-cheh 'bweh-nah*

6. TALKING ABOUT THE WEATHER

a. GENERAL WEATHER VOCABULARY

air	aire (*m*)	*'ah·ee-reh*
atmosphere	atmósfera	*aht-'mohs-feh-rah*
• **atmospheric conditions**	condiciones atmosféricas	*kohn-dee-see·'oh-nehs aht-mohs-'feh-ree-kahs*
climate	clima (*m*)	*'klee-mah*
• **continental**	continental (*adj*)	*kohn-tee-'nehn-tahl*
• **dry**	seco (*adj*)	*'seh-koh*
• **humid**	húmedo (*adj*)	*'oo-meh-doh*
• **Mediterranean**	mediterráneo (*adj*)	*meh-dee-teh-'rrah-neh-oh*
• **tropical**	tropical (*adj*)	*troh-pee-'kahl*
cloud	nube (*f*)	*'noo-beh*
• **cloudy**	nublado (*adj*)	*noo-'blah-doh*

> **to be daydreaming** = estar en las nubes

---

cold	frío (*adj, n*)	*'free·oh*
cool	fresco (*adj*)	*'frehs-koh*
dark	oscuro (*adj*)	*ohs-'koo-roh*
• **It's getting dark.**	Anochece.	*ah-noh-'cheh-seh*
drop (*e.g., of rain*)	gota	*'goh-tah*
dry	seco (*adj*)	*'seh-koh*
fog	neblina	*neh-'blee-nah*
• **foggy**	brumoso (*adj*)	*broo-'moh-soh*
freeze	helarse*	*eh-'lahr-seh*
	congelarse (*v*)	*kohn-heh-'lahr-seh*
• **frozen**	helado (*pp*)	*eh-'lah-doh*
hail	granizo	*grah-'nee-soh*
• **hail**	granizar (*v*)	*grah-nee-'sahr*
humid, damp	húmedo	*'oo-meh-doh*

• to be humid	ser* (estar*) húmedo	*sehr (ehs-'tahr) 'oo-meh-doh*
• humidity	humedad (f)	*oo-meh-'dahd*
hurricane	huracán (m)	*ooh-rah-'kahn*
ice	hielo	*ee·'eh-loh*
light	luz (f)	*loos*
lightning	relámpago	*reh-'lahm-pah-goh*
• lightning	relampaguear (v)	*reh-lahm-pah-geh-'ahr*
mild	templado (adj)	*tehm-'plah-doh*
• be mild	ser* (estar*) templado	*sehr (ehs-'tahr) tehm-'plah-doh*
moon	luna	*'loo-nah*
• full moon	luna llena	*'loo-nah 'yeh-nah*
• half moon	luna media	*'loo-nah 'meh-dee·ah*
• new moon	luna nueva	*'loo-nah 'nweh-bah*
mugginess	bochorno (m)	*boh-'chohr-noh*
• muggy	bochornoso (adj)	*boh-chohr-'noh-soh*
• be muggy	ser* (estar*) bochornoso	*sehr (ehs-'tahr) boh-chohr-'noh-soh*
rain	lluvia	*'yoo-bee·ah*
• rain	llover (v)	*yoh-'behr*
• It's rainy.	Está lluvioso.	*ehs-'tah yoo-bee·'oh-soh*
rainbow	arco iris (m)	*'ahr-koh 'ee-rees*
sea	mar (m/f)	*mahr*
shadow, shade	sombra	*'sohm-brah*
sky	cielo	*see·'eh-loh*
snow	nieve (f)	*nee·'eh-beh*
• snow	nevar*	*neh-'bahr*
storm	tormenta	*tohr-'mehn-tah*
	tempestad (f)	*tehm-pehs-'tahd*
sun	sol (m)	*sohl*
thunder	trueno	*'trweh-noh*
• thunder	tronar*	*troh-'nahr*

---

to quarrel with = tronar con

---

tornado	tornado	*tohr-'nah-doh*
weather	tiempo	*tee·'ehm-poh*
wind	viento	*bee·'ehn-toh*

b. REACTING TO THE WEATHER

How's the weather?	¿Qué tiempo hace?	*keh tee·'ehm-poh 'ah-seh*

• It's a bit cold.	Hace un poco de frío.	'ah-seh oon 'poh-koh deh 'free-oh
• It's terrible.	Hace mal tiempo.	'ah-seh mahl tee·'ehm-poh
• It's beautiful.	Hace muy buen tiempo.	'ah-seh mwee bwehn tee·'ehm-poh
• It's cloudy.	Está nublado.	eh-'stah noo-'blah-doh
• It's cold.	Hace frío.	'ah-seh 'free·oh
• It's cool.	Hace fresco.	'ah-seh 'frehs-koh
• It's hot.	Hace calor.	'ah-seh kah-'lohr
• It's humid.	Es (Está) húmedo.	ehs (ehs-'tah) 'oo-meh-doh
• It's mild.	Es (Está) templado.	ehs (ehs-'tah) tehm-'plah-doh
• It's muggy.	Es (Está) bochornoso.	ehs (ehs-'tah) boh-chohr-'noh-soh
• It's pleasant.	Es (Está) agradable.	ehs (ehs-'tah) ah-grah-'dah-bleh
• It's raining.	Está lloviendo.	ehs-'tah yoh-bee·'ehn-doh
• It's snowing.	Está nevando.	ehs-'tah neh-'bahn-doh
• It's sunny.	Hace sol.	'ah-seh sohl
• It's thundering.	Truena	'trweh-nah
• It's very cold.	Hace mucho frío.	'ah-seh 'moo-choh 'free·oh
• It's very hot.	Hace mucho calor.	'ah-seh 'moo-choh kah-'lohr
• It's windy.	Hace viento.	'ah-seh bee·'ehn-toh
• It's lightning.	Relampaguea.	reh-lahm-pah-'geh-ah
be cold	tener* frío	teh-'nehr 'free·oh
• I can't stand the cold.	No puedo soportar el frío.	noh 'pweh-doh soh-pohr-'tahr ehl 'free·oh
• I love the cold.	Me encanta el frío.	meh ehn-'kahn-tah ehl 'free·oh
be hot	tener* calor	teh-'nehr kah-'lohr
• I can't stand the heat.	No puedo soportar el calor.	noh 'pweh-doh soh-pohr-'tahr ehl kah-'lohr
• I love the heat.	Me encanta el calor.	meh ehn-'kahn-tah ehl kah-'lohr
catch a chill	enfriarse*	ehn-free·'ahr-seh
perspire	sudar (v)	soo-'dahr
warm up	calentarse*	kah-lehn-'tahr-seh

c. WEATHER-MEASURING INSTRUMENTS AND ACTIVITIES

barometer	barómetro	bah-'roh-meh-troh
• barometric pressure	presión barométrica (f)	preh-see·'ohn bah-roh-'meh-tree-kah

Celsius	Celsio	*'sehl-see·oh*
Fahrenheit	Fahrenheit	*fah-rehn-'heh·eet'*
mercury	mercurio	*mehr-'koo-ree·oh*
temperature	temperatura	*tehm-peh-rah-'too-rah*
• high (*temp*)	alta	*'ahl-tah*
• low	baja	*'bah-hah*
• maximum	máxima	*'mahk-see-mah*
• minimum	mínima	*'mee-nee-mah*
thermometer	termómetro	*tehr-'moh-meh-troh*
• boiling point	punto de ebullición	*'poon-toh deh eh-boo-yee-see·'ohn*
• melting point	punto de fusión	*'poon-toh deh foo-see·'ohn*
thermostat	termostato	*tehr-mohs-'tah-to*
weather forecast	pronóstico del tiempo	*proh-'nohs-tee-koh dehl tee·'ehm-poh*
weather report	boletín meteorológico	*boh-leh-'teen meh-teh·oh-oh-roh-'loh-hee-koh*
zero	cero	*'seh-roh*
• below zero	bajo cero	*'bah-hoh 'seh-roh*

7. COLORS

a. BASIC COLORS

What color is it?	¿De qué color es?	*deh keh koh-'lohr ehs*
• black	negro	*'neh-groh*
• blue	azul	*ah-'sool*
• dark blue	azul oscuro	*ah-'sool ohs-'koo-roh*
• navy blue	azul marino	*ah-'sool mah-'ree-noh*
• light blue	azul claro	*ah-'sool 'klah-roh*
• brown	marrón	*mah-'rrohn*
• gold	dorado	*doh-'rah-doh*
• gray	gris	*grees*
• green	verde	*'behr-deh*
• orange	anaranjado	*ah-nah-rahn-'hah-doh*
• pink	rosado	*roh-'sah-doh*
• purple	morado	*moh-'rah-doh*
• red	rojo	*'roh-hoh*
• silver	plateado	*plah-teh-'ah-doh*
• white	blanco	*'blahn-koh*
• yellow	amarillo	*ah-mah-'ree-yoh*

to blush	=	ponerse* rojo
to get as red as a beet	=	ponerse* de mil colores
to be very pessimistic	=	verlo todo negro

b. DESCRIBING COLORS

bright	vivo (*adj*)	*'bee-boh*
dark	oscuro (*adj*)	*ohs-'koo-roh*
dull	apagado (*adj*)	*ah-pah-'gah-doh*
light	claro (*adj*)	*'klah-roh*
lively	vivo (*adj*)	*'bee-boh*
opaque	opaco (*adj*)	*oh-'pah-koh*
pure	puro (*adj*)	*'poo-roh*
transparent	transparente (*adj*)	*trahns-pah-'rehn-teh*
vibrant	vibrante (*adj*)	*bee-'brahn-teh*

c. ADDITIONAL VOCABULARY: COLORS

color	color (*m*)	*koh-'lohr*
• color	colorear (*v*)	*koh-loh-reh-'ahr*
• colored	coloreado (*pp*)	*koh-loh-reh-'ah-doh*
• coloring	coloración (*f*)	*koh-loh-rah-see-'ohn*
• food coloring	coloración para comida (*f*)	*koh-loh-rah-see-'ohn 'pah-rah koh-'mee-dah*
crayon	creyón (*m*)	*kreh-'yohn*
• coloring book	libro para colorear	*'lee-broh 'pah-rah koh-loh-reh-'ahr*
painter	pintor (a)	*peen-'tohr (rah)*
• paint	pintar (*v*)	*peen-'tahr*
• paint	pintura (*f*)	*peen-'too-rah*
• canvas	lienzo	*lee-'ehn-soh*
pen	pluma	*'ploo-mah*
• felt pen	rotulador (*m*)	*roh-too-lah-'dohr*
tint (*hair dye*)	tinte (*m*)	*'teen-teh*
• tint	teñir*	*teh-'nyeer*

8. BASIC GRAMMAR

a. GRAMMATICAL TERMS

adjective	adjetivo	*ahd-heh-'tee-boh*
• demonstrative	demostrativo	*deh-mohs-trah-'tee-boh*
• descriptive	descriptivo	*dehs-kreep-'tee-boh*
• indefinite	indefinido	*een-deh-feh-'nee-doh*
• interrogative	interrogativo	*een-teh-rroh-gah-'tee-boh*
• possessive	posesivo	*poh-seh-'see-boh*
adverb	adverbio	*ahd-'behr-bee·oh*
alphabet	alfabeto	*ahl-fah-'beh-toh*

• accent	acento	*ah-'sehn-toh*
• consonant	consonante	*kohn-soh-'nahn-teh*
• letter	letra	*'leh-trah*
• phonetics	fonética	*foh-'neh-tee-kah*
• pronunciation	pronunciación (*f*)	*proh-noon-see·ah-see·'ohn*
• vowel	vocal (*f*)	*boh-'kahl*
article	artículo	*ahr-'tee-koo-loh*
• definite	definido	*deh-fee-'nee-doh*
• indefinite	indefinido (*adj*)	*een-deh-fee-'nee-doh*
clause	cláusula	*'clow-soo-lah*
• main	principal (*adj*)	*preen-see-'pahl*
• relative	relativo (*adj*)	*reh-lah-'tee-boh*
• subordinate	subordinado (*adj*)	*soo-bohr-dee-'nah-doh*
comparison	comparación (*f*)	*kohm-pah-rah-see·'ohn*
conjugation	conjugación (*f*)	*kohn-hoo-gah-see·'ohn*
conjunction	conjunción (*f*)	*kohn-hoon-see·'ohn*
discourse	discurso	*dees-'koor-soh*
• direct	directo (*adj*)	*dee-'rehk-toh*
• indirect	indirecto (*adj*)	*een-dee-'rehk-toh*
gender	género	*'heh-neh-roh*
• feminine	femenino	*feh-meh-'nee-noh*
• masculine	masculino	*mahs-koo-'lee-noh*
grammar	gramática	*grah-'mah-tee-kah*
interrogative	interrogativo (*adj*)	*een-teh-rroh-gah-'tee-boh*
mood	modo	*'moh-doh*
• imperative	imperativo	*eem-peh-rah-'tee-boh*
• indicative	indicativo	*een-dee-kah-'tee-boh*
• subjunctive	subjuntivo	*soob-hoon-'tee-boh*
noun	sustantivo	*soos-tahn-'tee-boh*
number	número	*'noo-meh-roh*
• plural	plural (*adj*)	*ploo-'rahl*
• singular	singular (*adj*)	*seen-goo-'lahr*
object	complemento	*kohm-pleh-'mehn-toh*
• direct	directo (*adj*)	*dee-'rehk-toh*
• indirect	indirecto (*adj*)	*een-dee-'rehk-toh*
participle	participio	*pahr-tee-'see-pee·oh*
• past	pasado (*adj*)	*pah-'sah-doh*
• present	presente (*adj*)	*preh-'sehn-teh*
person	persona	*pehr-'soh-nah*
• first	primera (*adj*)	*pree-'meh-rah*
• second	segunda (*adj*)	*seh-'goon-dah*
• third	tercera (*adj*)	*tehr-'seh-rah*
predicate	predicado	*preh-dee-'kah-doh*
pronoun	pronombre (*m*)	*proh-'nohm-breh*
• demonstrative	demostrativo (*adj*)	*deh-mohs-trah-'tee-boh*

• interrogative	interrogativo (*adj*)	*een-teh-rroh-gah-'tee-boh*
• object	complemento	*kohm-pleh-'mehn-toh*
• personal	personal (*adj*)	*pehr-soh-'nahl*
• possessive	posesivo (*adj*)	*poh-seh-'see-boh*
• reflexive	reflexivo (*adj*)	*reh-fleh-'ksee-boh*
• relative	relativo (*adj*)	*reh-lah-'tee-boh*
• subject	sujeto (*adj*)	*soo-'heh-toh*
sentence	frase (*f*)	*'frah-seh*
	oración (*f*)	*oh-rah-see-'ohn*
• active voice	voz activa (*f*)	*bohs ahk-'tee-bah*
• declarative	enunciativo (*adj*)	*eh-noon-see-ah-'tee-boh*
• interrogative	interrogativo (*adj*)	*een-teh-rroh-gah-'tee-boh*
• passive voice	voz pasiva (*f*)	*bohs pah-'see-bah*
spelling	deletreo	*deh-leh-'treh-oh*
subject	sujeto	*soo-'heh-toh*
tense	tiempo	*tee-'ehm-poh*
• conditional	condicional	*kohn-dee-see-oh-'nahl*
• future	futuro	*foo-'too-roh*
• imperfect	imperfecto	*eem-pehr-'fehk-toh*
• pluperfect	pluscuamperfecto	*ploos-kwahm-pehr-'fehk-toh*
• present	presente	*preh-'sehn-teh*
• present perfect	presente perfecto	*preh-'sehn-teh pehr-'fehk-toh*
• preterite	pretérito	*preh-'teh-ree-toh*
verb	verbo	*'behr-boh*
• conjugation	conjugación (*f*)	*kohn-hoo-gah-see-'ohn*
• ending	terminación (*f*)	*tehr-mee-nah-see-'ohn*
• gerund	gerundio	*heh-'roon-dee-oh*
• infinitive	infinitivo	*een-fee-nee-'tee-boh*
• intransitive	intransitivo	*een-trahn-see-'tee-boh*
• irregular	irregular	*ee-rreh-goo-'lahr*
• reflexive	reflexivo	*reh-fleh-'ksee-boh*
• regular	regular	*reh-goo-'lahr*
• transitive	transitivo	*trahn-see-'tee-boh*

b. DEFINITE ARTICLES

the	el (*m, s*)	*ehl*
	la (*f, s*)	*lah*
	los (*m, pl*)	*lohs*
	las (*f, pl*)	*lahs*

	SINGULAR	PLURAL
Masculine	el	los
Feminine	la	las

c. INDEFINITE ARTICLES

a, an	un (*m, s*)	*oon*
	una (*f, s*)	*'oo-nah*

	SINGULAR	PLURAL
Masculine	un	unos
Feminine	una	unas

d. DEMONSTRATIVE ADJECTIVES

this	este (*m, s*)	*'ehs-teh*
	esta (*f, s*)	*'ehs-tah*
that (*nearby*)	ese (*m, s*)	*'eh-seh*
	esa (*f, s*)	*'eh-sah*
that (*farther away*)	aquel (*m, s*)	*ah-'kehl*
	aquella (*f, s*)	*ah-'keh-yah*
these	estos (*m, pl*)	*'ehs-tohs*
	estas (*f, pl*)	*'ehs-tahs*
those (*nearby*)	esos (*m, pl*)	*'eh-sohs*
	esas (*f, pl*)	*'eh-sahs*
those (*farther away*)	aquellos (*m, pl*)	*ah-'keh-yohs*
	aquellas (*f, pl*)	*ah-'keh-yahs*

e. POSSESSIVE ADJECTIVES

my	mi (*m/f, s*)	*mee*
	mis (*m/f, pl*)	*mees*
your	tu (*m/f, s, fam*)	*too*
	tus (*m/f, pl*)	*toos*

your	su (*m/f, s pol*)	*soo*
	sus (*m/f, pl*)	*soos*
his, her, their	su (*m/f, s*)	*soo*
	sus (*m/f, pl*)	*soos*
our	nuestro (*m, s*)	*'nwehs-troh*
	nuestra (*f, s*)	*'nwehs-trah*
	nuestros (*m, pl*)	*'nwehs-trohs*
	nuestras (*f, pl*)	*'nwehs-trahs*

Adjective	Pronoun	
mi	el mío/la mía	
tu	el tuyo/la tuya	
su	el suyo/la suya	singular
nuestro/nuestra	el nuestro/la nuestra	
vuestro/vuestra	el vuestro/la vuestra	
mis	los míos/las mías	
tus	los tuyos/las tuyas	
sus	los suyos/las suyas	
nuestros/ nuestras	los nuestros/las nuestras	plural
vuestros/ vuestras	los vuestros/las vuestras	

Este es **mi** dibujo. ¿Cuál es el **tuyo**? = This is **my** drawing. Which one is **yours**?

f. POSSESSIVE PRONOUNS

mine	mío (*m, s*), mía (*f, s*)	*'mee-oh, 'mee-ah*
	míos, (*m, pl*), mías (*f, pl*)	*'mee-ohs, 'mee-ahs*
yours	tuyo (*m, s, fam*), tuya (*f, s, fam*)	*'too-yoh, 'too-yah*
	tuyos (*m, pl, fam*), tuyas (*f, pl, fam*)	*'too-yohs, 'too-yahs*
yours	suyo (*m, s, pol*), suya (*f, s, pol*)	*'soo-yoh, 'soo-yah*
	suyos (*m, s, pol*), suyas (*f, s, pol*)	*'soo-yohs, 'soo-yahs*
yours	vuestro (*m, s, fam*), vuestra (*f, s, fam*)	*'vwehs-troh, 'vwehs-trah*
	vuestros (*m, pl, fam*), vuestras (*f, pl, fam*)	*'vwehs-trohs, 'vwehs-trahs*

ours	nuestro (m, s),	noo·'ehs-troh, noo·'ehs-
	nuestra (f, s)	trah
	nuestros (m, pl),	noo·'ehs-trohs,
	nuestras (f, pl)	noo·'ehs-tras

g. PREPOSITIONS

among	entre	'ehn-treh
at	en, a	ehn, ah
besides	además de	ah-deh-'mahs deh
between	entre	'ehn-treh
for	por, para	pohr, 'pah-rah
from	de	deh
in	en	ehn
of	de	deh
on	en, sobre	ehn, 'soh-breh
	encima de	ehn-'see-mah deh
to	a	ah
with	con	kohn

h. SUBJECT PRONOUNS

I	yo	yoh
you	tú (s, fam)	too
you	usted (s, pol)	oos-'tehd
he	él	ehl
she	ella	'eh-yah
we	nosotros (m)	noh-'soh-trohs
	nosotras (f)	noh-'soh-trahs
you	vosotros (m, pl, fam)	boh-'soh-trohs
	vosotras (f, pl, fam)	boh-'soh-trahs
you	ustedes (pl, pol)	oos-'teh-dehs
they	ellos (m)	'eh-yohs
	ellas (f)	'eh-yahs

i. DIRECT OBJECT PRONOUNS

me	me	meh
you	te (s, fam)	teh
you	lo (m, pol)	loh
	la (f, pol)	lah
him	lo, le	loh, leh
her	la	lah

it	lo *(m, s)*	*loh*
	la *(f, s)*	*lah*
us	nos	*nohs*
you	os *(pl, fam)*	*ohs*
you	los *(m, pol)*	*lohs*
	las *(f, pol)*	*lahs*
them	los *(m, pl)*	*lohs*
	las *(f, pl)*	*lahs*

j. INDIRECT OBJECT PRONOUNS

to me	me	*meh*
to you	te *(s, fam)*	*teh*
to you	le *(s, pol)*	*leh*
to him	le	*leh*
to her	le	*leh*
to us	nos	*nohs*
to you	os *(pl, fam)*	*ohs*
to you	les *(pl, pol)*	*lehs*
to them	les	*lehs*

k. REFLEXIVE PRONOUNS

myself	me	*meh*
yourself	te *(s, fam)*	*teh*
yourself	se *(s, pol)*	*seh*
himself	se	*seh*
herself	se	*seh*
ourselves	nos	*nohs*
yourselves	os *(pl, fam)*	*ohs*
yourselves	se *(pl, pol)*	*seh*
themselves	se	*seh*

Adjective		Pronoun
cuyo (s), cuya (s)	= WHOSE =	de quién (es)

*Ése el cantante **cuya** música es muy popular hoy día.* = This is the singer whose music is very popular nowadays.

*Van Gogh es el artista **cuyas** pinturas tienen colores vibrantes.* = Van Gogh is the artist whose paintings have vibrant colors.

*Esta pluma azul, ¿**de quién es**?* = This blue pen, whose is it? *¿De quiénes son todos esos libros?* = Whose are all those books?

l. RELATIVE ADJECTIVE

whose	cuyo (*m, s*), cuya (*f, s*)	*'koo-yoh, 'koo-yah*
	cuyos (*m, pl*), cuyas (*f, pl*)	*'koo-yohs, 'koo-yahs*

m. RELATIVE PRONOUNS

that, which, who	que	*keh*
he, she, who	quien	*kee·'ehn*
whose	de quién	*deh kee·'ehn*
	de quiénes	*deh kee·'ehn-ehs*

n. OTHER PRONOUNS

everyone	todos	*'toh-dohs*
	todo el mundo	*'toh-doh ehl 'moon-doh*
everything	todo	*'toh-doh*
many	muchos (*m*)	*'moo-chohs*
	muchas (*f*)	*'moo-chahs*
no one	nadie	*'nah-dee·eh*
others	otros	*'oh-trohs*
some (*people*)	algunos (*m*)	*ahl-'goo-nohs*
	algunas (*f*)	*ahl-'goo-nahs*
someone	alguien	*'ahl-gee·ehn*
something	algo	*'ahl-goh*

> **some is better than none** = algo es algo

o. CONJUNCTIONS

after	después (de) que	*dehs-poo·'ehs (deh) keh*
although	aunque	*ah·'oon-keh*
and	y (e)	*ee, (eh)*
as	como	*'koh-moh*
as if	como si	*'koh-moh see*
because	porque	*'pohr-keh*
before	antes (de) que	*'ahn-tehs (deh) keh*
but	pero (sino que)	*'peh-roh ('see-noh keh)*
even though	aunque	*'ah·oon-keh*
if, whether	si	*see*

in case	en caso (de) que	*ehn 'ka-soh (deh) keh*
in order that, so that	para que	*'pah-rah keh*
	de modo que	*deh 'moh-doh keh*
provided that	con tal (de) que	*kohn tahl (deh) keh*
since	desde que	*'dehs-deh keh*
	puesto que	*poo·'ehs-toh keh*
unless	a menos que	*ah 'meh-nohs keh*
until	hasta que	*'ahs-tah keh*
while	mientras	*mee·'ehn-trahs*
without	sin	*seen*

9. REQUESTING INFORMATION

answer	respuesta	*rehs-'pwehs-tah*
• answer	responder (*v*)	*rehs-pohn-'dehr*
	contestar (*v*)	*kohn-tehs-'tahr*
ask	preguntar (*v*)	*preh-goon-'tahr*
• ask a question	hacer* una pregunta	*ah·'sehr 'oo-nah preh-'goon-tah*
Can you tell me . . . ?	¿Puede Ud. decirme . . . ?	*poo·'eh-deh oos-'tehd deh-'seer-meh*
How?	¿Cómo?	*'koh-moh*
How do you say . . . in Spanish?	¿Cómo se dice . . . en español?	*'koh-moh seh 'dee-seh ehn ehs-pah-nyohl*
How come . . . ?	¿Cómo es que . . . ?	*'koh-moh ehs keh*
How much?	¿Cuánto?	*'kwahn-toh*
I don't understand.	No comprendo.	*noh kohm-'prehn-doh*
	No entiendo.	*noh ehn-tee·'ehn-doh*
What?	¿Cómo?	*'koh-moh*
What does . . . mean?	¿Qué quiere decir . . . ?	*keh kee·'eh-reh deh-'seer*
When?	¿Cuándo?	*'kwahn-doh*
Where?	¿Dónde?	*'dohn-deh*
Which (one)?	¿Cuál?	*kwahl*
Who?	¿Quién? (*s*)	*kee·'ehn*
	¿Quiénes? (*pl*)	*kee·'ehn-ehs*
Why?	¿Por qué?	*pohr keh*

PEOPLE

10. FAMILY AND FRIENDS

a. FAMILY MEMBERS

aunt	tía	'tee-ah
brother	hermano	ehr-'mah-noh
• brother-in-law	cuñado	koo-'nyah-doh
cousin	primo(a)	'pree-moh (-mah)
dad	papá	pah-'pah
daughter	hija	'ee-hah
• daughter-in-law	nuera	'nweh-rah
	hija política	'ee-hah poh-'lee-tee-kah
family	familia	fah-'mee-lee-ah
father	padre	'pah-dreh
• father-in-law	suegro	'sweh-groh
grandchild	nieto(a)	nee-'eh-toh (-ah)
grandfather	abuelo	ah-'bweh-loh
grandmother	abuela	ah-'bweh-lah
great-aunt	tía abuela	'tee-ah ah-'bweh-lah
great grandchild	bisnieto(a)	bees-nee-'eh-toh (-tah)
great grandfather	bisabuelo	bees-ah-'bweh-loh
great grandmother	bisabuela	bees-ah-'bweh-lah
great-uncle	tío abuelo	'tee-oh ah-'bweh-loh
husband	marido	mah-'ree-doh
	esposo	ehs-'poh-soh
mom	mamá	mah-'mah
mother	madre	'mah-dreh
• mother-in-law	suegra	'sweh-grah
nephew	sobrino	soh-'bree-noh
niece	sobrina	soh-'bree-nah
parents	padres (m, pl)	'pah-drehs
relatives	parientes (m, pl)	pah-ree-'ehn-tehs
sister	hermana	ehr-'mah-nah
• sister-in-law	cuñada	koo-'nyah-dah
	hermana política	ehr-'mah-nah poh-'lee-tee-kah
son	hijo	'ee-hoh
• son-in-law	yerno	'yehr-noh
	hijo político	'ee-hoh poh-'lee-tee-koh
stepbrother	hermanastro	ehr-mah-'nahs-troh
stepdaughter	hijastra	ee-'hahs-trah
stepfather	padrastro	pah-'drahs-troh
stepmother	madrastra	mah-'drahs-trah

stepsister	hermanastra	*ehr-mah-'nahs-trah*
stepson	hijastro	*ee-'hahs-troh*
twin	gemelo(a)	*heh-'meh-loh (-lah)*
	mellizo(a)	*meh-'yee-soh (-sah)*
• twin brother	hermano gemelo	*ehr-'mah-noh heh-'meh-loh*
• twin sister	hermana gemela	*ehr-'mah-nah heh-'meh-lah*
uncle	tío	*'tee-oh*
wife	esposa	*ehs-'poh-sah*
	mujer (*f*)	*moo-'hehr*

b. FRIENDS

acquaintance	conocido(a)	*koh-noh-'see-doh (-dah)*
boyfriend	novio	*'noh-bee·oh*
	amigo	*ah-'mee-goh*
colleague	colega (*m/f*)	*koh-'leh-gah*
enemy	enemigo(a)	*eh-neh-'mee-goh (gah)*
fiancé	novio	*'noh-bee·oh*
fiancée	novia	*'noh-bee·ah*
friend	amigo(a)	*ah-'mee-goh (gah)*
• become friends	hacerse* amigos	*ah-'sehr-seh ah-'mee-gohs*
• between friends	entre amigos	*'ehn-treh ah-'mee-gohs*
• break off a friendship	romper una amistad	*rohm-'pehr 'oo-nah ah-mees-'tahd*
• close friends	amigos íntimos	*ah-'mee-gohs 'een-tee-mohs*
• family friend	amigo de familia	*ah-'mee-goh deh fah-'mee-lee·ah*
• friendship	amistad (*f*)	*ah-mees-'tahd*
girlfriend	novia	*'noh-bee·ah*
	amiga	*ah-'mee-gah*
lover	amante (*m/f*)	*ah-'mahn-teh*
• love affair	amorío	*ah-moh-'ree-oh*

11. DESCRIBING PEOPLE

a. GENDER AND APPEARANCE

attractive	atractivo (*adj*)	*ah-trahk-'tee-boh*
beautiful	hermoso (*adj*)	*ehr-'moh-soh*
• beauty	belleza	*beh-'yeh-sah*
big	grande (*adj*)	*'grahn-deh*

• **bigness**	grandeza	*grahn-'deh-sah*
• **make big**	engrandecer*	*ehn-grahn-deh-'sehr*
blond	rubio (*adj*)	*'roo-bee-oh*
body	cuerpo	*'kwehr-poh*
• **bodily physique**	físico	*'fee-see-koh*
boy	chico	*'chee-koh*
	muchacho	*moo-'chah-choh*
brunette	moreno (*adj*)	*moh-'reh-noh*
• **dark-haired**	de pelo oscuro	*deh 'peh-loh ohs-'koo-roh*
clean	limpio (*adj*)	*'leem-pee-oh*
curly	rizado (*adj*)	*ree-'sah-doh*
• **curly-haired**	de pelo rizado	*deh 'peh-loh ree-'sah-doh*
dirty	sucio (*adj*)	*'soo-see-oh*
elegant	elegante (*adj*)	*eh-leh-'gahn-teh*
• **elegance**	elegancia	*eh-leh-'gahn-see-ah*
• **elegantly**	elegantemente (*adv*)	*eh-leh-gahn-teh-'mehn-teh*
• **inelegant**	poco elegante (*adj*)	*'poh-koh eh-leh-'gahn-teh*
fat	gordo (*adj*)	*'gohr-doh*
• **become fat**	engordar (*v*)	*ehn-gohr-'dahr*
• **obesity**	obesidad (*f*)	*oh-beh-see-'dahd*
female (*sex*)	(sexo) femenino (*adj*)	*'seh-ksoh feh-meh-'nee-noh*
• **female** (*animals*)	hembra (*adj*)	*'ehm-brah*
• **a female voice**	una voz de mujer	*'oo-nah bohs deh moo-'hehr*
• **feminine**	femenino (*adj*)	*feh-meh-'nee-noh*
gentleman	caballero	*kah-bah-'yeh-roh*
	señor	*seh-'nyohr*
girl	chica	*'chee-kah*
	muchacha	*moo-'chah-chah*
handicapped	incapacitado (*adj*)	*een-kah-pah-see-'tah-doh*
health	salud (*f*)	*sah-'lood*
• **be in good health**	estar* bien de salud	*ehs-'tahr bee-'ehn deh sah-'lood*
• **healthy**	sano, saludable (*adj*)	*'sah-noh, sah-loo-'dah-bleh*
height	estatura	*ehs-tah-'too-rah*
• **How tall are you?**	¿Cuánto mide Ud.?	*'kwahn-toh 'mee-deh oos-'tehd*
• **I am . . . tall.**	Tengo . . . de alto.	*'tehn-goh deh 'ahl-toh*
• **of medium height**	de estatura mediana	*deh ehs-tah-'too-rah meh-dee-'ah-nah*

• short	bajo (*adj*)	*'bah-hoh*
• tall	alto (*adj*)	*'ahl-toh*
lady	señora	*seh-'nyoh-rah*
• young lady	señorita	*seh-nyoh-'ree-tah*
large	grande (*adj*)	*'grahn-deh*
male (*sex*)	(sexo) masculino	*'seh-ksoh mahs-koo-'lee-noh*
• male (*animals*)	macho (*n, adj*)	*'mah-choh*
• male (*person*)	varón (*n, adj*)	*bah-'rohn*
• virile	viril (*adj*)	*bee-'reel*
man	hombre (*m*)	*'ohm-breh*
• young man	joven	*'hoh-behn*
physical appearance	aspecto físico	*ah-'spehk-toh 'fee-see-koh*
red-haired	pelirrojo (*adj*)	*peh-lee-'roh-hoh*
sexy	atractivo (*adj*)	*ah-trahk-'tee-boh*
sick	enfermo (*adj*)	*ehn-'fehr-moh*
• sickness	enfermedad (*f*)	*ehn-fehr-meh-'dahd*
• become sick	enfermarse (*v*)	*ehn-fehr-'mahr-seh*
small, little	pequeño (*adj*)	*peh-'keh-nyoh*
strength	fuerza	*'fwehr-sah*
• strong	fuerte (*adj*)	*'fwehr-teh*
ugly	feo (*adj*)	*'feh-oh*
• ugliness	fealdad (*f*)	*feh-ahl-'dahd*
weak	débil (*adj*)	*'deh-beel*
• weakness	debilidad (*f*)	*deh-bee-lee-'dahd*
• become weak	debilitarse (*v*)	*deh-bee-lee-'tahr-seh*
weight	peso	*'peh-soh*
• heavy	pesado (*adj*)	*peh-'sah-doh*
• How much do you weigh?	¿Cuánto pesa Ud.?	*'kwahn-toh 'peh-sah oos-'tehd*
• I weigh . . .	Peso . . .	*'peh-soh*
• light	ligero (*adj*)	*lee-'heh-roh*
• skinny, thin	delgado (*adj*)	*dehl-'gah-doh*
	flaco (*adj*)	*'flah-koh*
• weigh oneself	pesarse (*v*)	*peh-'sahr-seh*
• pound	libra	*'lee-brah*
• kilo	kilo	*'kee-loh*
• become thin	adelgazar (*v*)	*ah-dehl-gah-'sahr*
• lose weight	perder* peso	*pehr-'dehr 'peh-soh*
• slim, slender	esbelto (*adj*)	*ehs-'behl-toh*
woman	mujer (*f*)	*moo-'hehr*

b. CONCEPTS OF AGE

adolescence	juventud (*f*)	*hoo-behn-'tood*
• adolescent, teenager	joven (*m/f*)	*'hoh-behn*

adult	adulto	*ah-'dool-toh*
age	edad (f)	*eh-'dahd*
baby	bebé (m/f)	*beh-'beh*
boy	chico	*'chee-koh*
	muchacho	*moo-'chah-choh*
child	niño(a)	*'nee-nyoh (-nyah)*
• children	niños(as)	*'nee-nyohs (-nyahs)*
elderly person	viejo(a)	*bee·'eh-hoh (-hah)*
• elderly people	personas de mayor edad	*pehr-'soh-nahs deh mah-'yohr eh-'dahd*
• have white hair	tener* canas	*teh-'nehr 'kah-nahs*
girl	chica	*'chee-kah*
	muchacha	*moo-'chah-chah*
old	viejo (adj)	*bee·'eh-hoh*
• become old	envejecerse*	*ehn-beh-heh-'sehr-seh*
• older	mayor	*mah-'yohr*
• older brother	hermano mayor	*ehr-'mah-noh mah-'yohr*
• older sister	hermana mayor	*ehr-'mah-nah mah-'yohr*
• How old are you?	¿Cuántos años tiene Ud.?	*'kwahn-tohs 'ah-nyohs tee·'eh-neh oos-'tehd*
• I am . . . old.	Tengo . . . años.	*'tehn-goh 'ah-nyohs*
• two-year old	de dos años	*deh dohs 'ah-nyohs*
• twenty-year old	de veinte años	*deh 'beh·een-teh 'ah-nyohs*
young	joven (m/f)	*'hoh-behn*
• younger	menor	*meh-'nohr*
• younger brother	hermano menor	*ehr-'mah-noh meh-'nohr*
• younger sister	hermana menor	*ehr-'mah-nah meh-'nohr*
• youthful	joven (adj)	*'hoh-behn*

c. MARRIAGE AND THE HUMAN LIFE CYCLE

anniversary	aniversario	*ah-nee-behr-'sah-ree·oh*
• golden anniversary	aniversario de oro	*ah-nee-behr-'sah-ree·oh deh 'oh-roh*
• silver anniversary	aniversario de plata	*ah-nee-behr-'sah-ree·oh deh 'plah-tah*
bachelor	soltero(a)	*sohl-'teh-roh (-rah)*
birth	nacimiento	*nah-see-mee·'ehn-toh*
• be born	nacer*	*nah-'sehr*
• I was born on the (day) of (month).	Nací el . . . de . . .	*nah-'see ehl deh*
birthday	cumpleaños (m)	*koom-pleh-'ah-nyohs*
• celebrate one's birthday	celebrar el cumpleaños	*seh-leh-'brahr ehl koom-pleh-'ah-nyohs*

• **Happy Birthday!**	¡Feliz cumpleaños!	*feh-'lees koom-pleh-'ah-nyohs*
bride	novia	*'noh-bee·ah*
death	muerte (*f*)	*'mwehr-teh*
• **die**	morir*	*moh-'reer*
divorce	divorciarse (*v*)	*dee-bohr-see·'ahr-seh*
• **divorce**	divorcio (*m*)	*dee-'bohr-see·oh*
• **divorced**	divorciado (*adj*)	*dee-bohr-see·'ah-doh*
engaged	prometido	*proh-meh-'tee-doh*
	comprometido	*kohm-proh-meh-'tee-doh*
• **become engaged**	prometerse (*v*)	*proh-meh-'tehr-seh*
	comprometerse	*kohm-proh-meh-'tehr-seh*
• **engagement**	noviazgo	*noh-bee·'ahs-goh*
• **engagement ring**	anillo de compromiso	*ah-'nee-yoh deh kohm-proh-'mee-soh*
fiancé	novio	*'noh-bee·oh*
fiancée	novia	*'noh-bee·ah*
get used to	acostumbrarse (*v*)	*ah-kohs-toom-'brahr-seh*
gift	regalo	*reh-'gah-loh*
• **give a gift**	regalar (*v*)	*reh-gah-'lahr*
go to school	asistir (*v*) a la escuela	*ah-sees-'teer ah lah ehs-'kweh-lah*
groom	novio	*'noh-bee·oh*
heredity	herencia	*eh-'rehn-see·ah*
• **inherit**	heredar (*v*)	*eh-reh-'dahr*
honeymoon	luna de miel	*'loo-nah deh mee·'ehl*
	viaje de novios	*bee·'ah-heh deh 'noh-bee·ohs*
husband	marido	*mah-'ree-doh*
kiss	besar (*v*)	*beh-'sahr*
• **kiss**	beso	*'beh-soh*
life	vida	*'bee-dah*
• **live**	vivir (*v*)	*bee-'beer*
love	querer*	*keh-'rehr*
	amar (*v*)	*ah-'mahr*
• **love**	amor (*m*)	*ah-'mohr*
• **fall in love**	enamorarse (*v*)	*eh-nah-moh-'rahr-seh*
• **in love**	enamorado (*adj*)	*eh-nah-moh-'rah-doh*
marriage, matrimony	matrimonio	*mah-tree-'moh-nee·oh*
• **get married**	casarse (*v*)	*kah-'sahr-seh*
• **marriage ceremony**	boda	*'boh-dah*
• **married**	casado (*adj*)	*kah-'sah-doh*
• **married couple**	matrimonio	*mah-tree-'moh-nee·oh*
• **marry (someone)**	casar (*v*)	*kah-'sahr*
• **unmarried**	soltero(a)	*sohl-'teh-roh (-rah)*
marital status	estado civil	*ehs-'tah-doh see-'beel*

pregnancy	embarazo	*ehm-bah-'rah-soh*
• **be pregnant**	estar* embarazada	*ehs-'tahr ehm-bah'rah- 'sah-dah*
• **give birth**	dar* a luz	*dahr ah loos*
• **have a baby**	tener* un niño	*teh-'nehr oon 'nee-nyoh*
raise (*someone*)	criar (*v*)	*kree-'ahr*
reception	recepción (*f*)	*reh-sehp-see-'ohn*
separation	separación (*f*) matrimonial	*seh-pah-rah-see-'ohn mah-tree-moh-nee-'ahl*
• **separate**	separarse (*v*)	*seh-pah-'rahr-seh*
• **separated**	separado (*adj*)	*seh-pah-'rah-doh*
spouse	esposo	*ehs-'poh-soh*
	esposa	*ehs-'poh-sah*
wedding	boda	*'boh-dah*
• **wedding dress**	traje de novia (*m*)	*'trah-heh deh 'noh-bee·ah*
• **wedding invitation**	invitación (*f*) de boda	*een-bee-tah-see-'ohn deh 'boh-dah*
• **wedding ring**	anillo de boda	*ah-'nee-yoh deh 'boh-dah*
widow	viuda	*bee-'oo-dah*
widower	viudo	*bee-'oo-doh*
wife	esposa	*ehs-'poh-sah*
	mujer	*moo-'hehr*

d. RELIGION AND RACE

> For nationalities, see Section 30.

agnostic	agnóstico	*ahg-'nohs-tee-koh*
atheism	ateísmo	*ah-teh·'ees-moh*
• **atheist**	ateísta (*m/f*)	*ah-teh-'ees-tah*
baptism	bautismo	*bow-'tees-moh*
• **baptized**	bautizado	*bow-tee-'sah-doh*
Baptist	bautista (*m/f*)	*bow-'tees-tah*
belief	creencia	*kreh-'ehn-see·ah*
• **believe**	creer (*v*)	*kreh-'ehr*
• **believer**	creyente (*m/f*)	*kreh-'yehn-teh*
Buddhism	budismo	*boo-'dees-moh*
• **Buddhist**	budista (*m/f*)	*boo-'dees-tah*
catechism	catecismo	*kah-teh-'sees-moh*
Catholic	católico	*kah-'toh-lee-koh*
• **Catholicism**	catolicismo	*kah-toh-lee-'sees-moh*

Christian	cristiano	*krees-tee·'ah-noh*
• **Christianity**	cristianismo	*krees-tee·ah-'nees-moh*
church	iglesia	*ee-'gleh-see·ah*
confirmation	confirmación (f)	*kohn-feer-mah-see·'ohn*
faith	fé (f)	*feh*
• **faithful**	fiel (adj)	*fee-'ehl*
God	Dios	*dee·'ohs*
Hindu	hindú (m/f)	*een·'dooh*
human	humano	*oo-'mah-noh*
• **human being**	ser humano	*sehr oo-'mah-noh*
• **humanity**	humanidad (f)	*oo-mah-nee·'dahd*
Islamic	islámico	*ees-'lah-mee-koh*
Jewish	judío	*hoo-'dee·oh*
• **Judaism**	judaísmo	*hoo-dah·'ees-moh*
lay person	laico	*'lah·ee-koh*
• **laity**	laicado	*lah·ee-'kah-doh*
Lutheran	luterano	*loo-teh-'rah-noh*
Mass	misa	*'mee-sah*
Methodist	metodista (m/f)	*meh-toh-'dees-tah*
minister	ministro	*mee-'nees-troh*
monk	monje (m)	*'mohn-heh*
mosque	mezquita	*mehs-'kee-tah*
Muslim	musulmán(a) (adj)	*moo-sool-'mahn (ah)*
myth	mito	*'mee-toh*
nun	monja	*'mohn-hah*
oriental	oriental (n, adj)	*oh-ree·ehn-'tahl*
pagan	pagano	*pah-'gah-noh*
people	gente (f)	*'hehn-teh*
person	persona	*pehr-'soh-nah*
pray	rezar (v)	*reh-'sahr*
	orar (v)	*oh-'rahr*
• **prayer**	oración (f)	*oh-rah-see·'ohn*
Presbyterian	presbiteriano	*prehs-bee-teh-ree·'ah-noh*
priest	cura (m)	*'koo-rah*
	sacerdote (m)	*sah-sehr-'doh-teh*
Protestantism	protestantismo	*proh-tehs-tahn-'tees-moh*
• **Protestant**	protestante	*proh-tehs-'tahn-teh*
rabbi	rabino	*rah-'bee-noh*
• **Rabbi**	rabí	*rah-'bee*
race	raza	*'rah-sah*
religion	religión (f)	*reh-lee-hee·'ohn*
• **religious**	religioso (adj)	*reh-lee-hee·'oh-soh*
rite	rito	*'ree-toh*
soul	alma (f)	*'ahl-mah*
spirit	espíritu (m)	*ehs-'pee-ree-too*
• **spiritual**	espiritual (adj)	*ehs-pee-ree-too·'ahl*

synagogue	sinagoga	*see-nah-'goh-gah*
temple	templo	*'tehm-ploh*
western	occidental (*adj*)	*ok-see-dehn-'tahl*

e. CHARACTERISTICS AND SOCIAL TRAITS

active	activo (*adj*)	*ahk-'tee-boh*
• activity	actividad (*f*)	*ahk-tee-bee-'dahd*
adapt	adaptar (*v*)	*ah-dahp-'tahr*
• adaptable	adaptable (*adj*)	*ah-dahp-'tah-bleh*
addict	adicto (*n*)	*ah-'deek-toh*
• addict (*oneself*)	enviciar(se) (*v*)	*ehn-bee-see-'ahr (-seh)*
affection	afecto	*ah-'fehk-toh*
	cariño (*adj*)	*kah-'ree-nyoh*
• affectionate	afectuoso (*adj*)	*ah-fehk-'twoh-soh*
	cariñoso (*adj*)	*kah-ree-'nyoh-soh*
aggressive	agresivo (*adj*)	*ah-greh-'see-boh*
• aggressiveness	agresividad (*f*)	*ah-greh-see-bee-'dahd*
altruism	altruismo	*ahl-'trwees-moh*
• altruistic, altruist	altruista (*m/f*)	*ahl-'trwees-tah*
ambition	ambición (*f*)	*ahm-bee-'see·ohn*
• ambitious	ambicioso (*adj*)	*ahm-bee-see·'oh-soh*
anger	ira	*'ee-rah*
	enojo	*eh-'noh-hoh*
• angry	enojado (*adj*)	*eh-noh-'hah-doh*
	enfadado (*adj*)	*ehn-fah-'dah-doh*
• become angry	enojarse (*v*)	*eh-noh-'hahr-seh*
	enfadarse (*v*)	*ehn-fah-'dahr-seh*
anxious	inquieto (*adj*)	*een-kee-'eh-toh*
• anxiousness	inquietud (*f*)	*een-kee·eh-'tood*
arrogant	arrogante (*adj*)	*ah-rroh-'gahn-teh*
artistic	artístico (*adj*)	*ahr-'tees-tee-koh*
astute	astuto (*adj*)	*ahs-'too-toh*
• astuteness	astucia	*ahs-'too-see·ah*
attractive	atractivo (*adj*)	*ah-trahk-'tee-boh*
avarice, greed	avaricia	*ah-bah-'ree-see·ah*
• avaricious	avaro (*adj*)	*ah-'bah-roh*
• greedy	avaricioso (*adj*)	*ah-bah-ree-see·'oh-soh*
bad, mean	malo (*adj*)	*'mah-loh*
• meanness	maldad (*f*)	*mahl-'dahd*
bold	audaz (*adj*)	*ow-'dahs*
brash	atrevido (*adj*)	*ah-treh-'bee-doh*
brilliant	brillante (*adj*)	*bree-'yahn-teh*
calm	tranquilo (*adj*)	*trahn-'kee-loh*
• calmness	tranquilidad (*f*)	*trahn-kee-lee-'dahd*

character	carácter (m)	kah-'rahk-tehr
• characteristic	característica	kah-rahk-teh-'rees-tee-kah
• characterize	caracterizar (v)	kah-rahk-teh-ree-'sahr
conformist	conformista (m/f)	kohn-fohr-'mees-tah
• nonconformist	disidente (m/f)	dee-see-'dehn-teh
conscience	conciencia	kohn-see-'ehn-see·ah
• conscientious	concienzudo (adj)	kohn-see-ehn-'soo-doh
conservative	conservador (-dora) (n, adj)	kohn-sehr-bah-'dohr (-doh-rah)
courage	valor (m)	bah-'lohr
• courageous	valiente (adj)	bah-lee-'ehn-teh
courteous	cortés (adj)	kohr-'tehs
• courtesy	cortesía	kohr-teh-'see·ah
• discourteous	descortés (adj)	dehs-kohr-'tehs
crazy, mad	loco (adj)	'loh-koh
• madness	locura	loh-'koo-rah
creativity	creatividad (f)	kreh-ah-tee-bee-'dahd
• create	crear (v)	kreh-'ahr
• creative	creativo (adj)	kreh-ah-'tee-boh
critical	crítico (adj)	'kree-tee-koh
cry	llorar (v)	yoh-'rahr
• crying	llanto	'yahn-toh
cultured	culto (adj)	'kool-toh
curiosity	curiosidad (f)	koo-ree·oh-see-'dahd
delicate	delicado (adj)	deh-lee-'kah-doh
diligence	diligencia	dee-lee-'hehn-see·ah
• diligent	diligente (adj)	dee-lee-'hehn-teh
diplomatic	diplomático (adj)	dee-ploh-'mah-tee-koh
dishonest	deshonesto (adj)	dehs-oh-'nehs-toh
• dishonesty	deshonestidad (f)	dehs-oh-nehs-tee-'dahd
disorganized	desorganizado (adj)	dehs-ohr-gah-nee-'sah-doh
dynamic	dinámico (adj)	dee-'nah-mee-koh
eccentric	excéntrico (adj)	ehks-'sehn-tree-koh
egoism	egoísmo	eh-goh·'ees-moh
• egoist, egoistic	egoísta (adj)	eh-goh·'ees-tah
eloquence	elocuencia	eh-loh-'kwehn-see·ah
• eloquent	elocuente (adj)	eh-loh 'kwehn-teh
energetic	enérgico (adj)	eh-'nehr-hee-koh
	vigoroso (adj)	bee-goh-'roh-soh
• energy	energía	eh-nehr-'hee·ah
envious	envidioso (adj)	ehn-bee-dee·'oh-soh
• envy	envidia	ehn-'bee-dee·ah
faithful	fiel (adj)	fee·'ehl
fascinate	fascinar (v)	fah-see-'nahr
• fascinating	fascinante (adj)	fah-see-'nahn-teh

• **fascination**	fascinación (f)	fah-see-nah-see-'ohn
	encanto	ehn-kahn-toh
fool, clown	tonto	'tohn-toh
	bufón (m)	boo-'fohn
• **foolish, silly**	tonto (adj)	'tohn-toh
friendly	amistoso (adj)	ah-mees-'toh-soh
funny	cómico (adj)	'koh-mee-koh
fussy	exigente (adj)	eks-ee-'hehn-teh
generosity	generosidad (f)	heh-neh-roh-see-'dahd
• **generous**	generoso (adj)	heh-neh-'roh-soh
gentle (*mild*)	suave (adj)	'swah-beh
gentle (*tame*)	manso (adj)	'mahn-soh
good, kind	bueno (adj)	'bweh-noh
	bondadoso (adj)	bohn-dah-'doh-soh
• **goodness, kindness**	bondad (f)	bohn-'dahd
graceful	gracioso (adj)	grah-see-'oh-soh
habit	hábito	'ah-bee-toh
happiness	felicidad (f)	feh-lee-see-'dahd
• **happy**	alegre (adj)	ah-'leh-greh
	contento (adj)	kohn-'tehn-toh
hate	odio	'oh-dee·oh
• **hate**	odiar (v)	oh-dee-'ee·ahr
• **hateful**	odioso (adj)	oh-dee-'oh-soh
honest	honesto (adj)	oh-'nehs-toh
	recto (adj)	'rehk-toh
• **honesty**	honradez (f)	ohn-rah-'dehs
humanitarian	humanitario (adj)	oo-mah-nee-'tah-ree·oh
• **humanitarianism**	humanitarismo	oo-mah-nee-tah-'rees-moh
humble	humilde (adj)	oo-'meel-deh
• **humility**	humildad (f)	oo-meel-'dahd
humor	humor (m)	oo-'mohr
• **sense of humor**	sentido del humor	sehn-'tee-doh dehl oo-'mohr
idealism	idealismo	ee-deh·ah-'lees-moh
• **idealist, idealistic**	idealista (m/f)	ee-deh·ah-lees-tah
	idealista (adj)	
imagination	imaginación (f)	ee-mah-hee-nah-see-'ohn
• **imaginative**	imaginativo (adj)	ee-mah-hee-nah-'tee-boh
impudence	insolencia	een-soh-'lehn-see·ah
• **impudent**	insolente (adj)	een-soh-'lehn-teh
impulse	impulso	eem-'pool-soh
• **impulsive**	impulsivo (adj)	eem-pool-'see-boh
indecision	indecisión (f)	een-deh-see-'see·ohn

• **indecisive**	indeciso (*adj*)	*een-deh-see-'see-boh*
independent	independiente (*adj*)	*een-deh-pehn-dee-'ehn-teh*
ingenious	ingenioso (*adj*)	*een-heh-nee-'oh-soh*
• **ingeniousness**	ingenio	*een-'heh-nee-oh*
innocence	inocencia	*ee-noh-'sehn-see-ah*
• **innocent**	inocente (*adj*)	*ee-noh-'sehn-teh*
intelligence	inteligencia	*een-teh-lee-'hehn-see-ah*
• **intelligent**	inteligente (*adj*)	*een-teh-lee-'hehn-teh*
irascible	colérico (*adj*)	*koh-'leh-ree-koh*
irony	ironía	*ee-roh-'nee-ah*
• **ironic**	irónico (*adj*)	*ee-'roh-nee-koh*
irritable	irritable (*adj*)	*ee-rree-'tah-bleh*
jealousy	celos (*m*)	*'seh-lohs*
• **jealous**	celoso (*adj*)	*seh-'loh-soh*
laugh	reírse*	*rreh-'eer-seh*
• **laughter**	risa	*rree-sah*
laziness	pereza	*peh-'reh-sah*
• **lazy**	perezoso (*adj*)	*peh-reh-'soh-soh*
liberal	liberal (*adj*)	*lee-beh-'rahl*
lively	vivo (*adj*)	*'bee-boh*
love	amor (*m*)	*ah-'mohr*
• **love**	amar (*v*)	*ah-'mahr*
	querer*	*keh-'rehr*
• **lovable**	amable (*adj*)	*ah-'mah-bleh*
• **loving**	cariñoso (*adj*)	*kah-ree-'nyoh-soh*
malicious	malévolo (*adj*)	*mah-'leh-boh-loh*
mischievous	travieso (*adj*)	*trah-bee-'eh-soh*
mood	humor (*m*)	*oo-'mohr*
• **bad mood**	mal humor	*mahl oo-'mohr*
• **good mood**	buen humor	*bwehn oo'-mohr*
neat	limpio (*adj*)	*'leem-pee-oh*
	ordenado (*adj*)	*ohr-deh-'nah-doh*
nice	simpático (*adj*)	*seem-'pah-tee-koh*
not nice, odious	antipático (*adj*)	*ahn-tee-'pah-tee-koh*
obstinate	obstinado (*adj*)	*ohbs-tee-'nah-doh*
optimism	optimismo (*adj*)	*ohp-tee-'mees-moh*
• **optimist**	optimista (*m/f*)	*ohp-tee-'mees-tah*
• **optimistic**	optimista (*adj*)	*ohp-tee-'mees-tah*
original	original (*adj*)	*oh-ree-hee-'nahl*
patience	paciencia	*pah-see-'ehn-see-ah*
• **impatient**	impaciente (*adj*)	*eem-pah-see-'ehn-teh*
• **patient**	paciente (*adj*)	*pah-see-'ehn-teh*
perfection	perfección (*f*)	*pehr-feks-see-'ohn*
• **perfect**	perfecto (*adj*)	*pehr-'fek-toh*
• **perfectionist**	perfeccionista (*adj*)	*pehr-fek-see-oh-'nees-tah*
personality	personalidad (*f*)	*pehr-soh-nah-lee-'dahd*

pessimism	pesimismo	peh-see-'mees-moh
• **pessimist**	pesimista (m/f)	peh-see-'mees-tah
• **pessimistic**	pesimista (adj)	peh-see-'mees-tah
picky	difícil (adj)	dee-'fee-seel
pleasant, likable	agradable (adj)	ah-grah-'dah-bleh
• **unpleasant**	desagradable (adj)	dehs-ah-grah-'dah-bleh
poor	pobre (adj)	'poh-breh
possessive	posesivo (adj)	poh-seh-'see-boh
presumptuous	presuntuoso (adj)	preh-soon-'twoh-soh
pretentious	pretencioso (adj)	preh-tehn-see-'oh-soh
proud	orgulloso (adj)	ohr-goo-'yoh-soh
prudent	prudente (adj)	proo-'dehn-teh
• **imprudent**	imprudente (adj)	eem-proo-'dehn-teh
rebellious	rebelde (adj)	reh-'behl-deh
refined	refinado (adj)	reh-fee-'nah-doh
reserved	reservado (adj)	reh-sehr-'bah-doh
rich	rico (adj)	'ree-koh
romantic	romántico (adj)	roh-'mahn-tee-koh
rough	áspero (adj)	'ahs-peh-roh
rude	descortés (adj)	dehs-kohr-'tehs
	mal educado (adj)	mahl eh-doo-'kah-doh
sad	triste (adj)	'trees-teh
• **sadness**	tristeza	trees-'teh-sah
sarcasm	sarcasmo	sahr-'kahs-moh
• **sarcastic**	sarcástico (adj)	sahr-'kahs-tee-koh
seduction	seducción (f)	seh-dook-see-'ohn
• **seductive**	seductivo (adj)	seh-dook-'tee-boh
selfish	egoísta (adj)	eh-goh-'ees-tah
self-sufficient	independiente (adj)	een-deh-pehn-dee-'ehn-teh
sensitive	sensible (adj)	sehn-'see-bleh
	sensitivo (adj)	sehn-see-'tee-boh
sentimental	sentimental (adj)	sehn-tee-mehn-'tahl
serious	serio (adj)	'seh-ree-oh
shrewd	sagaz (adj)	sah-'gahs
	listo (adj)	'lees-toh
• **shrewdness**	sagacidad (f)	sah-gah-see-'dahd
shy	tímido (adj)	'tee-mee-doh
simple	sencillo (adj)	sehn-'see-yoh
sincere	sincero (adj)	seen-'seh-roh
• **sincerity**	sinceridad (f)	seen-seh-ree-'dahd
sloppy	desorganizado (adj)	dehs-ohr-gah-nee-'sah-doh
smart	listo (adj)	'lees-toh
snobbish	presuntuoso (adj)	preh-soon-'twoh-soh
stingy	mezquino (adj)	mehs-'kee-noh
	tacaño (adj)	tah-'kah-nyoh

• stinginess	mezquindad (*f*)	mehs-keen-'dahd
strong	fuerte (*adj*)	'fwehr-teh
stubborn	terco (*adj*)	'tehr-koh
stupid	estúpido (*adj*)	ehs-'too-pee-doh
superstitious	supersticioso (*adj*)	soo-pehr-stee-see-'oh-soh
sweet	dulce (*adj*)	'dool-seh
traditional	tradicional (*adj*)	trah-dee-see-oh-'nahl
troublemaker	perturbador (*m*)	pehr-toor-bah-'dohr
vain	vanidoso (*adj*)	bah-nee-'doh-soh
versatile	versátil (*adj*)	behr-'sah-teel
weak	débil (*adj*)	'deh-beel
well-mannered	cortés (*adj*)	kohr-'tehs
	bien educado (*adj*)	bee-'ehn eh-doo-'kah-doh
willing	dispuesto (*adj*)	dees-'pwehs-toh
wisdom	sabiduría	sah-bee-doo-'ree·ah
• wise	sabio (*adj*)	'sah-bee·oh

f. BASIC PERSONAL INFORMATION

> For jobs and professions see Section 38

address	dirección, señas	dee-rehk-see-'ohn, 'seh-nyahs
• avenue	avenida	ah-beh-'nee-dah
• square	plaza	'plah-sah
• street	calle (*f*)	'kah-yeh
• Where do you live?	¿Dónde vive Ud.?	'dohn-deh 'bee-beh oos-'tehd
• I live on . . . street.	Vivo en la calle	bee-boh ehn lah 'kah-yeh
• house number	número de casa	'noo-meh-roh deh 'kah-sah
be from	ser* de	sehr deh
• city	ciudad (*f*)	see·oo-'dahd
• country	país (*m*)	pah-'ees
• state	estado	ehs-'tah-doh
• town	pueblo	'pweh-bloh
career	carrera	kah-'rreh-rah
date of birth	fecha de nacimiento	'feh-chah deh nah-see-mee-'ehn-toh
education	enseñanza	ehn-seh-'nyahn-sah
• go to school	asistir a la escuela	ah-sees-'teer ah lah ehs-'kweh-lah

• **finish school**	terminar la escuela	*tehr-mee-'nahr lah ehs-'kweh-lah*
• **university degree**	título universitario	*'tee-too-loh oo-nee-behr-see-'tah-ree-oh*
• **diploma**	diploma (*m*)	*dee-'ploh-mah*
• **register, enroll**	matricularse (*v*)	*mah-tree-koo-'lahr-seh*
identification	identificación (*f*)	*ee-dehn-tee-fee-kah-see-'ohn*
job	trabajo	*trah-'bah-hoh*
name	nombre (*m*)	*'nohm-breh*
• **first name**	nombre de pila	*'nohm-breh deh 'pee-lah*
• **family name surname**	apellido	*ah-peh-'yee-doh*
• **be called**	llamarse (*v*)	*yah-'mahr-seh*
• **How do you spell your name?**	¿Cómo se escribe (deletrea) su nombre?	*'koh-moh seh ehs-'kree-beh (deh-leh-treh-ah) soo 'nohm-breh*
• **Print your name.**	Escriba su nombre con letras de molde (imprenta).	*ehs-'kree-bah soo 'nohm-breh kohn 'leh-trahs deh 'mohl-deh (eem-'prehn-tah)*
• **What's your name?**	¿Cómo se llama Ud.?	*'koh-moh seh 'yah-mah oos-'tehd*
• **My name is . . .**	Me llamo . . .	*meh 'yah-moh*
• **sign**	firmar (*v*)	*feer-'mahr*
• **signature**	firma	*'feer-mah*
nationality	nacionalidad (*f*)	*nah-see·oh-nah-lee-'dahd*
place of birth	lugar de nacimiento	*loo-'gahr deh nah-see-mee·'ehn-toh*
place of employment	lugar de trabajo	*loo-'gahr deh trah-'bah-hoh*
profession	profesión (*f*)	*proh-feh-see·'ohn*
• **professional**	profesional (*adj*)	*proh-feh-see·oh-'nahl*
residence	residencia	*reh-see-'dehn-see·ah*
telephone number	número de teléfono	*'noo-meh-roh deh teh-'leh-foh-noh*
title	título	*'tee-too-loh*
• **Dr.**	Doctor(a) (Dr.)	*dohk-'tohr (-rah)*
• **Miss**	Señorita (Srta.)	*seh-nyoh-'ree-tah*
• **Mr.**	Señor (Sr.)	*seh-'nyohr*
• **Mrs.**	Señora (Sra.)	*seh-'nyoh-rah*
• **Prof.**	Profesor(a) (Prof.)	*proh-feh-sohr (-rah)*
work	trabajo	*trah-'bah-hoh*
• **work**	trabajar (*v*)	*trah-bah-'hahr*
• **line of work**	tipo de trabajo	*'tee-poh deh tra-'bah-hoh*

12. THE BODY

a. PARTS OF THE BODY

> See also Section 40.

ankle	tobillo	toh-'bee-yoh
arm	brazo	'brah-soh
beard	barba	'bahr-bah
blood	sangre (f)	'sahn-greh
body	cuerpo	'kwehr-poh
bone	hueso	'weh-soh
brain	cerebro	seh-'reh-broh
buttocks	trasero	trah-'seh-roh
calf	pantorrilla	pahn-toh-'rree-yah
cheek	mejilla	meh-'hee-yah
chest	pecho	'peh-choh
chin	barbilla	bahr-'bee-yah
ear	oreja	oh-'reh-hah
elbow	codo	'koh-doh
eye	ojo	'oh-hoh
eyebrow	ceja	'seh-hah
eyelash	pestaña	pehs-'tah-nyah
eyelid	párpado	'pahr-pah-doh
face	cara	'kah-rah
finger	dedo	'deh-doh
fingernail	uña	'oo-nyah
foot	pie (m)	'pee·eh
forehead	frente (f)	'frehn-teh
hair	pelo	'peh-loh
	cabello	kah-'beh-yoh
hand	mano (f)	'mah-noh
head	cabeza	kah-'beh-sah

Two heads are better than one. = Más ven cuatro ojos que dos.

word for word = al pie de la letra

to get on one's feet = levantar cabeza

---

heart	corazón (m)	koh-rah-'sohn
hip	cadera	kah-'deh-rah
index finger	dedo índice	'deh-doh 'een-dee-seh
jaw	mandíbula	mahn-'dee-boo-lah
knee	rodilla	roh-'dee-yah
knuckle	nudillo	noo-'dee-yoh

leg	pierna	*pee-'ehr-nah*
lip	labio	*'lah-bee-oh*
little finger	dedo meñique	*'deh-doh meh-'nyee-keh*
lung	pulmón (*m*)	*pool-'mohn*
middle finger	dedo medio	*'deh-doh 'meh-dee·oh*
mouth	boca	*'boh-kah*
muscle	músculo	*'moos-koo-loh*
mustache	bigote (*m*)	*bee-'goh-teh*
neck	cuello	*'kweh-yoh*
nose	nariz (*f*)	*nah-'rees*
nostril	nariz, narices (*f*)	*nah-'rees (ehs)*
ring finger	dedo anular	*'deh-doh ah-noo-'lahr*
shoulder	hombro	*'ohm-broh*
skin	piel (*f*)	*pee-'ehl*

FOCUS: Parts of the Body

stomach	estómago	ehs-'toh-mah-goh
thigh	muslo	'moos-loh
throat	garganta	gahr-'gahn-tah
thumb	pulgar (m)	pool-'gahr
toe	dedo del pie	'deh-doh dehl pee-'eh
tongue	lengua	'lehn-gwah
tooth	diente (m)	dee-'ehn-teh
	muela	moo-'eh-lah
waist	cintura	seen-'too-rah
wrist	muñeca	moo-'nyeh-kah

b. PHYSICAL STATES AND ACTIVITIES

be cold	tener* frío	teh-'nehr 'free·oh
be hot	tener* calor	teh-'nehr kah-'lohr
be hungry	tener* hambre	teh-'nehr 'ahm-breh
• hunger	hambre (f)	'ahm-breh
be sleepy	tener* sueño	teh-'nehr 'sweh-nyoh
be thirsty	tener* sed	teh-'nehr sehd
• thirst	sed (f)	sehd
be tired	estar cansado	ehs-'tahr kahn-'sah-doh
breathe	respirar (v)	rehs-pee-'rahr
drink	beber (v)	beh-'behr
eat	comer (v)	koh-'mehr
fall asleep	dormirse*	dohr-'meer-seh
feel badly	sentirse* mal	sehn-'teer-seh mahl
feel well	sentirse* bien	sehn-'teer-seh bee-'ehn
get up	levantarse (v)	leh-bahn-'tahr-seh
go to bed	acostarse*	ah-kohs-'tahr-seh
relax	relajarse (v)	reh-lah-'hahr-seh
rest	descansar (v)	dehs-kahn-'sahr
run	correr (v)	koh-'rrehr
sleep	dormir*	dohr-'meer
urinate	orinar (v)	oh-ree-'nahr
wake up	despertarse*	dehs-pehr-'tahr-seh
walk	andar (v)	ahn-'dahr

c. SENSORY PERCEPTION

blind (person)	ciego	see-'eh-goh
• blindness	ceguera	seh-'geh-rah
deaf (person)	sordo	'sohr-doh
• deafness	sordera	sohr-'deh-rah
flavor	sabor	sah-'bohr
• taste	probar*	proh-'bahr

hear	oír*	*oh-'eer*
• hearing	oído	*oh-'ee-doh*
listen (to)	escuchar (v)	*ehs-koo-'chahr*
look at	mirar (v)	*mee-'rahr*
mute (person)	mudo	*'moo-doh*
noise	ruido	*'rwee-doh*
• noisy	ruidoso	*rwee-'doh-soh*
perceive	percibir (v)	*pehr-see-'beer*
• perception	percepción (f)	*pehr-sehp-see-'ohn*
see	ver*	*behr*
• sight	vista	*'bees-tah*
sense, feel	sentirse*	*sehn-'teer-seh*
• sense	sentido	*sehn-'tee-doh*
smell	oler*	*oh-'lehr*
• sense of smell	olfato	*ohl-'fah-toh*
sound	sonido	*soh-'nee-doh*
touch	tocar (v)	*toh-'kahr*
• sense of touch	el sentido del tacto	*ehl sehn-'tee-doh dehl 'tahk-toh*

d. PERSONAL CARE

bald	calvo (adj)	*'kahl-boh*
bangs	flequillo	*fleh-'kee-yoh*
barber	barbero	*bahr-'beh-roh*
• barber shop	barbería	*bahr-beh-'ree-ah*
	peluquería	*peh-loo-keh-'ree-ah*
beautician	peluquero(a)	*peh-loo-'keh-roh (-rah)*
brush	cepillarse (v)	*seh-pee-'yahr-seh*
brush	cepillarse (v)	*seh-pee-'yahr-seh*
• brush	cepillo	*seh-'pee-yoh*
clean oneself	limpiarse (v)	*leem-pee-'ahr-seh*
clippers	maquinilla	*mah-kee-'nee-yah*
comb	peinarse (v)	*peh·ee-'nahr-seh*
comb one's hair	peinarse (v)	*peh·ee-'nahr-seh*
• comb	peine (m)	*'peh·ee-neh*
curls	bucles (m)	*'boo-klehs*
• loose curls	bucles flojos	*'boo-klehs 'floh-hohs*
curlers	rulos	*'roo-lohs*
	rizadores (m)	*ree-sah-'doh-rehs*
cut	cortar (v)	*kohr-'tahr*
cut one's hair	cortarse el pelo	*kohr-'tahr-seh ehl 'peh-loh*
dirty	sucio	*'soo-see·oh*
dry	secar (v)	*'seh-kahr*
dry oneself	secarse (v)	*seh-'kahr-seh*
frosted hair	pelo escarchado	*'peh-loh ehs-kahr-'chah-doh*

hair	pelo	*'peh-loh*
• permanent	permanente (*f*)	*pehr-mah-'nehn-teh*
haircut	corte (*m*) de pelo	*'kohr-teh deh 'peh-loh*
• in the back	por detrás	*pohr deh-'trahs*
• in the front	por delante	*pohr deh-'lahn-teh*
• on the sides	a los lados	*ah lohs 'lah-dohs*
• on top	de arriba	*deh ah-'rree-bah*
hairdresser	peluquero(a)	*peh-loo-'keh-roh (-rah)*
hairdryer	secador (*m*)	*seh-kah-'dohr*
hair spray	laca	*'lah-kah*
hygiene	higiene (*f*)	*ee-hee-'eh-neh*
• hygienic	higiénico (*adj*)	*ee-hee-'eh-nee-koh*
long	largo (*adj*)	*'lahr-goh*
makeup	maquillaje (*m*)	*mah-kee-'yah-heh*
• put on makeup	ponerse* el maquillaje	*poh-'nehr-seh ehl mah-kee-'yah-heh*
manicure	manicura	*mah-nee-'koo-rah*
mascara	rimel (*m*)	*ree-'mehl*
massage	masaje (*m*)	*mah-'sah-heh*
nail polish	esmalte para las uñas	*ehs-'mahl-teh 'pah-rah lahs 'oo-nyahs*
perfume	perfume (*m*)	*pehr-'foo-meh*
• put on perfume	ponerse* perfume	*poh-'nehr-seh pehr-'foo-meh*
permanent	permanente (*f*)	*pehr-mah-'nehn-teh*
razor	afeitadora	*ah-feh-ee-tah-'doh-rah*
• electric razor	afeitadora eléctrica	*ah-feh-ee-tah-'doh-rah eh-'lehk-tree-kah*
rinse	enjuague	*ehn-'hwah-geh*
scissors	tijeras	*tee-'heh-rahs*
set	arreglar (*v*)	*ah-rreh-'glahr*
shampoo	champú (*m*)	*chahm-'poo*
shave	afeitarse (*v*)	*ah-feh-ee-'tahr-seh*
short	corto (*adj*)	*'kohr-toh*
sideburn	patilla	*pah-'tee-yah*
soap	jabón (*m*)	*hah-'bohn*
toothbrush	cepillo de dientes	*seh-'pee-yoh deh dee-'ehn-tehs*
toothpaste	crema dental	*'kreh-mah dehn-'tahl*
	pasta dentífrica	*'pahs-tah dehn-'tee-free-kah*
touch up	retoque (*m*)	*reh-'toh-keh*
towel, handcloth	toalla	*toh-'ah-yah*
	paño	*'pah-nyoh*
trim	recortar (*v*)	*reh-kohr-'tahr*
wash	lavado	*lah-'bah-doh*
wash oneself	lavarse (*v*)	*lah-'bahr-seh*
• wash one's hair	lavarse el pelo	*lah-'bahr-seh ehl 'peh-loh*

THE PHYSICAL, PLANT, AND ANIMAL WORLDS

13. THE PHYSICAL WORLD

a. THE UNIVERSE

> For signs of the Zodiac see Section 5.

astronomy	astronomía	*ahs-troh-noh-'mee-ah*
comet	cometa (*m*)	*koh-'meh-tah*
cosmos	cosmos (*m*)	*'kohs-mohs*
eclipse	eclipse (*m*)	*eh-'kleep-seh*
• **lunar eclipse**	eclipse lunar	*eh-'kleep-seh loo-'nahr*
• **solar eclipse**	eclipse solar	*eh-'kleep-seh soh-'lahr*
galaxy	galaxia	*gah-'lahk-see-ah*
gravitation	gravitación	*grah-bee-tah-see-'ohn*
• **gravity**	gravedad (*f*)	*grah-beh-'dahd*
light	luz (*f*)	*loos*
• **infrared light**	luz infrarroja	*loos een-frah-'rroh-hah*
• **light year**	año luz	*'ah-nyoh loos*
• **ultraviolet light**	luz ultravioleta	*loos ool-trah-bee·oh-'leh-tah*
meteor	meteoro	*meh-teh-'oh-roh*
moon	luna	*'loo-nah*
• **full moon**	luna llena	*loo-nah 'yeh-nah*
• **moonbeam (ray)**	rayo de luna	*'rah-yoh deh 'loo-nah*
• **new moon**	luna nueva	*'loo-nah 'nweh-bah*
orbit	estar en órbita	*ehs-'tahr ehn 'ohr-bee-tah*
• **orbit**	órbita	*'ohr-bee-tah*
planet	planeta (*m*)	*plah-'neh-tah*
• **Earth**	Tierra	*tee-'eh-rrah*
• **Jupiter**	Júpiter (*m*)	*'hoo-pee-tehr*
• **Mars**	Marte (*m*)	*'mahr-teh*
• **Mercury**	Mercurio	*mehr-koo-'ree·oh*
• **Neptune**	Neptuno	*nehp-'too-noh*
• **Pluto**	Plutón (*m*)	*ploo-'tohn*
• **Saturn**	Saturno	*sah-'toor-noh*
• **Uranus**	Urano	*oo-'rah-noh*
• **Venus**	Venus (*m*)	*'beh-noos*
satellite	satélite (*m*)	*sah-'teh-lee-teh*

space	espacio	*ehs-'pah-see·oh*
• three-dimensional space	espacio tridimensional	*ehs-'pah-see·oh tree-dee-mehn-see·oh-'nahl*
star	estrella	*ehs-'treh-yah*
	astro	*ahs-troh*
sun	sol (*m*)	*sohl*
solar system	rayo de sol	*'ra-yoh de sohl*
• sunbeam (ray)	luz del sol	*loos dehl sohl*
• sunlight	sistema solar (*m*)	*sees-'teh-mah soh-'lahr*

---

to publish = sacar a luz

to give birth to = dar a luz

in the twilight = entre dos luces

my sweet = luz de mis ojos

| universe | universo | *oo-nee-'behr-soh* |
| world | mundo | *'moon-doh* |

b. THE ENVIRONMENT

See also Sections 13 and 44.

archipelago	archipiélago	*ahr-chee-pee-'eh-lah-goh*
atmosphere	atmósfera	*aht-'mohs-feh-rah*
• atmospheric	atmosférico (*adj*)	*aht-mohs-'feh-ree-koh*
basin	cuenca	*'kwehn-kah*
bay	bahía	*bah-'ee·ah*
beach	playa	*'plah-yah*
canal	canal (*m*)	*kah-'nahl*
cape	cabo	*'kah-boh*
cave	cueva	*'kweh-bah*
channel	cauce (*m*)	*'kow-seh*
cloud	nube (*f*)	*'noo-beh*
coast	costa	*'kohs-tah*
countryside	campo	*'kahm-poh*
	campiña	*kahm-'pee-nyah*
dam	dique	*'dee-keh*
	presa	*'preh-sah*
desert	desierto	*deh-see-'ehr-toh*
earthquake	terremoto	*teh-rreh-'moh-toh*
environment	ambiente (*m*)	*ahm-bee-'ehn-teh*

farmland	tierras de labrantío	tee-'eh-rrahs deh lah-brahn-'tee-oh
field	campo	'kahm-poh
forest	selva	'sehl-bah
	bosque	'bohs-keh
• **tropical forest**	selva tropical	'sehl-bah troh-pee-'kahl
grass	hierba	ee-'ehr-bah
gulf	golfo	'gohl-foh
hill	colina	koh-'lee-nah
	cerro	'seh-rroh
hurricane	huracán	oo-rah-'kahn
ice	hielo	ee-'eh-loh
island	isla	'ees-lah
jungle	selva	'sehl-bah
	jungla	'hoon-glah
lake	lago	'lah-goh
land	tierra	tee-'eh-rrah
	terreno	teh-'rreh-noh
landscape	paisaje (*m*)	pah-'eeh-sah-heh
layer	estrato	ehs-trah-toh
marsh	pantano	pahn-'tah-noh
• **wetland**	tierra pantanosa	tee-'eh-rrah pahn-tah-'noh-sah
meadow	prado	'prah-doh
mountain	montaña	mohn-'tah-nyah
• **mountain range**	cordillera	kohr-dee-'yeh-rah
• **mountainous**	montañoso (*adj*)	mohn-tah-'nyoh-soh
• **peak**	pico	'pee-koh
nature	naturaleza	nah-too-rah-'leh-sah
• **natural**	natural	nah-too-'rahl
ocean	océano	oh-'seh-ah-noh
• **Antarctic**	Antártico	ahn-'tahr-tee-koh
• **Arctic**	Artico	'ahr-tee-koh
• **Atlantic**	Atlántico	aht-'lahn-tee-koh
• **Indian**	Indio	'een-dee-oh
• **Pacific**	Pacífico	pah-'see-fee-koh
peninsula	península	peh-'neen-soo-lah
plain	llano	'yah-noh
pond	estanque (*m*)	ehs-'tahn-keh
	laguna	lah-'goo-nah
river	río	'ree-oh
• **flow**	fluir (*v*)	floo-'eer
• **navigable**	navegable (*adj*)	nah-beh-'gah-bleh
rock	roca	'roh-kah
	peña	'peh-nyah
sand	arena	ah-'reh-nah
sea	mar (*m*)	mahr

sky	cielo	*see·'eh-loh*
stone	piedra	*pee·'eh-drah*
strait	estrecho	*ehs-'treh-choh*
tide	marea	*mah-'reh-ah*
valley	valle (*m*)	*'bah-yeh*
vegetation	vegetación	*beh-heh-tah-see·'ohn*
volcano	volcán (*m*)	*bohl-'kahn*
• eruption	erupción (*f*)	*eh-roop-see·'ohn*
• lava	lava	*'lah-bah*
wave	ola	*'oh-lah*
woods	bosque (*m*)	*'bohs-keh*

c. MATTER AND THE ENVIRONMENT

> See also Section 44.

acid	ácido	*'ah-see-doh*
air	aire (*m*)	*'ah·ee·reh*
ammonia	amoniaco	*ah-moh-nee·'ah-koh*
atom	átomo	*'ah-toh-moh*
• charge	carga	*'kahr-gah*
• electron	electrón (*m*)	*eh-'lehk-tron*
• neutron	neutrón (*m*)	*neh·oo-'trohn*
• nucleus	núcleo	*'noo-kleh-oh*
• proton	protón (*m*)	*proh-'tohn*
brass	latón (*m*)	*lah-'tohn*
bronze	bronce (*m*)	*'brohn-ceh*
carbon	carbono	*kahr-'boh-noh*
chemical	producto químico	*proh-'dook-toh 'kee-mee-koh*
• chemistry	química	*'kee-mee-kah*
chlorine	cloro	*'kloh-roh*
clay	arcilla	*ahr-'see-yah*
coal	carbón (*m*)	*kahr-'bohn*
• coal mine	mina de carbón	*'mee-nah deh kahr-'bohn*
• coal mining	extracción del carbón (*f*)	*ehks-trahk-see·'ohn dehl kahr-'bohn*
compound	compuesto	*kohm-'pwehs-toh*
copper	cobre (*m*)	*'koh-breh*
cotton	algodón (*m*)	*ahl-goh-'dohn*
electricity	electricidad (*f*)	*eh-lehk-tree-see-'dahd*
• electrical	eléctrico (*adj*)	*eh-'lehk-tree-koh*

element	elemento	eh-leh-'mehn-toh
energy	energía	eh-nehr-'hee·ah
• fossil	fósil (adj)	'foh-seel
• nuclear	nuclear (adj)	noo-kleh-'ahr
• radioactive	radioactivo (adj)	rah-dee·oh-ahk-'tee-boh
• solar	solar (adj)	soh-'lahr
fiber	fibra	'fee-brah
fire	fuego	foo·'eh-goh
fuel	combustible (m)	kohm-boos-'tee-bleh
• fossil fuel	combustibles (m) de fósil	kohm-boos-'tee-blehs deh 'foh-seel
gas	gas (m)	gahs
• gasoline	gasolina	gah-soh-'lee-nah
• natural gas	gas natural	gahs nah-too-'rahl
gold	oro	'oh-roh
heat	calor (m)	kah-'lohr
heat (for home)	calefacción (f)	kah-leh-fahk-see·'ohn
hydrogen	hidrógeno	ee-'droh-heh-noh
industrial	industrial (adj)	een-doos-tree·'ahl
• industry	industria	een-'doos-tree·ah
iodine	yodo	'yoh-doh
iron	hierro	ee·'eh-rroh
laboratory	laboratorio	lah-boh-rah-'toh-ree·oh
lead	plomo	'ploh-moh
leather	de cuero (adj)	deh koo·'eh-roh
	de piel (adj)	deh pee·ehl
liquid	líquido	'lee-kee-doh
material	materia	mah-'teh-ree·ah
	material	mah-teh-ree·'ahl
matter	materia	mah-'teh-ree·ah
mercury	mercurio	mehr-'koo-ree·oh
metal	metal (m)	meh-'tahl
methane	metano	meh-'tah-noh
microscope	microscopio	mee-kroh-'skoh-pee·oh
mineral	mineral (m)	mee-neh-'rahl
molecule	molécula	moh-'leh-koo-lah
• model	modelo	moh-'deh-loh
• molecular	molecular (adj)	moh-leh-koo-'lahr
• molecular formula	fórmula molecular	'fohr-moo-lah moh-leh-koo-'lahr
• structure	estructura	ehs-trook-'too-rah
natural resources	recursos naturales	rreh-'koor-sohs nah-too-rah-lehs
organic	orgánico (adj)	ohr-'gah-nee-koh
• inorganic	inorgánico (adj)	een-ohr-'gah-nee-koh
oxygen	oxígeno	ohks-'ee-heh-noh
particle	partícula	pahr-'tee-koo-lah

petroleum	petróleo	peh-'troh-leh-oh
physical	físico (adj)	'fee-see-koh
• physics	física	'fee-see-kah
plastic	plástico (n, adj)	'plahs-tee-koh
platinum	platino	plah-'tee-noh
pollution	contaminación (f)	kohn-tah-mee-nah-see-'ohn
salt	sal (f)	sahl
silk	seda	'seh-dah
silver	plata	'plah-tah
smoke	humo	'oo-moh
sodium	sodio	'soh-dee-oh
steel	acero	ah-'seh-roh
• stainless steel	acero inoxidable	ah-'seh-roh een-ohks-ee-'dah-bleh
substance	substancia	soob-'stahn-see-ah
sulphur	azufre (m)	ah-'soo-freh
• sulphuric acid	ácido sulfúrico	'ah-see-doh sool-'foo-ree-koh
textile	textil	tehks-'teel
	tejido	teh-'hee-doh
tin	estaño	ehs-'tah-nyoh
vapor	vapor (m)	bah-'pohr
water	agua (f)	'ah-gwah
wool	lana	'lah-nah

d. CHARACTERISTICS OF MATTER

artificial	artificial (adj)	ahr-tee-fee-see-'ahl
authentic	auténtico (adj)	ow-'tehn-tee-koh
elastic	elástico (adj)	eh-'lahs-tee-koh
fake	falso (adj)	'fahl-soh
hard	duro (adj)	'doo-roh
heavy	pesado (adj)	peh-'sah-doh
light	ligero (adj)	lee-'heh-roh
malleable	maleable (adj)	mah-leh-'ah-bleh
opaque	opaco (adj)	oh-'pah-koh
pure	puro (adj)	'poo-roh
resistant	resistente (adj)	reh-sees-'tehn-teh
robust	robusto (adj)	roh-'boos-toh
rough	áspero (adj)	'ahs-peh-roh
smooth	liso (adj)	'lee-soh
soft	blando (adj)	'blahn-doh
soluble	soluble (adj)	soh-'loo-bleh
stable	estable (adj)	ehs-'tah-bleh

strong	fuerte (*adj*)	*'fwehr-teh*
synthetic	sintético (*adj*)	*seen-'teh-tee-koh*
transparent	transparente (*adj*)	*trahns-pah-'rehn-teh*
weak	débil (*adj*)	*'deh-beel*

e. GEOGRAPHY

> For names of countries, cities, etc., see Section 30.

Antarctic Circle	Círculo Antártico	*'seer-koo-loh ahn-'tahr-tee-koh*
Arctic Circle	Círculo Artico	*'seer-koo-loh 'ahr-tee-koh*
area	área (*f*)	*'ah-reh-ah*
border	frontera	*frohn-'teh-rah*
city	ciudad (*f*)	*see-oo-'dahd*
• capital	capital (*f*)	*kah-pee-'tahl*
continent	continente (*m*)	*kohn-tee-'nehn-teh*
• continental	continental (*adj*)	*kohn-tee-nehn-'tahl*
country	país (*m*)	*pah·'ees*
equator	ecuador (*m*)	*eh-kwah-'dohr*
geography	geografía	*heh-oh-grah-'fee-ah*
• geographical	geográfico (*adj*)	*heh-oh-'grah-fee-koh*
globe	globo	*'gloh-boh*
hemisphere	hemisferio	*eh-mees-'feh-ree-oh*
• hemispheric	hemisférico (*adj*)	*eh-mees-'feh-ree-koh*
latitude	latitud (*f*)	*lah-tee-'tood*
longitude	longitud (*f*)	*lohn-hee-'tood*
locate	localizar (*v*)	*loh-kah-lee-'zahr*
• location	localización (*f*)	*loh-kah-lee-sah-see·'ohn*
• be located	estar* ubicado (situado)	*ehs'-tahr oo-bee-'kah-doh (see-'twah-doh)*
map	mapa (*m*)	*'mah-pah*
meridian	meridiano (*adj*)	*meh-ree-dee·'ah-noh*
• prime meridian	primer meridiano	*pree-'mehr meh-ree-dee·'ah-noh*
nation	nación (*f*)	*nah-see·'ohn*
• national	nacional (*adj*)	*nah-see·oh-'nahl*
pole	polo	*'poh-loh*
• North Pole	Polo Norte	*'poh-loh 'nohr-teh*
• South Pole	Polo Sur	*'poh-loh soor*
province	provincia	*proh-'been-see·ah*
region	región (*f*)	*reh-hee·'ohn*
state	estado	*ehs-'tah-doh*

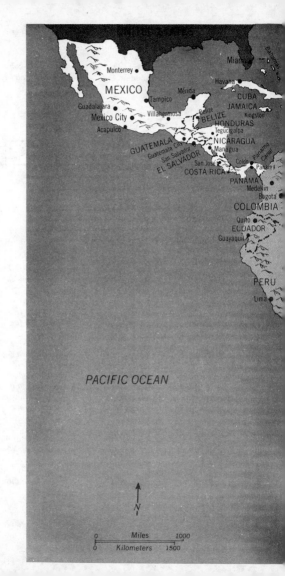

territory	territorio	teh-rree-'toh-ree·oh
tropic	trópico	'troh-pee-koh
• **Tropic of Cancer**	trópico de Cáncer	'troh-pee-koh deh 'kahn-sehr
• **Tropic of Capricorn**	trópico de Capricornio	'troh-pee-koh deh kah-pree-'kohr-nee·oh
• **tropical**	tropical	troh-pee-'kahl
zone	zona	'soh-nah

14. *PLANTS*

a. GENERAL VOCABULARY

agriculture	agricultura	ah-gree-kool-'too-rah
bloom	florecer (v)	floh-reh-'sehr
botanical	botánico (adj)	boh-'tah-nee-koh
• **botany**	botánica	boh-'tah-nee-kah
branch	rama	'rah-mah
bud	brote (m)	'broh-teh
• **in bud**	en capullo	ehn kah-'poo-yoh
bulb	bulbo	'bool-boh
bush	arbusto	ahr-'boos-toh
cell	célula	'seh-loo-lah
• **nucleus**	núcleo	'noo-kleh-oh
chlorophyll	clorofila	kloh-roh-'fee-lah
cultivate	cultivar (v)	kool-tee-'bahr
• **cultivation**	cultivo	kool-'tee-boh
dig	cavar (v)	kah-'bahr
flower	florecer (v)	floh-reh-'sehr
foliage	follaje (m)	foh-'yah-heh
gather	recoger (v)	reh-koh-'hehr
grain	grano	'grah-noh
greenhouse	invernadero	een-behr-nah-'deh-roh
hedge	seto vivo	'seh-toh 'bee-boh
horticulture	horticultura	ohr-tee-kool-'too-rah
leaf	hoja	'oh-hah
look after	cuidar (v)	kwee-'dahr
membrane	membrana	mehm-'brah-nah
organism	organismo	ohr-gah-'nees-moh
photosynthesis	fotosíntesis (f)	foh-toh-'seen-teh-sees
plant	planta	'plahn-tah
• **plant**	plantar (v)	plahn-'tahr
	sembrar*	sehm-'brahr
pollen	polen (m)	'poh-lehn
reproduce	reproducir*	reh-proh-doo-'seer
• **reproduction**	reproducción (f)	reh-proh-dook-see-'ohn
ripe	maduro (adj)	mah-'doo-roh

root	raíz (f)	rah-'ees
rotten	podrido (adj)	poh-'dree-doh
seed	semilla	seh-'mee-yah
• seed	sembrar*	sehm-'brahr
species	especie (f)	ehs-'peh·see·eh
stem	tallo	'tah-yoh
	pedúnculo	peh-'doon-koo-loh
transplant	trasplantar (v)	trahs-plahn-'tahr
• transplant	trasplante (m)	trahs-'plahn-teh
trunk	tronco	'trohn-koh
water	regar*	reh-'gahr
wheat	trigo	'tree-goh

b. FLOWERS

carnation	clavel (m)	klah-'behl
cyclamen	ciclamen (m)	see-'klah-mehn
dahlia	dalia	'dah-lee·ah
flower	flor (f)	flohr
• bouquet of flowers	ramo de flores	'rah-moh deh 'floh-rehs
• flowerbed	macizo	mah-'see-soh
	arriate (m)	ah-rree-'ah-teh
• pick flowers	recoger* flores	reh-koh-'gehr 'floh-rehs
• wilted flower	flor marchita	flohr mahr-'chee-tah
geranium	geranio	heh-'rah-nee·oh
gladiolus	gladiolo	glah-dee-'oh-loh
lily	azucena	ah-soo-'seh-nah
orchid	orquídea	ohr-'kee-deh·ah
petal	pétalo	'peh-tah-loh
petunia	petunia	peh-'too-nee·ah
poppy	amapola	ah-mah-'poh-lah
rose	rosa	'roh-sah
thorn	espina	ehs-'pee-nah
tulip	tulipán (m)	too-lee-'pahn
violet	violeta	bee·oh-'leh-tah

c. TREES

beech tree	haya	'ah-yah
cypress tree	ciprés (m)	see-'prehs
fir tree	abeto	ah-'beh-toh
fruit tree	frutero	froo-'teh-roh
• apple tree	manzano	mahn-'zah-noh
• cherry tree	cerezo	seh-'reh-soh
• fig tree	higuera	ee-'geh-rah

• **lemon tree**	limonero	*lee-moh-'neh-roh*
• **olive tree**	olivo	*oh-'lee-boh*
• **orange tree**	naranjo	*nah-'rahn-hoh*
• **peach tree**	duraznero	*doo-rahs-'neh-ro*
	melocotonero	*meh-loh-koh-toh-'neh-roh*
• **pear tree**	peral (*m*)	*peh-'rahl*
• **walnut tree**	nogal (*m*)	*noh-'gahl*
maple tree	arce (*m*)	*'ahr-seh*
oak tree	roble (*m*)	*'roh-bleh*
palm tree	palma	*'pahl-mah*
pine tree	pino	*'pee-noh*
poplar tree	álamo	*'ah-lah-moh*
tree	árbol (*m*)	*'ahr-bohl*

d. FRUITS

apple	manzana	*mahn-'zah-nah*
apricot	albaricoque (*m*)	*ahl-bah-ree-'koh-keh*
banana	banana	*bah-'nah-nah*
	plátano	*'plah-tah-noh*
blackberry	zarzamora	*sahr-sah-'moh-rah*
cherry	cereza	*seh-'reh-sah*
chestnut	castaña	*kah-'stah-nyah*
citrus	fruta agria	*'froo-tah 'ah-gree·ah*
• **citric**	cítrico (*adj*)	*'see-tree-koh*
date	dátil (*m*)	*'dah-teel*
dried fruit	frutas secas	*'froo-tahs 'seh-kahs*
fig	higo	*'ee-goh*
fruit	fruta	*'froo-tah*
grapefruit	toronja	*toh-'rohn-hah*
	pomelo	*poh-'meh-loh*
grapes	uvas	*'oo-bahs*
lemon	limón	*lee-'mohn*
mandarin orange	mandarina	*mahn-dah-'ree-nah*
melon	melón	*meh-'lohn*
olive	oliva	*oh-'lee-bah*
orange	naranja	*nah-'rahn-hah*
peach	durazno	*doo-'rahs-noh*
	melocotón	*meh-loh-koh-'tohn*
peanut	cacahuete (*m*)	*kah-kah-'weh-teh*
	maní (*m*)	*mah-'nee*
pear	pera	*'peh-rah*
pineapple	piña	*'pee-nyah*
plum	ciruela	*see-'rweh-lah*
prune	ciruela pasa	*see-'rweh-lah 'pah-sah*
raspberry	frambuesa	*frahm-'bweh-sah*

strawberry	fresa	*'freh-sah*
walnut	nuez (*f*)	*'nwehs*
watermelon	sandía	*sahn-'dee-ah*

e. VEGETABLES AND HERBS

artichoke	alcachofa	*ahl-kah-'choh-fah*
asparagus	espárrago	*ehs-'pah-rrah-goh*
basil	albahaca	*al-bah-'ah-kah*
beans	frijoles (*m, pl*)	*free'hoh-lehs*
	habas (*f, pl*)	*'ah-bahs*
beet	remolacha	*reh-moh-'lah-chah*
broccoli	brécol (*m*)	*'breh-kohl*
	bróculi (*m*)	*'broh-koo-lee*
cabbage	col (*f*)	*kohl*
	repollo	*reh-'poh-yoh*
carrot	zanahoria	*sah-nah-'oh-ree·ah*
cauliflower	coliflor (*f*)	*koh-lee-'flohr*
celery	apio	*'ah-pee·oh*
corn	maíz (*m*)	*mah-'ees*
cucumber	pepino	*peh-'pee-noh*
eggplant	berenjena	*beh-rehn-'heh-nah*
fennel	hinojo	*ee-'noh-hoh*
garden	jardín (*m*)	*hahr-'deen*
• vegetable garden	huerta	*'wehr-tah*
garlic	ajo	*'ah-hoh*
grass	césped (*m*)	*'sehs-pehd*
	hierba	*ee·'ehr-bah*
green pepper	pimiento verde	*pee-mee-'ehn-toh 'vehr-deh*
lentil	lenteja	*lehn-'teh-hah*
lettuce	lechuga	*leh-'choo-gah*
lima bean	frijol de media luna (*m*)	*free-'hohl deh 'meh-dee·ah 'loo-nah*
mint	menta	*'mehn-tah*
mushroom	seta	*'seh-tah*
	hongo	*'ohn-goh*
onion	cebolla	*seh-'boh-yah*
parsley	perejil (*m*)	*peh-reh-'heel*
pea	guisante (*m*)	*gee-'sahn-teh*
potato	papa	*'pah-pah*
	patata	*pah-'tah-tah*
pumpkin	calabaza	*kah-lah-'bah-sah*
radish	rábano	*'rah-bah-noh*
rhubarb	ruibarbo	*rwee-'bahr-boh*
rosemary	romero	*roh-'meh-roh*
spinach	espinaca	*ehs-pee-'nah-kah*

string bean	judía verde	*hoo-'dee-ah 'behr-deh*
tomato	tomate (*m*)	*toh-'mah-teh*
turnip	nabo	*'nah-boh*
vegetable	legumbre (*f*)	*leh-'goom-breh*
	vegetal (m, adj)	*beh-heh-'tahl*
zucchini	calabacín (*m*)	*kah-lah-bah-'seen*

15. *THE ANIMAL WORLD*

a. ANIMALS

animal	animal (*m*)	*ah-nee-'mahl*
bat	murciélago	*moor-see-'eh-lah-goh*
bear	oso	*'oh-soh*
beast	bestia	*'behs-tee-ah*
buffalo	búfalo	*'boo-fah-loh*
bull	toro	*'toh-roh*
camel	camello	*kah-'meh-yoh*
cat	gato	*'gah-toh*
• meow	maullar*	*mow-'yahr*
cow	vaca	*'bah-kah*
deer	venado	*beh-'nah-doh*
dog	perro	*'peh-rroh*
• bark	ladrar (*v*)	*lah-'drahr*
donkey	burro	*'boo-rroh*
elephant	elefante (*m*)	*eh-leh-'fahn-teh*
farm	granja	*'grahn-hah*
	hacienda	*ah-see-'ehn-dah*
• barn	establo	*ehs-'tah-blo*
• farmer	campesino	*kahm-peh-'see-noh*
	labrador (*m*)	*lah-brah-'dohr*
• fence	cerca	*'sehr-kah*
fox	zorro	*'soh-rroh*
giraffe	jirafa	*hee-'rah-fah*
goat	cabra	*'kah-brah*
hare	liebre (*f*)	*lee-'eh-breh*
hippopotamus	hipopótamo	*ee-poh-'poh-tah-moh*
horse	caballo	*kah-'bah-yoh*
• neigh	relinchar (*v*)	*reh-leen-'chahr*
hunter	cazador (*m*)	*kah-sah-'dohr*
• hunt	cazar (*v*)	*kah-'sahr*
• hunting	caza	*kah-sah*
hyena	hiena	*ee-·'eh-nah*
lamb	cordero	*kohr-'deh-roh*
leopard	leopardo	*leh-oh-'pahr-doh*

lion	león	*leh-'ohn*
• roar	rugir*	*roo-'heer*
mammal	mamífero	*mah-'mee-feh-roh*
mole	topo	*'toh-poh*
monkey	mono	*'moh-noh*
mouse	ratón (*m*)	*rah-'tohn*
mule	mulo	*'moo-loh*
ox	buey (*m*)	*bwehy*
paw	pata	*'pah-tah*
pet	animal doméstico	*ah-nee-'mahl doh-'mehs-tee-koh*
pig	cerdo	*'sehr-doh*
primate	primate (*m*)	*pree-'mah-teh*
rabbit	conejo	*koh-'neh-hoh*
rat	rata	*'rah-tah*
rhinoceros	rinoceronte (*m*)	*ree-noh-seh-'rohn-teh*
sheep	carnero	*kahr-'neh-roh*
	oveja	*oh-'beh-hah*
• bleat	balar (*v*)	*bah-'lahr*
tail	cola	*'koh-lah*

> **to line up** = hacer cola

tiger	tigre	*'tee-greh*
vertebrate	vertebrado	*behr-teh-'brah-doh*
• invertebrate	invertebrado	*een-behr-teh-'brah-doh*
wild animal	animal salvaje	*ah-nee-'mahl sahl-'bah-heh*
wolf	lobo	*'loh-boh*
• howl	aullar*	*ow-'yahr*
zebra	cebra	*'seh-brah*
zoo	parque (*m*) zoológico	*'pahr-keh soh-oh-'loh-hee-koh*
• zoological	zoológico (*adj*)	*soh-oh-'loh-hee-koh*
• zoology	zoología	*soh-oh-loh-'hee-ah*

b. BIRDS AND FOWL

albatross	albatros (*m*)	*ahl-'bah-trohs*
beak	pico	*'pee-koh*
bird	pájaro	*'pah-hah-roh*
blackbird	mirlo	*'meer-loh*
dove	paloma	*pah-'loh-mah*
duck	pato	*'pah-toh*
eagle	águila (*f*)	*'ah-gee-lah*

feather	pluma	'ploo-mah
• plumage	plumaje (*m*)	ploo-'mah-heh
goose	ánsar	'ahn-sahr
	ganso (*m*)	'gahn-soh
hen	gallina	gah-'yee-nah
nightingale	ruiseñor (*m*)	rwee-seh-'nyohr
ostrich	avestruz (*f*)	ah-beh-'stroos
owl	buho	'boo-oh
parakeet	perico	peh-'ree-koh
parrot	loro	'loh-roh
pelican	pelícano	peh-'lee-kah-noh
pigeon	pichón	pee-'chohn

---

to kill two birds with one stone = matar dos pájaros en un tiro

---

rooster	gallo	'gah-yoh
seagull	gaviota	gah-bee-'oh-tah
sparrow	gorrión (*m*)	goh-rree-'ohn
swan	cisne (*m*)	'sees-neh
turkey	pavo	'pah-boh
vulture	buitre (*m*)	'bwee-treh
wing	ala	'ah-lah

c. FISH, REPTILES, AMPHIBIANS, AND MARINE MAMMALS

amphibian	anfibio (*n, adj*)	ahn-'fee-bee-oh
codfish	bacalao	bah-kah-'lah-oh
crocodile	cocodrilo	koh-koh-'dree-loh
dolphin	delfín (*m*)	dehl-'feen
eel	anguila	ahn-'gee-lah
fish	pez (in water)	pehs
	pescado (food)	pehs-'kah-doh
• fin	aleta	ah-'leh-tah
• fishbone	espina	ehs-'pee-nah
• fish	pescar (*v*)	pehs-'kahr
• fisherman	pescador (*m*)	pehs-kah-'dohr
• fishing	pesca	'pehs-kah
• fishing rod	caña de pescar	'kah-nyah deh pehs-'kahr
• hook	anzuelo	ahn-soo·'eh-loh

frog	rana	*'rah-nah*
goldfish	carpa dorada	*'kahr-pah doh-'rah-dah*
hake	merluza	*mehr-'loo-sah*
octopus	pulpo	*'pool-poh*
red snapper	huachinango	*wah-chee-'nahn-goh*
reptile	reptil (*m*)	*rehp-'teel*
salamander	salamandra	*sah-lah-'mahn-drah*
sardine	sardina	*sahr-'dee-nah*
shark	tiburón (*m*)	*tee-boo-'rohn*
snake	serpiente (*f*)	*sehr-pee-'ehn-teh*
sole fish	lenguado	*lehn-'gwah-doh*
swordfish	pez espada (*m*)	*pehs ehs-'pah-dah*
toad	sapo	*'sah-poh*
trout	trucha	*'troo-chah*
tuna	atún (*m*)	*ah-'toon*
turtle	tortuga	*tohr-'too-gah*
whale	ballena	*bah-'yeh-nah*

FOCUS: Some Common Animals

el gato   la vaca   el caballito   el perro

el tigre   el león   el venado   el caballo

el lobo   el cerdo   el elefante   el oso

d. INSECTS AND OTHER INVERTEBRATES

ant	hormiga	*ohr-'mee-gah*
bedbug	chinche (*f*)	*'cheen-cheh*
bee	abeja	*ah-'beh-hah*
bug	insecto	*een-'sehk-toh*
butterfly	mariposa	*mah-ree-'poh-sah*
caterpillar	oruga	*oh-'roo-gah*
cockroach	cucaracha	*koo-kah-'rah-chah*
cricket	grillo	*'gree-yoh*
firefly	luciérnaga	*loo-see·'ehr-nah-gah*
flea	pulga	*'pool-gah*
fly	mosca	*'mohs-kah*
grasshopper	saltamontes (*m*)	*sahl-tah-'mohn-tehs*
	chapulín (*m*)	*chah-poo-'leen*
insect	insecto	*een-'sehk-toh*
louse	piojo	*pee-'oh-hoh*
metamorphosis	metamorfosis (*f*)	*meh-tah-mohr-'foh-sees*
mosquito	mosquito	*mohs-'kee-toh*
moth	polilla	*poh-'lee-yah*
scorpion	alacrán (*m*)	*ah-lah-'krahn*
spider	araña	*ah-'rah-nyah*
termite	comején (*m*)	*koh-meh-'hehn*
tick	garrapata	*gah-rrah-'pah-tah*
wasp	avispa	*ah-'bees-pah*
worm	gusano	*goo-'sah-noh*

COMMUNICATING, FEELING, AND THINKING

16. BASIC SOCIAL EXPRESSIONS

a. GREETINGS AND FAREWELLS

Good afternoon.	Buenas tardes.	*'bweh-nahs 'tahr-dehs*
Good evening.	Buenas tardes.	*'bweh-nahs 'tahr-dehs*
Good morning.	Buenos días.	*'bweh-nohs 'dee·ahs*
Good night.	Buenas noches.	*'bweh-nahs 'noh-chehs*
Good bye.	Adiós.	*ah-dee·'ohs*
Hello.	Hola.	*'oh-lah*
How are you?	¿Cómo está Ud.? *(pol)*	*'koh-moh ehs-'tah oos-'tehd*
	¿Cómo estás? *(fam)*	*'koh-moh ehs-'tahs*
	¿Qué tal?	*keh tahl*
How's it going?	¿Cómo le va?	*'koh-moh leh bah*
Badly.	Mal.	*mahl*
Fine.	Bien.	*bee·'ehn*
Quite well.	Bastante bien.	*bahs-'tahn-teh bee·'ehn*
So, so.	Regular.	*reh-goo-'lahr*
Very well.	Muy bien.	*mwee bee·'ehn*
Pleased to meet you.	Mucho gusto en conocerlo(la).	*'moo-choh 'goos-toh ehn koh-noh-'sehr-loh (-lah)*
See you.	Hasta luego.	*'ahs-tah 'lweh-goh*
• **See you seen.**	Hasta pronto.	*'ahs-tah 'prohn-toh*
• **See you Sunday.**	Hasta el domingo.	*'ahs-tah ehl doh-'meen-goh*
• **See you tomorrow.**	Hasta mañana.	*'ahs-tah mah-'nyah-nah*
Shake hands with . . .	Dar la mano a . . .	*dahr lah 'mah-noh ah*
• **handshake**	apretón de manos *(m)*	*ah-preh-'tohn deh 'mah-nohs*

b. FORMS OF ADDRESS AND INTRODUCTIONS

A pleasure.	Mucho gusto.	*'moo-choh 'goos-toh*
• **The pleasure is mine.**	El gusto es mío.	*ehl 'goos-toh ehs 'mee·oh*
• **Likewise.**	Igualmente.	*ee-'gwahl-'mehn-teh*

Allow me to introduce myself.	Permítame presentarme.	*pehr-'mee-tah-meh preh-sehn-'tahr-meh*
Allow me to introduce you to . . .	Permítame presentarlo(la) a . . .	*pehr-'mee-tah-meh preh-sehn-'tahr-loh (-lah) ah*
be on a first-name basis	tutear (v)	*too-teh-'ahr*
calling card	tarjeta de visita	*tahr-'heh-tah deh bee-'see-tah*
Come in. (Enter)	Pase Ud.	*'pah-seh oos-'tehd*
	Pasen Uds. (pl)	*'pah-sehn oos-'teh-dehs*
Delighted.	Encantado(a)	*ehn-kahn-'tah-doh (-dah)*
introduce oneself	presentarse (v)	*preh-sehn-'tahr-seh*
• **introduction**	presentación	*preh-sehn-tah-see-'ohn*
know someone	conocer*	*koh-noh-'sehr*
title	título	*'tee-too-loh*
• **Dr.**	Doctor(a) (Dr.)	*dohk-'tohr(ah)*
• **Miss**	Señorita (Srta.)	*seh-nyoh-'ree-tah*
• **Mr.**	Señor (Sr.)	*seh-'nyohr*
• **Mrs.**	Señora (Sra.)	*seh-'nyoh-rah*
What's your name?	¿Cómo se llama Ud.?	*'koh-moh seh 'yah-mah oos-'tehd*
• **My name is . . .**	Me llamo . . .	*meh 'yah-moh*
• **I'm . . .**	Soy . . .	*soy*

c. COURTESY

Bless you. (*after a sneeze*)	Salud.	*sah-'lood*
Cheers.	Salud.	*sah-'lood*
Congratulations.	Enhorabuena.	*ehn-oh-rah-'bweh-nah*
	Felicitaciones.	*feh-lee-see-tah-see-'oh-nehs*
Don't mention it.	No hay de qué.	*noh 'ah·ee deh keh*
Eat up.	Buen apetito.	*bwehn ah-peh-'tee-toh*
	Buen provecho.	*bwehn proh-'beh-choh*
Excuse me.	Perdón.	*pehr-'dohn*
	Discúlpeme.	*dees-'kool-peh-meh*
Good luck.	Buena suerte.	*'bweh-nah 'swehr-teh*
Happy Birthday.	Feliz cumpleaños.	*feh-'lees koom-pleh-'ah-nyohs*
Happy New Year.	Feliz Año Nuevo.	*feh-'lees 'ah-nyoh 'nweh-boh*
Have a good holiday.	¡Qué pase(n) buenas vacaciones!	*keh 'pahn-sehn 'bweh-nahs bah-kah-see-'oh-nehs*

Have a good time.	¡Diviértase!	dee-bee-'ehr-tah-seh
	¡Diviértanse! (pl)	dee-bee-'ehr-tahn-seh
Have a good trip.	Buen viaje.	bwehn bee-'ah-heh
Many thanks.	Muchas gracias.	'moo-chahs 'grah-see·ahs
May I come in?	¿Puedo pasar?	'pweh-doh pah-'sahr
May I help you?	¿En qué puedo servirlo(la)?	ehn keh 'pweh-doh sehr-'beer-loh (-lah)
Merry Christmas.	Feliz Navidad.	feh-'lees nah-bee-'dahd
No!	¡No!	noh
OK	Está bien.	ehs-'tah bee-'ehn
Please.	Por favor.	pohr fah-'bohr
Yes.	Sí.	see
You're welcome.	De nada.	deh 'nah-dah
Thank you.	Gracias.	'grah-see·ahs

17. SPEAKING AND TALKING

a. SPEECH ACTIVITIES AND TYPES

advice	consejo	kohn-'seh-hoh
• advise	aconsejar (v)	ah-kohn-seh-'hahr
allude	aludir (v)	ah-loo-'deer
analogy	analogía	ah-nah-loh-'gee-ah
announce	anunciar (v)	ah-noon-see-'ahr
• announcement	anuncio	ah-'noon-see-oh
answer	responder (v)	rehs-pohn-'dehr
	contestar (v)	kohn-tehs-'tahr
• answer	respuesta	rehs-'pwehs-tah
argue	reñir*	reh-'nyeer
• argument	disputa	dees-'poo-tah
articulate	articular (v)	ahr-tee-koo-'lahr
ask	preguntar (v)	preh-goon-'tahr
beg to do something	rogarle* hacer una cosa	roh-'gahr-leh ah-'sehr 'oo-nah 'koh-sah
call	llamar (v)	yah-'mahr
change the subject	cambiar (v) de tema	kahm-bee-'ahr deh 'teh-mah
chat	charlar (v)	chahr-'lahr
communicate	communicar (v)	koh-moo-nee-'kahr
• communication	communicación (f)	koh-moo-nee-kah-see-'ohn
compare	comparar (v)	kohm-pah-'rahr
• comparison	comparación (f)	kohm-pah-rah-see-'ohn
conclude	concluir*	kohn-'klweer
• conclusion	conclusión (f)	kohn-kloo-see-'ohn
congratulate	felicitar (v)	feh-lee-see-'tahr

conversation	conversación (f)	kohn-behr-sah-see·'ohn
debate	debatir (v)	deh-bah-'teer
• debate	debate (m)	deh-'bah-teh
declare	declarar (v)	deh-klah-'rahr
deny	negar*	neh-'gahr
describe	describir (v)	dehs-kree-'beer
• description	descripción (f)	dehs-kreep-see·'ohn
dictate	dictar (v)	deek-'tahr
digress	divagar (v)	dee-bah-'gahr
discuss	discutir (v)	dees-koo-'teer
• discussion	discusión (f)	dees-koo-see·'ohn
emphasize	enfatizar (v)	ehn-fah-tee-'sahr
• emphasis	énfasis (m)	'ehn-fah-sees
excuse oneself	disculparse (v)	dees-kool-'pahr-seh
• excuse	excusa	ehks-'koo-sah
explain	explicar (v)	ehks-plee-'kahr
• explanation	explicación (f)	ehks-plee-kah-see·'ohn
express oneself	expresarse (v)	ehks-preh-'sahr-seh
• express	expresar (v)	ehks-preh-'sahr
• expression	expresión (f)	ehks-preh-see·'ohn
figure of speech	figura retórica	fee-'goo-rah reh-'toh-ree-kah
• allegory	alegoría	ah-leh-goh-'ree·ah
• literal	literal (adj)	lee-teh-'rahl
• metaphor	metáfora	meh-'tah-foh-rah
• symbol	símbolo	'seem-boh-loh
gossip	chismear (v)	chees-meh-'ahr
• gossip	chisme (m)	'chees-meh
hesitate	vacilar (v)	bah-see-'lahr
• hesitation	vacilación (f)	bah-see-lah-see·'ohn
identify	identificar (v)	ee-dehn-tee-fee-'kahr
indicate, point out	señalar (v)	seh-'nyah-lahr
• indication	indicación (f)	een-dee-kah-see·'ohn
inform	avisar (v)	ah-bee-'sahr
interrupt	interrumpir (v)	een-teh-rroom-'peer
• interruption	interrupción (f)	een-teh-rroop-see·'ohn
invite	invitar (v)	een-bee-'tahr
• invitation	invitación (f)	een-bee-tah-see·'ohn
jest	bromear (v)	broh-meh-'ahr
joke	chiste (m)	'chees-teh
• tell a joke	contar* un chiste	kohn-'tahr oon 'chees-teh
keep quiet	callarse (v)	kah-'yahr-seh
lecture	conferencia	kohn-feh-'rehn-see·ah
• lecture	dar* una conferencia	dahr 'oo-nah kohn-feh-'rehn-see·ah
lie	mentir*	mehn-'teer
• lie	mentira	mehn-'tee-rah

listen to	escuchar (v)	ehs-koo-'chahr
malign, speak badly	hablar (v) mal de	ah-'blahr mahl deh
mean	querer* decir (v)	keh-'rehr-deh-'seer
	significar (v)	seeg-nee-fee-'kahr
• meaning	significado	seeg-nee-fee-'kah-doh
mention	mencionar (v)	mehn-see·oh-'nahr
mumble	mascullar (v)	mahs-koo-'yahr
murmur	murmurar (v)	moor-moo-'rahr
nag	regañar (v)	reh-gah-'nyahr
offend	ofender (v)	oh-fehn-'dehr
oral	oral (adj)	oh-'rahl
• orally	oralmente (adv)	oh-rahl-'mehn-teh
order	mandar (v)	mahn-'dahr
• order	mandato	mahn-'dah-toh
outspoken	franco (adj)	'frahn-koh
praise	alabar (v)	ah-lah-'bahr
pray	rezar (v)	reh-'sahr
	orar (v)	oh-'rahr
• prayer	oración (f)	oh-rah-see·'ohn
preach	predicar (v)	preh-dee-'kahr
• sermon	sermón (m)	sehr-'mohn
predict	predecir*	preh-deh-'seer
promise	prometer (v)	proh-meh-'tehr
• promise	promesa	proh-'meh-sah
pronounce	pronunciar (v)	proh-noon-see·'ahr
• pronunciation	pronunciación (f)	proh-noon-see·ah-see·'ohn
propose	proponer*	proh-poh-'nehr
recommend	recomendar*	reh-koh-mehn-'dahr
relate	relatar (v)	reh-lah-'tahr
repeat	repetir*	reh-peh-'teer
• repetition	repetición (f)	reh-peh-tee-see·'ohn
report	relatar (v)	reh-lah-'tahr
• report	informe (m)	een-'fohr-meh
reproach	reprochar (v)	reh-proh-'chahr
request	pedir*	peh-'deer
• request	petición (f)	peh-tee-see·'ohn
rhetoric	retórica	reh-'toh-ree-kah
• rhetorical	retórico (adj)	reh-'toh-ree-koh
• rhetorical question	pregunta retórica	preh-'goon-tah reh-'toh-ree-kah
rumor	rumor (m)	roo-'mohr
• Rumor has it that . . .	Se dice que . . .	seh 'dee-seh keh
say, tell	decir*	deh-'seer
shout, yell	gritar (v)	gree-'tahr
• shout, yell	grito	'gree-toh

shut up	callarse (v)	kah-'yahr-seh
silence	silencio	see-'lehn-see·oh
• silent	silencioso (adj)	see-lehn-see-'oh-soh
speak, talk	decir*	deh-'seer
• speech, talk	discurso	dees-'koor-soh
state	declarar (v)	deh-klah-'rahr
• statement	declaración (f)	deh-klah-rah-see-'ohn
story	cuento	'kwehn-toh
• tell a story	contar*	kohn-'tahr
suggest	sugerir*	soo-heh-'reer
summarize	resumir (v)	reh-soo-'meer
• summary	resumen	reh-'soo-mehn
swear (in court)	jurar (v)	hoo-'rahr
swear (profanity)	maldecir*	mahl-deh-'seer
thank	agradecer*	ah-grah-deh-'sehr
threaten	amenazar (v)	ah-meh-nah-'sahr
• threat	amenaza	ah-meh-'nah-sah
toast	brindar (v)	breen-'dahr
• toast	brindis (m)	'breen-dees
translate	traducir*	trah-doo-'seer
• translation	traducción (f)	trah-dook-see-'ohn
utter	pronunciar (v)	proh-noon-see-'ahr
vocabulary	vocabulario	boh-kah-boo-'lah-ree·oh
warn	advertir*	adh-behr-'teer
• warning	aviso	ah-'bee-soh
	advertencia	ahd-behr-'tehn-see-ah
whisper	cuchichear (v)	koo-chee-cheh-'ahr
	susurrar (v)	soo-soo-'rrahr
word	palabra	pah-'lah-brah
	vocablo	boh-'kah-bloh
yawn	bostezar (v)	bohs-teh-'sahr
• yawn	bostezo	bohs-'teh-soh

b. USEFUL EXPRESSIONS

actually	en realidad	ehn reh-ah-lee-'dahd
as a matter of fact	en realidad	ehn reh-ah-lee-'dahd
	de hecho	deh 'eh-choh
briefly	brevemente (adv)	breh-beh-'mehn-teh
by the way	a propósito	ah proh-'poh-see-toh
Go ahead.	¡Adelante!	ah-deh-'lahn-teh
I didn't understand.	No entendí.	noh ehn-tehn-'dee
How do you say . . .	¿Cómo se dice . . .	'koh-moh seh 'dee-seh
in Spanish?	en español?	ehn ehs-pah-'nyohl
I'm sure that . . .	Estoy seguro(a) de	ehs-'toy seh-'goo-roh
	que . . .	(-rah) deh keh

Isn't it so?	¿verdad?	*behr-'dahd*
It seems that . . .	Parece que . . .	*pah-'reh-seh keh*
It's not true.	No es verdad.	*noh ehs behr-'dahd*
It's obvious that . . .	Es obvio que . . .	*ehs 'ohb-bee·oh keh*
It's true!	¡Es verdad!	*ehs behr-'dahd*
Listen!	¡Escuche!	*ehs-'koo-cheh*
now	ahora	*ah-'oh-rah*
to sum up	en resumen	*ehn reh-'soo-mehn*
You don't say!	¡No me digas!	*noh me 'dee-gahs*
Who knows?	¿Quién sabe?	*kee-'ehn 'sah-beh*

18. THE TELEPHONE

a. TELEPHONES AND ACCESSORIES

answering machine	contestador automático	*kohn-tehs-tah-'dohr ow-toh-'mah-tee-koh*
cable	cable (*m*)	*'kah-bleh*
fax machine	fax (*m*)	*fahks*
intercom	interfono	*een-tehr-'foh-noh*
plug	clavija	*klah-'bee-hah*
receiver, earphone	auricular (*m*)	*ow-ree-koo-'lahr*
	receptor (*m*)	*reh-seph-'tohr*
telecommunication	telecomunicación (*f*)	*teh-leh-koh-moo-nee-kah-see·'ohn*
• telecommunications satellite	satélite de telecomunicación	*sah-'teh-lee-teh deh teh-leh-koh-moo-nee-kah-see·'ohn*
telephone	teléfono	*teh-'leh-foh-noh*
• outlet (*telephone*)	toma	*'toh-mah*
• pay telephone	teléfono público	*teh-'leh-foh-noh 'poo-blee-koh*
• portable telephone	teléfono remoto	*teh-'leh-foh-noh reh-'moh-toh*
• telephone book	guía de teléfonos	*'gee·ah deh teh-'leh-foh-nohs*
• telephone booth	cabina telefónica	*kah-'bee-nah teh-leh-'foh-nee-kah*
telex machine	télex (*m*)	*'teh-lehks*
token	ficha	*'fee-chah*
• slot (*for tokens*)	ranura	*rah-'noo-rah*
yellow pages	páginas amarillas	*'pah-hee-nahs ah-mah-'ree-yahs*

b. USING THE TELEPHONE

answer	responder a (v)	rehs-pohn-'dehr ah
	contestar a (v)	kohn-tehs-'tahr ah
area code	zona telefónica	'soh-nah teh-leh-'foh-nee-kah
collect call	llamada de cobro revertido	yah-'mah-dah deh 'koh-broh reh-behr-'tee-doh
dial	marcar (v)	mahr-'kahr
• dial direct	marcar directo (m)	mahr-'kahr dee-'rehk-toh
fax	fax (m)	fahks
hang up	colgar*	kohl-'gahr
information	información (f)	een-fohr-mah-see-'ohn
long-distance call	llamada de larga distancia	yah-'mah-dah deh 'lahr-gah dees-'tahn-see-ah
make a call	hacer* una llamada	ah-'sehr 'oo-nah yah-'mah-dah
• Hello	Aló (Latin America)	ah-'loh
	Bueno (Mexico)	'bweh-noh
	Diga (Spain)	'dee-gah
• Is . . . in?	¿Está . . . ?	ehs-'tah
• This is . . .	Habla . . .	'ah-blah
• Who's speaking?	¿De parte de quién?	deh 'pahr-teh deh kee·'ehn
• Wrong number.	Número equivocado.	'noo-meh-roh eh-kee-boh-'kah-doh
message	mensaje (m)	mehn-'sah-heh
operator	telefonista (m, f), operador(a)	teh-leh-foh-'nees-tah, oh-peh-rah-'dohr (-rah)
phone	llamar (v) por teléfono	yah-'mahr pohr teh-'leh-foh-noh
ring	sonar*	soh-'nahr
telephone bill	cuenta telefónica	'kwehn-tah teh-leh-'foh-nee-kah
telephone line	línea telefónica	'lee-neh-ah teh-leh-'foh-nee-kah
• busy (line)	ocupada	oh-koo-'pah-dah
• free (line)	libre	'lee-breh
telephone number	número de teléfono	'noo-meh-roh deh teh-'leh-foh-noh
telex	télex (m)	'teh-lehks

19. LETTER WRITING

a. FORMAL SALUTATIONS/CLOSINGS

Dear Sir(s)	Estimado(s) señor(es):	*ehs-tee-'mah-doh(s) seh-'nyohr (-'nyoh-rehs)*
Dear Madam	Estimada señora:	*ehs-tee-'mah-dah seh-'nyoh-rah*
To Whom It May Concern:	A quien corresponda	*ah kee-'ehn koh-rrehs-'pohn-dah*
Attentively,	Atentamente,	*ah-tehn-tah-'mehn-teh*
Attentively yours,	De usted atentamente,	*deh oos-'tehd ah-tehn-tah-'mehn-teh*
Sincerely,	Sinceramente	*seen-seh-rah-'mehn-teh*

b. FAMILIAR SALUTATIONS/CLOSINGS

Dear . . .	Querido(a)	*keh-'ree-doh (-dah)*
With love	Con cariño	*kohn kah-'ree-nyoh*
Affectionately	Cariñosamente	*kah-ree-nyoh-sah-'mehn-teh*
With much love	Con mucho cariño	*kohn 'moo-choh kah-'ree-nyoh*
A kiss	Un beso	*oon 'beh-soh*
A hug	Un abrazo	*oon ah-'brah-soh*

c. PARTS OF A LETTER/PUNCTUATION

body	cuerpo	*'kwehr-poh*
closing	despedida	*dehs-peh-'dee-dah*
date	fecha	*'feh-chah*
heading	membrete (m)	*mehm-'breh-teh*
place	lugar (m)	*loo-'gahr*
punctuation	puntuación (f)	*poon-twah-see-'ohn*
• accent	acento	*ah-'sehn-toh*
• apostrophe	apóstrofe (m)	*ah-'pohs-troh-feh*
• asterisk	asterisco	*ahs-teh-'rees-koh*
• bracket	paréntesis (m)	*pah-'rehn-teh-sees*
• capital letter	mayúscula	*mah-'yohs-koo-lah*
• colon	dos puntos	*dohs 'poon-tohs*
• comma	coma	*'koh-mah*
• exclamation mark	signo de admiración	*'seeg-noh deh ahd-mee-rah-see-'ohn*
• hyphen	guión (m)	*gee-'ohn*
• italics	bastardilla	*bahs-tahr-'dee-yah*
• period	punto	*'poon-toh*

• **question mark**	signo de interrogación	*'seeg-noh deh een-teh-rroh-gah-see·'ohn*
• **quotation mark**	comillas	*koh-'mee-yahs*
• **semicolon**	punto y coma	*'poon-toh ee 'koh-mah*
• **small letter**	minúscula	*mee-'noos-koo-lah*
• **square bracket**	corchete (*m*)	*kohr-'cheh-teh*
• **underlining**	subrayado	*soob-rrah-'yah-doh*
salutation	salutación (*f*)	*sah-loo-tah-see·'ohn*
	saludo	*sah-'loo-doh*
signature	firma	*'feer-mah*
• **sign**	firmar (*v*)	*feer-'mahr*
text	texto	*'tehks-toh*
• **abbreviation**	abreviatura	*ah-breh-bee·ah-'too-rah*
• **letter** (*of the alphabet*)	letra	*'leh-trah*
• **line**	línea	*'lee-ne·ah*
• **margin**	margen (*m*)	*'mahr-hehn*
• **P.S.**	PD (posdata)	*pohs-'dah-tah*
• **paragraph**	párrafo	*'pah-rrah-foh*
• **phrase**	frase (*f*)	*'frah-seh*
• **sentence**	oración (*f*)	*oh-rah-see·'ohn*
• **spelling**	ortografía	*ohr-toh-grah-'fee·ah*
• **word**	palabra	*pah-'lah-brah*
	vocablo	*boh-'kah-bloh*

FOCUS: Letters

Madrid, 24 junio 1990	**Place and date** lugar y fecha
Estimados señores:	**Salutation** Saludo
En respuesta a su carta con fecha de	**Body of the letter** Texto de la carta
De usted atentamente,	**Complimentary close** Despedida
José González	**Signature** Firma

d. WRITING MATERIALS AND ACCESSORIES

adhesive tape	cinta adhesiva	*'seen-tah ahd-eh-'see-bah*
computer	computadora	*kohm-poo-tah-'doh-rah*
	ordenador (*m*)	*ohr-deh-nah-'dohr*
envelope	sobre (*m*)	*'soh-breh*
eraser	goma de borrar	*'goh-mah deh boh-'rrahr*
glue	pegamento	*peh-gah-'mehn-toh*
ink	tinta	*'teen-tah*
letter	carta	*'kahr-tah*
letterhead	papel con membrete (*m*)	*pah-'pehl kohn mehm-'breh-teh*
marker	marcador (*m*)	*mahr-kah-'dohr*
pad	bloc (*m*)	*blohk*
page	página	*'pah-hee-nah*
paper	papel (*m*)	*pah-'pehl*
paper clip	sujetapapeles (*m*)	*soo-heh-tah-pah-'peh-lehs*
pen	pluma	*'ploo-mah*
• **ballpoint pen**	bolígrafo	*boh-'lee-grah-foh*
• **felt pen**	rotulador (*m*)	*roh-too-lah-'dohr*
pencil	lápiz (*m*)	*'lah-pees*
ruler	regla	*'reh-glah*
scissors	tijeras (*f*)	*tee-'heh-rahs*
staple	grapa	*'grah-pah*
• **stapler**	engrapador (*m*)	*ehn-grah-pah-'dohr*
string	cordel (*m*)	*kohr-'dehl*
typewriter	máquina de escribir	*'mah-kee-nah deh ehs-kree-'beer*
• **carriage**	carro	*'kah-rroh*
• **keyboard**	teclado	*teh-'klah-doh*
• **margin**	margen (*m*)	*'mahr-hehn*
• **ribbon**	cinta de máquina de escribir	*'seen-tah deh 'mah-kee-nah deh ehs-kree-'beer*
• **space bar**	espaciador (*m*)	*ehs-pah-see·ah-'dohr*
• **tab**	tabulador (*m*)	*tah-boo-lah-'dohr*
word processor	procesador de texto (*m*)	*proh-seh-sah-'dohr deh 'tehks-toh*

For additional computer terms, see Section 42.

e. AT THE POST OFFICE

abroad	al extranjero	*ahl ehks-trahn-'heh-roh*
address	dirección (*f*)	*dee-rehk-see·'ohn*
	señas	*'seh-nyahs*
• **return address**	dirección del remitente (*m*)	*dee-rehk-see·'ohn dehl reh-mee-'tehn-teh*
addressee	destinatario	*dehs-tee-nah-'tah-ree·oh*
airmail	por avión	*pohr ah-bee-'yohn*
business letter	carta comercial	*'kahr-tah koh-mehr-see·'ahl*
clerk	dependiente	*deh-pehn-dee·'ehn-teh*
clerk's window	ventanilla	*behn-tah-'nee-yah*
correspondence	correspondencia	*koh-rrehs-pohn-'dehn-see·ah*
courier	mensajero	*mehn-sah-'heh-roh*
envelope	sobre (*m*)	*'soh-breh*
letter carrier	cartero	*kahr-'teh-roh*
mail	correo	*koh-'rreh-oh*
• **mail**	echar (*v*) al correo	*eh-'chahr ahl koh-'rreh-oh*
mail delivery	distribución (*f*) de correo	*dees-tree-boo-see·'ohn deh koh-'rreh-oh*
mailbox	buzón (*m*)	*boo-'sohn*
money order	giro postal	*'hee-roh pohs-'tahl*
note	nota	*'noh-tah*
package	paquete (*m*)	*pah-'keh-teh*
postcard	tarjeta postal	*tahr-'heh-tah pohs-'tahl*
postal code	código postal	*'koh-dee-goh pohs-'tahl*
postal rate	tarifa postal	*tah-'ree-fah pohs-'tahl*
printed matter	impresos	*eem-'preh-sohs*
registered letter	carta certificada	*'kahr-tah sehr-tee-fee-'kah-dah*
receive	recibir (*v*)	*reh-see-'beer*
reply	responder	*rehs-pohn-'dehr*
	contestar (*v*)	*kohn-tehs-'tahr*
send	mandar (*v*)	*mahn-'dahr*
sender	remitente (*m*)	*reh-mee-'tehn-teh*
special delivery	correo urgente	*koh-'rreh-oh oor-'hehn-teh*
	entrega inmediata	*ehn-'treh-gah een-meh-dee·'ah-tah*
stamp	estampilla	*ehs-tahm-'pee-yah*
	sello	*'seh-yoh*
	timbre (*m*)	*'teem-breh*
wait for	esperar (*v*)	*ehs-peh-'rahr*
write	escribir (*v*)	*ehs-kree-'beer*

FOCUS: How to Address an Envelope

Sr. Antonio González Ruiz
Avenida Cinco de Mayo 537
Guadalajara, Jalisco
México

NOTE: The street number follows the street name.

---

20. THE MEDIA

a. PRINT MEDIA

advertising	publicidad (*f*)	*poo-blee-see-'dahd*
	propaganda	*proh-pah-'gahn-dah*
appendix	apéndice (*m*)	*ah-'pehn-dee-seh*
atlas	atlas (*m*)	*'aht-lahs*
author	autor(a)	*ow-'tohr (-ah)*
book	libro	*'lee-broh*
comics	tiras cómicas	*'tee-rahs 'koh-mee-kahs*
cover	portada	*pohr-'tah-dah*
essay	ensayo	*ehn-'sah·yoh*
fiction	ficción	*feehk-'see·ohn*
• **non-fiction**	literatura no novelesca	*lee-teh-rah-'too-rah noh noh-beh-'lehs-kah*
index	índice (*m*)	*'een-dee-seh*
magazine	revista	*reh-'beehs-tah*
• **article**	artículo	*ahr-'tee-koo-loh*
• **criticism**	crítica	*'kree-tee-kah*
• **daily newspaper**	diario	*dee-'ah-ree·oh*
• **editor**	redactor (*m*)	*reh-dahk-'tohr*
• **editorial**	editorial (*m*)	*eh-dee-toh-ree-'ahl*
• **front page**	primera plana	*pree-'meh-rah 'plah-nah*
• **headline**	titular (*m*)	*tee-too-'lahr*
• **illustration**	ilustración (*f*)	*een-loos-trah-see-'ohn*
• **interview**	entrevista	*ehn-treh-'bees-tah*
• **journalist**	periodista (*m/f*)	*peh-ree·oh-'dees-tah*
• **news**	noticias	*noh-'tee-see·ahs*
• **obituary**	obituario	*oh-bee-'twah-ree·oh*
• **obituaries**	necrología (*f, pl*)	*neh-kroh-loh-'hee-ah*
• **photo(graph)**	foto(grafía)	*'foh-toh (foh-toh-grah-'fee-ah)*
• **reader**	lector(a)	*lehk-'tohr (-rah)*

• **reporter**	reportero	*reh-pohr-'teh-roh*
• **review**	reseña	*reh-'seh-nyah*
note	nota	*'noh-tah*
• **footnote**	nota	*'noh-tah*
novel	novela	*noh-'beh-lah*
• **adventure**	aventura	*ah-behn-'too-rah*
• **best seller**	éxito de librería	*'ehks-ee-toh deh lee-breh-'ree-ah*
• **mystery**	misterio	*mees-'teh-ree-oh*
• **plot**	trama	*'trah-mah*
• **romance**	romántica	*roh-'mahn-tee-kah*
page	página	*'pah-hee-nah*
pamphlet, brochure	folleto	*foh-'yeh-toh*
play	drama (*m*)	*'drah-mah*
	obra de teatro	*'oh-brah deh teh-'ah-troh*
• **comedy**	comedia	*koh-'meh-dee·ah*
• **drama**	drama (*m*)	*'drah-mah*
• **tragedy**	tragedia	*trah-'heh-dee·ah*
poem, poetry	poema (*m*)	*poh-'eh-mah*
	poesía	*poh-eh-'see·ah*
print	impresión (*f*)	*eem-preh-see-'ohn*
• **in print**	publicado	*poo-blee-'kah-doh*
	impreso	*eem-'preh-soh*
• **out of print**	agotado	*ah-goh-'tah-doh*
• **printing**	imprenta	*eem-'prehn-tah*
• **typography**	tipografía	*tee-poh-grah-'fee·ah*
publish	publicar (*v*)	*poo-blee-'kahr*
• **publisher**	editor (*m*)	*eh-dee-'tohr*
read	leer (*v*)	*leh-'ehr*
reference book	libro de consulta	*'lee-broh deh kohn-'sool-tah*
• **definition**	definición (*f*)	*deh-fee-nee-see-'ohn*
• **dictionary**	diccionario	*deek-see-oh-'nah-ree·oh*
• **encyclopedia**	enciclopedia	*ehn-see-kloh-'peh-dee·ah*
science fiction	ciencia ficción	*see-'ehn-see·ah feek-see-'ohn*
short story	cuento	*'kwehn-toh*
text	texto	*'tehks-toh*
title	título	*'tee-too-loh*
turn (pages), leaf through	hojear (*v*)	*oh-heh-'ahr*
write	escribir (*v*)	*ehs-kree-'beer*

b. ELECTRONIC MEDIA

antenna	antena	*ahn-'teh-nah*
audio equipment	equipo auditivo	*eh-'kee-poh ow-dee-'tee-boh*
• **cassette**	casete (*m*)	*kah-'seh-teh*
• **cassette player**	tocacintas (*m*)	*toh-kah-'seen-tahs*
• **compact disc**	disco compacto	*'dees-koh kohm-'pahk-toh*
• **headphones**	auriculares (*m*)	*ow-ree-koo-'lah-rehs*
• **loudspeaker**	altavoz (*m*)	*'ahl-tah-'bohs*
• **microphone**	micrófono	*mee-'kroh-foh-noh*
• **play (a record)**	tocar (*v*)	*toh-'kahr*
• **receiver, tuner**	receptor (*m*)	*reh-sehp-'tohr*
• **record**	disco	*'dees-koh*
• **record**	grabar (*v*)	*grah-'bahr*
• **record player**	tocadiscos (*m*)	*toh-kah-'dees-kohs*
• **speaker**	altavoz (*m*)	*ahl-tah-'bohs*
• **stereo(phonic)**	estereofónico (*adj*)	*ehs-teh-reh-oh-'foh-nee-koh*
• **tape recorder**	grabadora	*grah-bah-'doh-rah*
program	programa (*m*)	*proh-'grah-mah*
projector	proyector (*m*)	*proh-yehk-'tohr*
• **slide projector**	proyector de diapositivas	*proh-yehk-'tohr deh dee·ah-poh-see-'tee-bahs*
radio	radio	*'rah-dee·oh*
• **car radio**	radio	*'rah-dee·oh*
• **listen to**	escuchar (*v*)	*ehs-koo-'chahr*
• **news report**	noticias	*noh-'tee·see·ahs*
• **newscast**	noticiario	*noh-tee-see-'ah-ree·oh*
• **pocket radio**	radio de bolsillo	*'rah-dee·oh deh bohl-see-yoh*
• **station**	estación (*f*)	*ehs-tah-see-'ohn*
show	función (*f*)	*foon-see-'ohn*
television	televisión (*f*)	*teh-leh-bee-see-'ohn*
• **be on the air**	estar* transmitiendo	*ehs-'tahr trahns-mee-tee-'ehn-doh*
• **channel**	canal (*m*)	*kah-'nahl*
• **closed circuit**	circuito cerrado	*seer-'kwee-toh seh-'rrah-doh*
• **commercial**	anuncio	*ah-'noon-see·oh*
• **documentary**	documentario	*doh-koo-mehn-'tah-ree·oh*
• **interview**	entrevista	*ehn-tre-'bees-tah*
• **look at, watch**	mirar (*v*)	*mee-'rahr*
• **network**	cadena	*kah-'deh-nah*
• **remote control**	control remoto	*kohn-'trohl reh-'moh-toh*

• series	serie (f)	'seh-ree·eh
• soap opera	telenovela	teh-leh-noh-'beh-lah
• television set	televisor (m)	teh-leh-bee-'sohr
• transmission	transmisión (f)	trahns-mee-see·'ohn
• VCR	grabadora de videocasete	grah-bah-'doh-rah deh bee-deh·oh·oh-kah-'seh-teh
	videocasetera	bee-deh·oh-kah-seh-'teh-rah
• video game	juego eléctronico	hoo·'eh-goh eh-lehk-'troh-nee-koh
• videocassette	videocasete (m)	bee-deh-oh-kah-'seh-teh
• videotape	cinta (magnética) de video	'seen-tah (mahg-'neh-tee-ka) deh 'bee-deh·oh
turn off	apagar (v)	ah-pah-'gahr
turn on	poner*	poh-'nehr
walkie-talkie	radioteléfono portátil	rah-dee·oh-teh-'leh-foh-noh pohr-'tah-teel

21. FEELINGS

a. MOODS/ATTITUDES/EMOTIONS

affection	cariño	kah-'ree-nyoh
agree	estar de acuerdo	ehs-'tahr deh ah-'kwehr-doh
anger	enojo	eh-'noh-hoh
	ira	'ee-rah
anxiety, anxiousness	ansia	'ahn-see·ah
• anxious	ansioso (adj)	ahn-see·'oh-soh
	inquieto (adj)	een-kee·'eh-toh
assure	asegurar (v)	ah-seh-goo-'rahr
attitude	actitud (f)	ahk-tee-'tood
be able to	poder*	poh-'dehr

> Where there's a will, there's a way = Querer es poder

bore	aburrir (v)	ah-boo-'rreer
• become bored	aburririse (v)	ah-boo-'rreer-seh
• bored	aburrido (adj)	ah-boo-'rree-doh
• boredom	aburrimiento	ah-boo-rree-mee·'ehn-toh
complain	quejarse (v)	keh-'hahr-seh
• complaint	queja	'keh-hah

cry	llorar (v)	yoh-'rahr
• crying	llanto	'yahn-toh
depressed	deprimido (adj)	deh-pree-'mee-doh
• depression	depresión (f)	deh-preh-see-'ohn
desperate	desesperado (adj)	deh-sehs-peh-'rah-doh
• desperation	desesperación (f)	deh-sehs-peh-rah-see-'ohn
disagree	no estar* de acuerdo	noh ehs-'tahr deh ah-'kwehr-doh
• disagreement	desacuerdo	deh-sah-'kwehr-doh
• be against	estar* en contra de	ehs-'tahr ehn 'kohn-trah deh
disappoint	decepcionar (v)	deh-sehp-see-oh-'nahr
• disappointed	decepcionado (adj)	deh-sehp-see-oh-'nah-doh
dissatisfaction	descontento	dehs-kohn-'tehn-toh
• dissatisfied	descontento	dehs-kohn-'tehn-toh
encourage	animar (v)	ah-nee-'mahr
	estimular (v)	ehs-tee-moo-'lahr
faith, trust	fe (f)	feh
	confianza	kohn-fee-'ahn-sah
• trust	tener* confianza	teh-'nehr kohn-fee-'ahn-sah
feel	sentirse*	sehn-'teer-seh
• feel like	tener* ganas de	teh-'nehr 'gah-nahs deh
flatter	adular (v)	ah-doo-'lahr
• flattery	adulación (f)	ah-doo-lah-see-'ohn
fun, enjoyment	alegría	ah-leh-'gree·ah
	diversión (f)	dee-behr-see-'ohn
• have fun	divertirse*	dee-behr-'teer-seh
happiness	felicidad (f)	feh-lee-see-'dahd
• happy	feliz (adj)	feh-'lees
	contento (adj)	kohn-'tehn-toh
have to	tener* que	teh-'nehr keh
hope	esperar (v)	ehs-peh-'rahr
• hope	esperanza	ehs-peh-'rahn-sah
indifference	indiferencia	een-dee-feh-'rehn-see·ah
• indifferent	indiferente (adj)	een-dee-feh-'rehn-teh
joy	alegría	ah-leh-'gree·ah
laugh	reír*	reh-'eer
• laughter	risa	'ree-sah

He who laughs last laughs best = El que ríe al último ríe mejor.

matter	importar (v)	eem-pohr-'tahr
mood	humor (m)	oo-'mohr
• bad mood	mal humor	mahl oo-'mohr
• good mood	buen humor	bwehn oo-'mohr
need	necesitar (v)	neh-seh-see-'tahr
• need	necesidad (f)	neh-seh-see-'dahd
patience	paciencia	pah-see-'ehn-see·ah
• have patience	tener* paciencia	teh-'nehr pah-see-'ehn-see·ah
relief	alivio	ah-'lee-bee·oh
• relieve	aliviar (v)	ah-lee-bee-'ahr
	liberar (v)	lee-beh-'rahr
sad	triste (adj)	'trees-teh
• sadness	tristeza	trees-'teh-sah
• become sad	entristecerse*	ehn-trees-teh-'sehr-seh
satisfaction	satisfacción (f)	sah-tees-fahks-see-'ohn
• satisfied	satisfecho (adj)	sah-tees-'feh-choh
shame	vergüenza	behr-'gwehn-sah
• be ashamed	tener* vergüenza	teh-'nehr behr-'gwehn-sah
smile	sonreír*	sohn-reh·'eer
• smile	sonrisa	sohn-'ree-sah
sorrow	dolor (m)	doh-'lohr
	pena	'peh-nah
surprise	sorpresa	sohr-'preh-sah
• surprise	sorprender (v)	sohr-prehn-'dehr
• surprise	sorprendido (adj)	sohr-prehn-'dee-doh
sympathy (over a death)	pésame (m)	'peh-sah-meh
	condolencia	kohn-doh-'lehn-see·ah
• sympathetic	compasivo (adj)	kohm-pah-'see-boh
thankfulness	agradecimiento	ah-grah-deh-see-mee-'ehn-toh
• thankful	agradecido (adj)	ah-grah-deh-'see-doh
• thank	agradecer*	ah-grah-deh-'sehr
tolerance	tolerancia	toh-leh-'rahn-see·ah
• tolerate	tolerar (v)	toh-leh-'rahr
want to	querer*	keh-'rehr

b. LIKES AND DISLIKES

accept	aceptar (v)	ah-sehp-'tahr
• acceptable	aceptable (adj)	ah-sehp-'tah-bleh
• unacceptable	inaceptable (adj)	een-ah-sehp-'tah-bleh
approval	aprobación (f)	ah-proh-bah-see-'ohn
• approve	aprobar*	ah-proh-'bahr

be fond of	estar* encariñado con	ehs-'tahr ehn-kah-ree-'nyah-doh kohn
	ser* aficionado a	sehr ah-fee-see-oh-'nah-doh ah
detest	detestar (v)	deh-tehs-'tahr
	odiar (v)	oh-dee-'ahr
disgust	disgusto	dees-'goos-toh
• disgusted	disgustado (adj)	dees-goos-'tah-doh
hate	odiar (v)	oh-dee-'ahr
• hatred	odio	'oh-dee-oh
kiss	besar (v)	beh-'sahr
• kiss	beso	'beh-soh
like	gustarle a uno	goos-'tahr-leh ah 'oo-noh
• dislike	tener* aversión a	teh-'nehr ah-behr-see-'ohn ah
• liking	cariño	kah-'ree-nyo
love	amar (v)	ah-'mahr
	querer*	keh-'rehr
• love	amor (m)	ah-'mohr
mediocre	mediocre (adj)	meh-dee-'oh-kreh
pleasant	agradable (adj)	ah-grah-'dah-bleh
• unpleasant	desagradable (adj)	dehs-ah-grah-'dah-bleh
prefer	preferir*	preh-feh-'reer

c. EXPRESSING EMOTIONS

Are you joking?	¿Habla en serio?	'ah-blah ehn 'seh-ree-oh
Be careful.	Tenga cuidado.	'tehn-gah 'kwee-'dah-doh
Enough.	¡Basta!	'bahs-tah
Good heavens!	¡Dios mío!	dee-'ohs 'mee-oh
How fortunate!	¡Qué suerte!	keh 'swehr-teh
I can't stand him!	¡No puedo soportarlo!	noh 'pweh-doh soh-pohr-'tahr-loh
I don't believe it!	¡No lo puedo creer!	noh loh 'pweh-doh kre-'ehr
I don't feel like . . .	No tengo ganas de . . .	noh 'tehn-goh 'gah-nahs deh
I wish . . .	Ojalá . . .	oh-hah-'lah
I'm serious.	Hablo en serio.	'ah-bloh ehn 'seh-ree-oh
I'm sorry.	Lo siento.	loh see-'ehn-toh
Impossible.	Imposible.	eem-poh-'see-bleh
It doesn't matter	No importa.	noh eem-'pohr-tah
My God!	¡Dios mío!	dee-'ohs 'mee-oh
Poor man!	¡Pobrecito!	poh-breh-'see-toh
Poor woman!	¡Pobrecita!	poh-breh-'see-tah
Quiet!	¡Silencio!	see-'lehn-see-oh

Really?	¿De veras?	*deh 'beh-rahs*
Shut up!	¡Cállense!	*'kah-yehn-seh*
Thank goodness!	¡Gracias a Dios!	*'grah-see·ahs ah dee·'ohs*
Too bad!	¡Qué lástima!	*keh 'lahs-tee-mah*
Ugh!	¡Uf!	*oof*
Unbelievable!	¡Increíble!	*een-kreh-'ee-bleh*
Unfortunately!	Desafortunadamente.	*dehs-ah-fohr-too-nah-dah-'mehn-teh*
What a bore!	¡Qué bárbaro(a)!	*keh 'bahr-bah-roh (-rah)*
	¡Qué lata!	*keh 'lah-tah*

22. THINKING

a. DESCRIBING THOUGHT

complicated	complicado (*adj*)	*kohm-plee-'kah-doh*
concept	concepto	*kohn-'sehp-toh*
conscience	conciencia	*kohn-see-'ehn-see·ah*
conscientious	concienzudo (*adj*)	*kohn-see-ehn-'soo-doh*
difficult	difícil (*adj*)	*dee-'fee-seel*
doubt	duda	*'doo-dah*
easy	fácil (*adj*)	*'fah-seel*
existence	existencia	*ehks-ees-'tehn-see·ah*
hypothesis	hipótesis (*f*)	*ee-'poh-teh-sees*
idea	idea	*ee-'deh-ah*
ignorant	ignorante (*adj*)	*eeg-noh-'rahn-teh*
imagination	imaginación (*f*)	*ee-mah-hee-nah-see·'ohn*
interesting	interesante (*adj*)	*een-teh-reh-'sahn-teh*
judgment	juicio	*'hwee-see·oh*
knowledge	conocimiento	*koh-noh-see-mee·'ehn-toh*
knowledgeable	informado (*adj*)	*een-fohr-'mah-doh*
mind	mente (*f*)	*'mehn-teh*
opinion	opinión (*f*)	*oh-pee-nee·'ohn*
• in my opinion	a mi parecer	*ah mee pah-reh-'sehr*
problem	problema (*m*)	*proh-'bleh-mah*
• No problem.	Sin (ningún) problema	*seen (neen-'goon) proh-'bleh-mah*
reason	razón (*f*)	*rah-'sohn*
simple	sencillo (*adj*)	*sehn-'see-yoh*
thought	pensamiento	*pehn-sah-mee·'ehn-toh*
wisdom	sabiduría	*sah-bee-doo-'ree·ah*

b. BASIC THOUGHT PROCESSES

agree	estar* de acuerdo	ehs-'tahr deh ah-'kwehr-doh
be interested in	tener* interés en	teh-'nehr een-teh-'rehs ehn
be right	tener* razón	teh-'nehr rah-'sohn
be wrong	no tener* razón	noh teh-'nehr rah-'sohn
believe	creer (v)	kreh-'ehr
convince	convencer*	kohn-behn-'sehr
demonstrate	demostrar*	deh-mohs-'trahr
doubt	dudar (v)	doo-'dahr
forget	olvidarse de (v)	ohl-bee-'dahr-seh deh
imagine	imaginar (v)	ee-mah-hee-'nahr
know	saber*	sah-'behr
	conocer*	koh-noh-'sehr
learn	aprender (v)	ah-prehn-'dehr
persuade	persuadir (v)	peh-swah-'deer
reason	razonar (v)	rah-son-'nahr
reflect	reflexionar (v)	reh-fleh-ksee·oh-'nahr
	meditar (v)	meh-dee-'tahr
remember	recordar*	reh-kohr-'dahr
study	estudiar (v)	ehs-too-dee·'ahr
think	pensar*	pehn-'sahr
understand	comprender (v)	kohm-prehn-'dehr
	entender*	ehn-tehn-'dehr
• What do you think?	¿Qué opina Ud.?	keh oh-'pee-nah oos-'tehd

DAILY LIFE

23. AT HOME

a. PARTS OF THE HOUSE

attic	ático	'ah-tee-koh
balcony	balcón (m)	bahl-'kohn
basement	sótano	'soh-tah-noh
bathtub	bañera	bah-'nyeh-rah
ceiling	techo	'teh-choh
chimney	chimenea	chee-meh-'neh-ah
corridor	pasillo	pah-'see-yoh
door	puerta	'pwehr-tah
doorbell	timbre (m)	'teem-breh
entrance	entrada	ehn-'trah-dah
faucet	grifo	'gree-foh
fireplace	chimenea	chee-meh-'neh-ah
floor	suelo	'sweh-loh
floor (level)	piso	'pee-soh
garage	garaje (m)	gah-'rah-heh
garden	jardín (m)	har-'deen
ground floor	planta baja	'plahn-tah 'bah-hah
house	casa	'kah-sah
mailbox	buzón (m)	boo-'sohn
pantry	despensa	dehs-'pehn-sah
porch	portal	pohr-'tahl
	terraza cubierta	teh-'rrah-sah koo-bee·'ehr-tah
roof	tejado	teh-'hah-doh
shelf	estante (m)	ehs-'tahn-teh
shower	ducha	'doo-chah
sink	lavabo	lah-'bah-boh
stairs	escalera	ehs-kah-'leh-rah
switch	interruptor (m)	een-teh-rroop-'tohr
terrace	terraza	teh-'rrah-sah
toilet	retrete (m)	reh-'treh-teh
	excusado	ehks-coo-'sah-doh
wall (inside)	pared (f)	pah-'rehd
wall (exterior)	muro	'moo-roh
window	ventana	behn-'tah-nah
window ledge, sill	antepecho	ahn-teh-'peh-choh
yard	patio	'pah-tee·oh

b. ROOMS

bathroom	cuarto de baño	*kwahr-toh deh 'bah-nyoh*
bedroom	alcoba	*ahl-'koh-bah*
	cuarto	*'kwahr-toh*
	habitacion (*f*)	*ah-bee-tah-see·'ohn*
closet, cupboard	armario	*ahr-'mah-ree·oh*
dining room	comedor (*m*)	*koh-meh-'dohr*
hall	vestíbulo	*behs-'tee-boo-loh*
kitchen	cocina	*koh-'see-nah*
living room	sala (de estar)	*'sah-lah (deh ehs-'tahr)*
room	cuarto	*'kwahr-toh*
washroom	servicios	*sehr-'bee-see·ohs*
wine cellar	bodega	*boh-'deh-gah*

c. FURNITURE AND DECORATION

armchair	sillón (*m*)	*see-'yohn*
ashtray	cenicero	*seh-nee-'seh-roh*
bed	cama	*'kah-mah*
bedside table	mesilla de noche	*meh-'see-yah deh 'noh-cheh*
bookcase	estante (*m*)	*ehs-'tahn-teh*
carpet, rug	alfombra	*ahl-'fohm-brah*
chair	silla	*'see-yah*
chest of drawers, dresser	cómoda	*'koh-moh-dah*
curtain	cortina	*kohr-'tee-nah*
cushion	cojín (*m*)	*koh-'heen*
decor	decoración (*f*)	*deh-koh-rah-see·'ohn*
drawer	cajón (*m*)	*kah-'hohn*
dresser	tocador (*m*)	*toh-kah-'dohr*
furniture	muebles (*m*)	*'mweh-blehs*
• **piece of furniture**	mueble (*m*)	*'mweh-bleh*
lamp	lámpara	*'lahm-pah-rah*
mirror	espejo	*ehs-'peh-hoh*
painting	pintura	*peen-'too-rah*
	cuadro	*'kwah-droh*
sofa	sofá (*m*)	*soh-'fah*
stool	banquillo	*bahn-'kee-yoh*
table	mesa	*'meh-sah*
• **coffee table**	mesa de centro	*'meh-sah deh 'sehn-troh*
• **end table**	mesa auxiliar	*'meh-sah ow-ksee-lee·'ahr*
upholstery	tapizado	*tah-pee-'sah-doh*

venetian blinds	persianas	*pehr-see-'ah-nahs*
wallpaper	empapelado	*ehm-pah-peh-'lah-doh*
writing desk	escritorio	*ehs-kree-'toh-ree-oh*

d. APPLIANCES AND COMMON HOUSEHOLD ITEMS

bag	saco	*'sah-koh*
	bolsa	*'bohl-sah*
barrel	barril (*m*)	*bah-'rreel*
basket	cesta	*'sehs-tah*
	canasta	*kah-'nahs-tah*
blanket	manta	*'mahn-tah*
blender	licuadora	*lee-kwah-'doh-rah*
bottle	botella	*boh-'teh-yah*
bowl	tazón (*m*)	*tah-'sohn*
box	caja	*'kah-hah*
broom	escoba	*ehs-'koh-bah*
can	lata	*'lah-tah*
case	estuche (*m*)	*ehs-'too-cheh*
clothes hanger	percha	*'pehr-chah*
	gancho	*'gahn-choh*
coffee pot	cafetera	*kah-feh-'teh-rah*
colander	colador (*m*)	*koh-lah-'dohr*
corkscrew	sacacorchos (*m*)	*sah-kah-'kohr-chohs*
cup	taza	*'tah-sah*
dishwasher	lavaplatos (*m*)	*lah-bah-'plah-tohs*
dryer	secador (*m*)	*seh-kah-'dohr*
flour sifter	cernidor (*m*) de harina	*sehr-nee-'dohr deh ah-'ree-nah*
fork	tenedor (*m*)	*teh-neh-'dohr*
freezer	congelador (*m*)	*kohn-geh-lah-'dohr*
frying pan	sartén (*f*)	*sahr-'tehn*
glass (*drinking*)	vaso	*'bah-soh*
grater	rallador (*m*)	*rah-yah-'dohr*
iron	plancha	*'plahn-chah*
kettle	hervidor (*m*)	*ehr-bee-'dohr*
	cafetera	*kah-feh-'teh-rah*
key	llave (*f*)	*'ya-beh*
knife	cuchillo	*koo-'chee-yoh*
• **blade**	hoja	*'oh-hah*
• **handle**	mango	*'mahn-goh*
ladle	cucharón (*m*)	*koo-chah-'rohn*
lid	tapa	*'tah-pah*
measuring cups	juego de tazas de medir	*'hweh-goh deh 'tah-sahs deh meh-'deer*
measuring spoons	juego de cucharitas de medir	*'hweh-goh deh koo-chah-'ree-tahs deh meh-'deer*

microwave oven	horno de microondas	*'ohr-noh deh mee-kroh-'ohn-dahs*
mixer	batidora	*bah-tee-'doh-rah*
napkin	servilleta	*sehr-bee-'yeh-tah*
pail	cubo	*'koo-boh*
pan	cacerola	*kah-seh-'roh-lah*
pillow	almohada	*ahl-moh-'ah-dah*
plate	plato	*'plah-toh*
pot	olla	*'oh-yah*
radio	radio	*'rah-dee·oh*
refrigerator	nevera	*neh-'beh-rah*
	frigorífico	*free-goh-'ree-fee-koh*
	refrigerador (m)	*reh-free-heh-rah-'dohr*
saucer	platillo	*plah-'tee-yoh*
sewing machine	máquina de coser	*'mah-kee-nah deh koh-'sehr*
sheet (*bed*)	sábana	*'sah-bah-nah*
skillet	sartén (*f*)	*sahr-'tehn*
spatula	espátula	*ehs-'pah-too-lah*
spoon	cuchara	*koo-'chah-rah*
• **teaspoon**	cucharita	*koo-char-'ree-tah*
• **teaspoonful**	cucharadita	*koo-chah-rah-'dee-tah*
stove	estufa	*ehs-'too-fah*
tablecloth	mantel (*m*)	*mahn-'tehl*
teapot	tetera	*teh-'teh-rah*
television set	televisor (*m*)	*teh-leh-bee-'sohr*
toaster	tostador (*m*)	*tohs-'tah-'dohr*
tools	herramientas	*eh-rrah-mee-'ehn-tahs*
toothpick	palillo	*pah-'lee-yoh*
tray	bandeja	*bahn-'deh-hah*
utensils	utensilios (*m, pl*)	*oo-tehn-'see-lee·ohs*
vacuum cleaner	aspirador (a) (*m/f*)	*ahs-pee-rah-'dohr (-rah)*
vase	florero	*floh-'reh-roh*
washing machine	lavadora	*lah-bah-'doh-rah*

e. SERVICES

air conditioning	aire (*m*) acondicionado	*'ah-ee-reh ah-kohn-dee-see·oh-'nah-doh*
electricity	electricidad (*f*)	*eh-lehk-tree-see-'dahd*
	horno	*'ohr-noh*
furnace	calorífero	*kah-loh-'ree-feh-roh*
gas	gas (*m*)	*gahs*
heating	calefacción (*f*)	*kah-leh-fahk-see-'ohn*
telephone	teléfono	*teh-'leh-foh-noh*
water	agua (*f*)	*'ah-gwah*

f. ADDITIONAL HOUSEHOLD VOCABULARY

at home	en casa	*ehn 'kah-sah*
build	construir*	*kohns-'trweer*
buy	comprar (v)	*kohm-'prahr*
clean	limpiar (v)	*leem-pee-'ahr*
clear the table	quitar (v) la mesa	*kee-'tahr lah 'meh-sah*
decorate	decorar (v)	*deh-koh-'rahr*
live (in)	vivir (v) (en)	*bee-'beer (ehn)*
make the bed	hacer* la cama	*ah-'sehr lah 'kah-mah*
move	mudarse (v)	*moo-'dahr-seh*
paint	pintar (v)	*peen-'tahr*
put a room in order	arreglar (v) un cuarto	*ah-rreh-'glahr oon 'kwahr-toh*
restore	restaurar (v)	*rehs-tow-'rahr*
sell	vender (v)	*behn-'dehr*
set the table	poner* la mesa	*poh-'nehr lah 'meh-sah*
wash	lavar (v)	*lah-'bahr*
• **wash the clothes**	lavar la ropa	*lah-'bahr lah 'roh-pah*
• **wash the dishes**	lavar los platos	*lah-'bahr lohs 'plah-tohs*

g. LIVING IN AN APARTMENT

apartment	apartamento	*ah-pahr-tah-'mehn-toh*
	piso	*'pee-soh*
apartment house	casa de pisos	*'kah-sah deh 'pee-sohs*
building	edificio	*eh-dee-'fee-see-oh*
condominium	condominio	*kohn-doh-'mee-nee-oh*
elevator	ascensor (m)	*ah-sehn-'sohr*
ground floor	planta baja	*'plahn-tah 'bah-hah*
landlord	propietario	*proh-pee-eh-'tah-ree-oh*
	patrón	*pah-'trohn*
rent	alquilar (v)	*ahl-kee-'lahr*
• **rent**	alquiler (m)	*ahl-kee-'lehr*
tenant	arrendatario	*ah-rrehn-dah-'tah-ree-oh*
	inquilino	*een-kee-'lee-noh*

24. EATING AND DRINKING

a. MEALS

breakfast	desayuno	*deh-sah-'yoo-noh*
• **eat breakfast**	desayunar(se) (v)	*deh-sah-yoo-'nahr (seh)*
dinner	cena	*'seh-nah*
• **eat dinner**	cenar (v)	*seh-'nahr*

food	comida	koh-'mee-dah
lunch	almuerzo	ahl-'mwehr-soh
• eat lunch	almorzar*	ahl-mohr-'sahr
meal	comida	koh-'mee-dah
snack	bocadillo	boh-kahn-'dee-yoh
• snack	comer (se) (v)	koh-'mehr (-seh) oon
	un bocadillo	boh-kah-'dee-yoh

b. PREPARATION OF FOOD

baked	asado (adj)	ah-'sah-doh
boiled	guisado (adj)	gee-'sah-doh
broiled	a la parrilla	ah lah pah-'rree-yah
medium	a término medio	ah 'tehr-mee-noh 'meh-dee·oh
rare	poco asado (adj)	'poh-koh ah-'sah-doh
well-done	bien asado (adj)	bee·'ehn ah-'sah-doh

c. MEAT AND POULTRY

bacon	tocino	toh-'see-noh
beefsteak	bistec (m)	bees-'tehk
chicken	pollo	'poh-yoh
goat	cabrito	kah-'bree-toh
ham	jamón (m)	hah-'mohn
lamb	cordero	kohr-'deh-roh
liver	hígado	'ee-gah-doh
pork	cerdo	'sehr-doh
• pork chops	chuletas de cerdo	choo-'leh-tahs deh 'sehr-doh
sausage	salchicha	sahl-'chee-chah
turkey	pavo	'pah-boh
veal	ternera	tehr-'neh-rah

d. FISH, SEAFOOD, AND SHELLFISH

anchovy	anchoa	ahn-'choh-ah
clam	almeja	ahl-'meh-hah
codfish	bacalao	bah-kah-'lah-oh
eel	anguila	ahn-'gee-lah
fish	pescado	pehs-'kah-doh
herring	arenque (m)	ah-'rehn-keh
lobster	langosta	lahn-'gohs-tah
mussels	mejillones (m)	meh-hee-'yoh-nehs

oyster	ostra	*'ohs-trah*
salmon	salmón (*m*)	*sahl-'mohn*
sardine	sardina	*sahr-'dee-nah*
seafood	pescado y marisco	*pehs-'kah-doh ee mah-'rees-koh*
shellfish	marisco (s)	*mah-'rees-koh (s)*
shrimp	gambas	*'gahm-bahs*
sole	lenguado	*lehn-'gwah-doh*
squid	camarones (*m*)	*kah-mah-'roh-nehs*
	calamares (*m*)	*kah-lah-'mah-rehs*
trout	trucha	*'troo-chah*
tuna	atún (*m*)	*ah-'toon*

e. VEGETABLES

artichoke	alcachofa	*ahl-kah-'choh-fah*
asparagus	espárrago	*ehs-'pah-rrah-goh*
beans	frijoles (*m*)	*free-'hoh-lehs*
beet	remolacha	*reh-moh-'lah-chah*
broccoli	brécol (*m*)	*'breh-kohl*
	bróculi (*m*)	*'broh-koo-lee*
cabbage	col (*m*)	*kohl*
	repollo	*reh-'poh-yoh*
carrot	zanahoria	*sah-nah-'oh-ree-ah*
cauliflower	coliflor (*f*)	*koh-lee-'flohr*
celery	apio	*'ah-pee-oh*
cucumber	pepino	*peh-'pee-noh*
eggplant	berenjena	*beh-rehn-'heh-nah*
lettuce	lechuga	*leh-'choo-gah*
mushroom	champiñone (*m*)	*chahm-pee-'nyoh-neh*
	hongo	*'ohn-goh*
olive	aceituna	*ah-seh'ee-'too-nah*
onion	cebolla	*seh-'boh-yah*
pea	guisante (*m*)	*gee-'sahn-teh*
potato	papa	*'pah-pah*
	patata	*pah-'tah-tah*
spinach	espinaca	*ehs-pee-'nah-kah*
string bean	judía verde	*hoo-'dee-ah 'behr-deh*
tomato	tomate (*m*)	*toh-'mah-teh*
vegetables	verduras	*behr-'doo-rahs*
	legumbres (*f*, *pl*)	*leh-'goom-brehs*

f. FRUITS

apple	manzana	*mahn-'sah-nah*
apricot	albaricoque (*m*)	*ahl-bah-ree-'koh-keh*

banana	banana	*bah-'nah-nah*
	plátano	*'plah-tah-noh*
blueberry	mirtilo	*meer-'tee-loh*
cherry	cereza	*seh-'reh-sah*
date	dátil (*m*)	*'dah-teel*
fig	higo	*'ee-goh*
fruit	fruta	*'froo-tah*
grapefruit	toronja	*toh-'rohn-hah*
	pomelo	*poh-'meh-loh*
grapes	uvas	*'oo-bahs*
lemon	limón (*m*)	*lee-'mohn*
orange	naranja	*nah-'rahn-hah*
peach	melocotón (*m*)	*meh-loh-koh-'tohn*
	durazno	*doo-'rahs-noh*
peanut	cacahuete (*m*)	*kah-kah-'weh-teh*
	maní (*m*)	*mah-'nee*
pineapple	piña	*'pee-nyah*
plum	ciruela	*see-'rweh-lah*
prune	ciruela pasa	*see-'rweh-lah 'pah-sah*
raspberry	frambuesa	*frahm-'bweh-sah*
strawberry	fresa	*'freh-sah*
tangerine	mandarina	*mahn-dah-'ree-nah*
watermelon	sandía	*sahn-'dee·ah*

g. MEAL AND MENU COMPONENTS

aperitif	aperitivo	*ah-peh-ree-'tee-boh*
appetizer	tapa	*'tah-pah*
	bocadillo	*boh-kah-'dee-yoh*
broth	caldo	*'kahl-doh*
cake	torta	*'tohr-tah*
course	plato	*'plah-toh*
cutlet	chuleta	*choo-'leh-tah*
dessert	postre (*m*)	*'pohs-treh*
filet	filete (*m*)	*fee-'leh-teh*
French fries	papas fritas	*'pah-pahs 'free-tahs*
menu	menú (*m*)	*meh-'noo*
	lista de platos	*'lees-tah deh 'plah-tohs*
pie	pastel (*m*)	*pahs-'tehl*
pudding	budín (*m*)	*booh-'deen*
salad	ensalada	*ehn-sah-'lah-dah*
sandwich	torta (*Mexico*)	*'tohr-tah*
	bocadillo (*Spain*)	*boh-kah-'dee-yoh*
	emparedado (*Latin America*)	*ehm-pah-reh-'dah-doh*
soup	sopa	*'soh-pah*

h. DAIRY PRODUCTS, EGGS, AND RELATED FOODS

butter	mantequilla	*mahn-teh-'kee-yah*
cheese	queso	*'keh-soh*
cream	crema	*'kreh-mah*
dairy product	productos lácteos	*proh-'dook-tohs 'lahk-teh-ohs*
egg	huevo	*'weh-boh*
ice cream	helado	*eh-'lah-doh*
margarine	margarina	*marh-gah-'ree-nah*
milk	leche (*f*)	*'leh-cheh*
omelette	tortilla (*Spain*)	*tohr-'tee-yah*
whipped cream	crema batida	*'kreh-mah bah-'tee-dah*
yogurt	yogur (*m*)	*yoh-'goor*

i. GRAINS AND GRAIN PRODUCTS

barley	cebada	*seh-'bah-dah*
biscuit	bizcocho	*bees-'koh-choh*
bread	pan (*m*)	*pahn*
cookie	galleta	*gah-'yeh-tah*
corn	maíz (*m*)	*mah-'ees*
flour	harina	*'ah-'ree-nah*
noodles	fideos	*fee-'deh-ohs*
oat	avena	*ah-'beh-nah*
pastry	pastel (*m*)	*pahs-'tehl*
rice	arroz (*m*)	*ah-'rrohs*
wheat	trigo	*'tree-goh*
• **whole wheat bread**	pan integrado	*pahn een-teh-'grah-doh*

j. CONDIMENTS AND SPICES

basil	albahaca	*ahl-bah-'ah-kah*
garlic	ajo	*'ah-hoh*
herb	hierba	*'ee·ehr-bah*
	yerba	*'yehr-bah*
honey	miel (*f*)	*mee·ehl*
horseradish	rábano picante	*'rah-bah-noh pee-'kahn-teh*
jam, marmalade	mermelada	*mehr-meh-'lah-dah*
ketchup	salsa de tomate	*'sahl-sah deh toh-'mah-teh*
mayonnaise	mayonesa	*mah-yoh-'neh-sah*
mint	menta	*'mehn-tah*
mustard	mostaza	*mohs-'tah-sah*

oil	aceite (*m*)	*ah-'seh·ee-teh*
parsley	perejil (*m*)	*peh-reh-'heel*
pepper	pimienta	*pee-mee-'ehn-tah*
rosemary	romero	*roh-'meh-roh*
salt	sal (*f*)	*sahl*
spice	especia	*ehs-'peh-see·ah*
sugar	azúcar (*m*)	*ah-'soo-kahr*
vinegar	vinagre (*m*)	*bee-'nah-greh*

k. DRINKS

alcoholic drink	bebida alcohólica	*beh-'bee-dah ahl-koh-'oh-lee-kah*
beer	cerveza	*sehr-'beh-sah*
coffee	café (*m*)	*kah-'feh*
• instant coffee	café instantáneo	*kah-'feh een-stahn-'tah-neh-oh*
drink	bebida	*beh-'bee-dah*
juice	jugo	*'hoo-goh*
	zumo	*'soo-moh*
liqueur	licor (*m*)	*lee-'kohr*
milk	leche (*f*)	*'leh-cheh*
mineral water	agua mineral (*f*)	*'ah-gwah mee-neh-'rahl*
soft drink	refresco	*reh-'frehs-koh*
tea	té (*m*)	*teh*
water	agua (*f*)	*'ah-gwah*
whiskey	whiski (*m*)	*'wees-kee*
wine	vino	*'bee-noh*

l. AT THE TABLE

bottle	botella	*boh-'teh-yah*
bowl	tazón (*m*)	*tah-'sohn*
cup	taza	*'tah-sah*
fork	tenedor (*m*)	*teh-neh-'dohr*
glass (*drinking*)	vaso	*'bah-soh*
knife	cuchillo	*koo-'chee-yoh*
napkin	servilleta	*sehr-bee-'yeh-tah*
plate	plato	*'plah-toh*
saucer	platillo	*pla-'tee-yoh*
spoon	cuchara	*koo-'chah-rah*
table	mesa	*'meh-sah*
tablecloth	mantel (*m*)	*mahn-'tehl*
teaspoon	cucharita	*koo-'chah-'ree-tah*
toothpick	palillo	*pahl-'lee-yoh*

tray	bandeja	*bahn-'deh-hah*
wineglass	vaso para vino	*'bah-soh 'pah-rah 'bee-noh*
	copa	*'koh-pah*

Cheers! = ¡Salud!

Enjoy your meal! = ¡Buen provecho!

---

m. DINING OUT

bartender	cantinero	*kahn-tee-'neh-roh*
bill, check	cuenta	*'kwehn-tah*
cafeteria	cafetería	*kah-feh-teh-'ree-ah*
cover charge	precio del cubierto	*'preh-see·oh dehl koo-bee·'ehr-toh*
fixed price	precio fijo	*'preh-see·oh 'fee-hoh*
price	precio	*'preh-see·oh*
reservation	reservación (f)	*reh-sehr-bah-see-'ohn*
• reserved	reservado (adj)	*reh-sehr-'bah-doh*
restaurant	restaurante (m)	*rehs-tow-'rahn-teh*
service	servicio	*sehr-'bee-see·oh*
snack bar	bar	*bahr*
	cafetería	*kah-feh-teh-'ree-ah*
tip	propina	*proh-'pee-nah*
• tip	dar* una propina	*dahr 'oo-nah proh-'pee-nah*
waiter	camarero	*kah-mah-'reh-roh*
	mesero	*meh-'seh-roh*
waitress	camarera	*kah-mah-'reh-rah*
wine list	lista de vinos	*'lees-tah deh 'bee-nohs*

n. BUYING FOOD AND DRINK

bakery	panadería	*pah-nah-deh-'ree-ah*
butcher shop	carnicería	*kahr-nee-seh-'ree-ah*
dairy	lechería	*leh-cheh-'ree-ah*
fish store	pescadería	*pehs-kah-deh-'ree-ah*
fruit store	frutería	*froo-teh-'ree-ah*
grocery store	tienda de comestibles	*'tee·ehn-dah deh koh-mehs-'tee-blehs*
ice cream parlor	heladería	*eh-lah-deh-'ree-ah*
market	mercado	*mehr-'kah-doh*
pastry shop	pastelería	*pahs-teh-leh-'ree-ah*
supermarket	supermercado	*soo-pehr-mehr-'kah-doh*

o. FOOD AND DRINK: ACTIVITIES

add up the bill	sumar (v) la cuenta	soo-'mahr lah 'kwehn-tah
be hungry	tener* hambre	teh-'nehr 'ahm-breh
be thirsty	tener* sed	teh-'nehr sehd
clear the table	quitar (v) la mesa	kee-'tahr lah 'meh-sah
	limpiar (v) la mesa	leem-pee·'ahr lah 'meh-sah
cook	cocinar (v)	koh-see-'nahr
cost	costar*	kohs-'tahr
cut	cortar (v)	kohr-'tahr
drink	beber (v)	beh-'behr
	tomar (v)	toh-'mahr
eat	comer (v)	koh-'mehr
have a snack	merendar*	meh-rehn-'dahr
have dinner	cenar (v)	seh-'nahr
have lunch	almorzar*	ahl-mohr-'sahr
order	pedir*	peh-'deer
peel	pelar (v)	peh-'lahr
pour	verter*	behr-'tehr
serve	servir*	sehr-'beer
set the table	poner* la mesa	poh-'nehr lah 'meh-sah
shop for food	comprar (v) comestibles	kohm-'prahr koh-mehs-'tee-blehs
slice	rebanar (v)	reh-bah-'nahr
	tajar (v)	tah-'hahr
toast	tostar*	tohs-'tahr
weigh	pesar (v)	peh-'sahr

p. DESCRIBING FOOD AND DRINK

appetizing	apetitoso (adj)	ah-peh-tee-'toh-soh
bad	malo (adj)	'mah-loh
baked	asado al horno (adj)	ah-'sah-doh ahl 'ohr-noh
cheap	barato (adj)	bah-'rah-toh
cold	frío (adj)	'free-oh
expensive	caro (adj)	'kah-roh
fried	frito (adj)	'free-toh
good	bueno (adj)	'bweh-noh
hot	caliente (adj)	kah-lee·'ehn-teh
mild	suave (adj)	'swah-beh
salty	salado (adj)	sah-'lah-doh
sour	agrio (adj)	'ah-gree·oh

spicy	picante (*adj*)	*pee-'kahn-teh*
sweet	dulce (*adj*)	*'dool-seh*
tasty	sabroso (*adj*)	*sah-'broh-soh*
with ice	con hielo	*kohn ee·'eh-loh*

25. SHOPPING AND ERRANDS

a. GENERAL VOCABULARY

antique	antigüedad (*f*)	*ahn-tee-gweh-'dahd*
bag	saco	*'sah-koh*
	bolsa	*'bohl-sah*
become	hacerse*	*ah-'sehr-seh*
bill	cuenta	*'kwehn-tah*
• bill	facturar (*v*)	*fahk-too-'rahr*
bring	traer*	*trah-'ehr*
buy	comprar (*v*)	*kohm-'prahr*
cash register	caja registradora	*'kah-hah reh-hees-trah-'doh-rah*
• cashier	cajero	*kah-'heh-roh*
change (*money*)	cambiar (*v*)	*kahm-bee-'ahr*
cost	costar*	*kohs-'tahr*
• How much does it cost?	¿Cuánto cuesta?	*'kwahn-toh 'kwehs-tah*
• How much is it?	¿Cuánto es?	*'kwahn-toh ehs*

> It costs an arm and a leg = Cuesta un ojo de la cara

counter	mostrador (*m*)	*mohs-trah-'dohr*
customer	cliente (*m/f*)	*klee·'ehn-teh*
department (*in store*)	departamento	*deh-pahr-tah-'mehn-toh*
entrance	entrada	*ehn-'trah-dah*
elevator	ascensor (*m*)	*ah-sehn-'sohr*
escalator	escalera movediza	*ehs-kah-leh-'rah moh-beh-'dee-sah*
exchange (*of merchandise*)	canje (*m*)	*'kahn-heh*
• exchange	canjear (*v*)	*kahn-'heh-ahr*
exit	salida	*sah-'lee-dah*
gift	regalo	*reh-'gah-loh*
lack	faltar (*v*)	*fahl-'tahr*
look for something	buscar (*v*) algo	*boos-'kahr 'ahl-goh*
package	paquete (*m*)	*pah-'keh-teh*

pay	pagar (*v*)	*pah-'gahr*
• **cash**	en efectivo	*ehn eh-fehk-'tee-boh*
• **check**	cheque (*m*)	*'cheh-keh*
• **credit card**	tarjeta de crédito	*tahr-'heh-tah deh 'kreh-dee-toh*
price	precio	*'preh-see·oh*
• **discount**	descuento	*dehs-'kwehn-toh*
• **expensive**	caro (*adj*)	*'kah-roh*
• **fixed price**	precio fijo	*'preh-see·oh 'fee-hoh*
• **inexpensive**	barato (*adj*)	*bah-'rah-toh*
• **reduced price**	precio reducido	*'preh-see·oh reh-doo-'see-doh*
• **tag, label**	etiqueta	*eh-tee·'keh-tah*
purchase	comprar (*v*)	*kohm-'prahr*
• **purchase**	compra	*kohm-prah*
refund	reembolso	*rreh-ehm-'bohl-soh*
• **refund**	reembolsar (*v*)	*rreh-ehm-bohl-'sahr*
return	devolución (*f*)	*deh-boh-loo-see·'ohn*
• **return** (*an object*)	devolver*	*deh-bohl-'behr*
sale	venta	*'behn-tah*
• **for sale**	de venta	*deh 'behn-tah*
	se vende	*seh 'behn-deh*
• **on sale**	de venta	*deh 'behn-tah*
shop	ir* de compras	*eer deh 'kohm-prahs*
• **shop**	tienda	*tee·'ehn-dah*
souvenir	recuerdo	*reh-'kwehr-doh*
spend	gastar (*v*)	*gahs-'tahr*
store	tienda	*tee·'ehn-dah*
• **closed**	cerrado (*adj*)	*seh-'rrah-doh*
• **closing time**	hora de cerrar	*'oh-rah deh seh-'rrahr*
• **department store**	almacén (*m*)	*ahl-mah-'sehn*
• **open**	abierto (*adj*)	*ah-'bee·ehr-toh*
• **opening hour**	hora de abrir	*'oh-rah deh ah-'breer*
• **store clerk**	dependiente (a)	*deh-pehn-dee·'ehn-teh (-tah)*
take	tomar (*v*)	*toh-'mahr*
• **take back**	devolver*	*deh-bohl-'behr*

b. HARDWARE

battery (*radios, etc.*)	pila	*'pee-lah*
• **battery** (*car*)	batería	*bah-teh-'ree·ah*
cable	cable (*m*)	*'kah-bleh*
clamp	abrazadera	*ah-brah-sah-'deh-rah*
drill	taladro	*tah-'lah-droh*

• drill	taladrar (v)	tah-lah-'drahr
electrical	eléctrico (adj)	eh-'lehk-tree-koh
file	lima	'lee-mah
flashlight	linterna	leen-'tehr-nah
fuse	fusible (m)	foo-'see-bleh
hammer	martillo	mahr-'tee-yoh
hardware store	ferretería	feh-rreh-teh-'ree-ah
insulation wire	alambre (m) aislante	ah-'lahm-breh ah·ees-'lahn-teh
light bulb	bombilla	bohm-'bee-yah
• fluorescent	fluorescente (adj)	flwoh-reh-'sehn-teh
• neon light	alumbrado de neón	ah-loom-'brah-doh deh neh-'ohn
masking tape	cinta adhesiva	'seen-tah ahd-eh-'see-bah
mechanical	mecánico (adj)	meh-'kah-nee-koh
nail	clavo	'kla-boh
• nail	clavar (v)	klah-'bahr
nut	tuerca	'twehr-kah
outlet (electrical)	toma	'toh-mah
paintbrush	brocha	'broh-chah
pick	piqueta	pee-'keh-tah
pincers	tenazas	teh-'nah-sahs
plane	cepillo	seh-'pee-yoh
pliers	alicates (m)	ah-lee-'kah-tehs
plug	enchufe (m)	ehn-'choo-feh
plumbing	fontanería	fohn-tah-neh-'ree-ah
punch	punzón (m)	poon-'sohn
saw	sierra	see-'eh-rrah
screwdriver	destornillador (m)	dehs-tohr-nee-yah-'dohr
• screw	tornillo	tohr-'nee-yoh
• screw	atornillar (v)	ah-tohr-nee-'yahr
• unscrew	destornillar (v)	dehs-tohr-nee-'yahr
shovel	pala	'pah-lah
tool	herramienta	eh-rrah-mee-'ehn-tah
transformer	transformador (m)	trahns-fohr-mah-'dohr
wire	alambre (m)	ah-'lahm-breh
wrench	llave inglesa	'yah-beh een-'gleh-sah

c. STATIONERY

adhesive tape	cinta adhesiva	'seen-tah ahd-eh-'see-bah
ballpoint pen	bolígrafo	boh-'lee-grah-foh
briefcase	cartera, portafolio (m)	kahr-'teh-rah, pohr-tah-'foh-lee·oh
envelope	sobre (m)	'soh-breh

marker	marcador (*m*)	*mahr-kah-'dohr*
note pad	bloc de papel (*m*)	*blohk deh pah-'pehl*
paper	papel (*m*)	*pah-'pehl*
pen	pluma	*'ploo-mah*
pencil sharpener	sacapuntas (*m*)	*sah-kah-'poon-tahs*
sheet (*of paper*)	hoja	*'oh-hah*
staple	grapa	*'grah-pah*
• stapler	engrapador (*m*)	*ehn-grah-pah-'dohr*
stationery store	papelería	*pah-peh-leh-'ree-ah*
string	cordel (*m*)	*kohr-'dehl*
writing paper	papel (*m*) de escribir	*pah-'pehl deh ehs-kree-'beer*

d. PHOTO/CAMERA

camera	cámara	*'kah-mah-rah*
• movie camera	cámara cinematográfica	*'kah-mah-rah cee-neh-mah-toh-'grah-fee-kah*
• video camera	cámara de vídeo	*'kah-mah-rah deh 'vee-deh-oh*
darkroom	cámara oscura	*'kah-mah-rah ohs-'koo-rah*
	cuarto oscuro	*'kwahr-toh ohs-'koo-roh*
develop	revelar (*v*)	*reh-beh-'lahr*
enlargement	ampliación (*f*)	*ahm-plee·ah-see·'ohn*
• enlarge	ampliar (*v*)	*ahm-plee-'ahr*
film	película	*peh-'lee-koo-lah*
• roll of film	rollo de película	*'roh-yoh deh peh-'lee-koo-lah*
flash	flash (*m*)	*flahsh*
glossy finish	con acabado brillante	*kohn ah-kah-'bah-doh bree-'yahn-teh*
matte finish	con acabado mate	*kohn ah-kah-'bah-doh 'mah-teh*
photo (graph)	foto (grafía) (*f*)	*'foh-toh (grah-'fee-ah)*
• black and white	en blanco y negro	*ehn 'blahn-koh ee 'neh-groh*
• clear	clara (*adj*)	*'klah-rah*
• focus	enfocar (*v*)	*ehn-foh-'kahr*
• in color	en colores	*ehn koh-'loh-rehs*
• in focus	enfocada (*adj*)	*ehn-foh-'kah-dah*
• out of focus	fuera de foco	*'fweh-rah deh 'foh-koh*
• take a picture	sacar (*v*) una foto	*sah-'kahr 'oo-nah 'foh-toh*
• It (the picture) turned out badly.	Salió mal.	*sah-lee-'oh mahl*

• It (the picture) turned out well.	Salió bien.	*sah-lee-'oh bee-'ehn*
print	prueba positiva	*'prweh-bah poh-see-'tee-bah*
screen	pantalla	*pahn-'tah-yah*
slide	diapositiva	*dee-ah-poh-see-'tee-bah*
zoom	zoom (*m*)	*soom*

e. TOBACCO

cigar	puro	*'poo-roh*
	cigarro	*see-'gah-rroh*
cigarette	cigarrillo	*see-gah-'rree-yoh*
lighter	mechero	*meh-'cheh-roh*
	encendedor (*m*)	*ehn-sehn-deh-'dohr*
matches	fósforos	*'fohs-foh-rohs*
	cerillas	*seh-'ree-yahs*
pipe	pipa	*'pee-pah*
tobacco	tabaco	*tah-'bah-koh*
tobacco shop	tabaquería	*tah-bah-keh-'ree-ah*

f. COSMETICS/TOILETRIES

bath oil	aceite (*m*) de baño	*ah-'seh-ee-teh deh 'bah-nyoh*
blade	hoja	*'oh-hah*
blush, rouge	colorete (*m*)	*koh-loh-'reh-teh*
bobbypins	horquillas	*ohr-'kee-yahs*
brush	cepillo	*seh-'pee-yoh*
cologne	colonia	*koh-'loh-nee-ah*
comb	peine (*m*)	*'peh-ee-neh*
cosmetics/perfume store	perfumería	*pehr-foo-meh-'ree-ah*
cream	crema	*'kreh-mah*
curler	rizador (*m*)	*ree-sah-'dohr*
deodorant	desodorante (*m*)	*dehs-oh-doh-'rahn-teh*
electric razor	afeitadora eléctrica	*ah-feh-ee-tah-'doh-rah eh-'lehk-tree-kah*
face powder	polvos para la cara	*'pohl-bohs 'pah-rah lah 'kah-rah*
hair dryer	secador (*m*)	*seh-kah-'dohr*
lipstick	lápiz (*m*) de labios	*'lah-pees deh 'lah-bee-ohs*
lotion	loción (*f*)	*loh-see-'ohn*
makeup	maquillaje (*m*)	*mah-kee-'yah-heh*
mascara	rimel (*m*)	*ree-'mehl*

nail clippers	cortauñas (m)	kohr-tah-'oo-nyahs
nail polish	esmalte (m) para las uñas	ehs-'mahl-teh 'pah-rah lahs 'oo-nyahs
perfume	perfume (m)	pehr-'foo-meh
razor	navaja de afeitar	nah-'bah-hah deh ah-feh·ee-'tahr
shampoo	champú (m)	chahm-'poo
shaving cream	crema de afeitar	'kreh-mah deh ah-feh·ee-'tahr
soap	jabón (m)	hah-'bohn
talcum powder	talco	'tahl-koh
tweezers	pinzas	'peen-sahs

g. LAUNDRY

button	botón (m)	boh-'tohn
• buttonhole	ojal (m)	oh-'hahl
clean	limpiar (v)	leem-pee-'ahr
clothes	ropa	'roh-pah
• clothes basket	cesta para la ropa sucia	'sehs-tah 'pah-rah lah 'roh-pah 'soo-see·ah
• clothespin	pinza	'peen-sah
dirty	sucio (adj)	'soo-see·oh
dry cleaner	tintorería	teen-toh-reh-'ree-ah
hole	agujero	ah-goo-'heh-roh
iron	planchar (v)	plahn'-chahr
• iron	plancha	'plahn-chah
• ironing board	tabla de planchar	'tah-blah deh plahn-'chahr
• scorch	chamuscar (v)	chah-moos-'kahr
laundry	lavandería	lah-vahn-deh-'ree-ah
lining (of a coat)	forro	'foh-rroh
mend	remendar*	reh-mehn-'dahr
pocket	bolsillo	bohl-'see-yoh
sew	coser (v)	koh-'sehr
sleeve	manga	'mahn-gah
soap powder	jabón de polvo	hah-'bohn deh 'pohl-boh
spot, stain	mancha	'mahn-chah
starch	almidón (m)	ahl-mee-'dohn
• starched	almidonado (adj)	ahl-mee-doh-'nah-doh
stitch	coser (v)	koh-'sehr
wash	lavar (v)	lah-'bahr
• washable	lavable (adj)	lah-'bah-bleh
wear	llevar (v)	yeh-'bahr
zipper	cremallera	kreh-mah-'yeh-rah

h. PHARMACY/DRUGSTORE

antibiotic	antibiótico	*ahn-tee-bee-'oh-tee-koh*
aspirin	aspirina	*ahs-pee-'ree-nah*
bandage	venda	*'behn-dah*
condom	condón (*m*)	*kohn-'dohn*
	hule (*m*)	*'oo-leh*
cortisone	cortisona	*kohr-tee-'soh-nah*
dental floss	hilo dental	*'ee-loh dehn-'tahl*
drugstore/pharmacy	farmacia	*fahr-'mah-see·ah*
injection	inyección (*m*)	*een-yehk-see-'ohn*
insulin	insulina	*een-soo-'lee-nah*
laxative	laxante (*m*)	*lahk-'sahn-teh*
medicine	medicina	*meh-dee-'see-nah*
ointment	ungüento	*oon-'gwehn-toh*
penicillin	penicilina	*peh-nee-see-'lee-nah*
pharmacist	farmacéutico (a)	*fahr-mah-'seh·oo-tee-koh (-kah)*
pill	píldora	*'peel-doh-rah*
powder	polvo	*'pohl-boh*
prescription	receta	*reh-'seh-tah*
sanitary napkins	servilletas higiénicas	*sehr-bee-'yeh-tahs ee-hee-'eh-nee-kahs*
sodium bicarbonate	bicarbonato de sodio	*bee-kahr-boh-'nah-toh deh 'soh-dee·oh*
suppository	supositorio	*soo-poh-see-'toh-ree·oh*
syrup	jarabe (*m*)	*hah-'rah-beh*
tablet	pastilla	*pahs-'tee-yah*
tampons	tapones (*m*)	*tah-'poh-nehs*
thermometer	termómetro	*tehr-'moh-meh-troh*
tincture of iodine	tintura de yodo	*teen-'too-rah deh 'yoh-doh*
tissue	pañuelo de papel	*pah-nee·oh-'eh-loh deh pah-'pehl*
toothbrush	cepillo de dientes	*seh-'pee-yoh deh dee-'ehn-tehs*
toothpaste	pasta dentífrica	*'pahs-tah dehn-'tee-free-kah*
vitamin	vitamina	*bee-tah-'mee-nah*

i. JEWELRY

amethyst	amatista	*ah-mah-'teehs-tah*
artificial	artificial (*adj*)	*ahr-tee-fee-see-'ahl*
bracelet	pulsera	*pool-'seh-rah*
brooch	broche (*m*)	*'broh-cheh*
carat	quilate (*m*)	*kee-'lah-teh*

chain	cadena	*kah-'deh-nah*
charm	dije (*m*)	*'dee-heh*
diamond	diamante (*m*)	*dee·ah-'mahn-teh*
earring	arete (*m*)	*ah-'reh-teh*
	pendiente (*m*)	*pehn-dee·'ehn-teh*
emerald	esmeralda	*ehs-meh-'rahl-dah*
false	falso (*adj*)	*'fahl-soh*
fix	reparar (*v*)	*reh-pah-'rahr*
gold	oro	*'oh-roh*
ivory	marfil (*m*)	*mahr-'feel*
jewel	joya	*'hoh-yah*
jewelry store	joyería	*ho-yeh-'ree-ah*
necklace	collar (*m*)	*koh-'yahr*
opal	ópalo	*'oh-pah-loh*
pearl	perla	*'pehr-lah*
precious	precioso (*adj*)	*preh-see·'oh-soh*
ring (*with stone*)	sortija	*sohr-'tee-hah*
ring (*without stone*)	anillo	*ah-'nee-yoh*
ruby	rubí (*m*)	*roo-'bee*
sapphire	zafiro	*sah-'fee-roh*
silver	plata	*'plah-tah*
topaz	topacio	*toh-'pah-see·oh*
true	verdadero (*adj*)	*behr-dah-'deh-roh*
watch, clock	reloj (*m*)	*reh-'loh*
• **alarm clock**	despertador (*m*)	*desh-pehr-tah-'dohr*
• **dial**	esfera	*ehs-'feh-rah*
• **hand**	mano (*f*)	*'mah-noh*
	manecilla	*mah-neh-'see-yah*
• **spring**	muelle (*m*)	*'mweh-yeh*
• **wind**	dar* cuerda a	*dahr 'kwehr-dah ah*
• **wristband**	muñequera	*moo-nyeh-'keh-rah*
	correa	*koh-'rreh-ah*

j. MUSIC

cassette	casete (*m*)	*kah-'seh-teh*
classical music	música clásica	*'moo-see-kah 'klah-see-kah*
compact disk	disco compacto	*'dees-koh kohm-'pahk-toh*
composer	compositor (a)	*kohm-poh-see-'tohr (-rah)*
dance music	música de baile	*'moo-see-kah deh 'bah·ee-leh*
jazz	jazz (*m*)	*yahs*
music	música	*'moo-see-kah*
record	disco	*'dees-koh*
rock music	música rock	*'moo-see-kah rohk*

singer	cantante (*m/f*)	*kahn-'tahn-teh*
song	canción (*f*)	*kahn-see·'ohn*
tape	cinta	*'seen-tah*

k. CLOTHING

articles of clothing	prendas de vestir	*'prehn-dahs deh behs-'teer*
bathing suit	traje (*m*) de baño	*'trah-heh deh 'bah-nyoh*
belt	cinturón (*m*)	*seen-too-'rohn*
blouse	blusa	*'bloo-sah*
bra	sostén (*m*)	*sohs-'tehn*
briefs	calzoncillos	*kahl-sohn-'see-yohs*
changing room	vestuario	*behs-'twah-ree·oh*
clothing store	tienda de ropa	*tee·'ehn-dah deh 'roh-pah*
coat	abrigo	*ah-'bree-goh*
dress	vestido	*behs-'tee-doh*
fashion	moda	*'moh-dah*
fur coat	abrigo de piel	*ah-'bree-goh deh pee·'ehl*
glove	guante (*m*)	*'gwahn-teh*
handkerchief	pañuelo	*pah-'nyweh-loh*
hat	sombrero	*sohm-'breh-roh*
jacket	chaqueta	*chah-'keh-tah*
pajamas	pijamas	*pee-'hah-mahs*
panties	bragas	*'brah-gahs*
pants	pantalones (*m*)	*pahn-tah-'loh-nehs*
raincoat	impermeable (*m*)	*eem-pehr-meh-'ah-bleh*
scarf	bufanda	*boo-'fahn-dah*
shirt	camisa	*kah-'mee-sah*
shorts (*underwear*)	calzoncillos	*kahl-sohn-'see-yohs*
size	talla	*'tah-yah*
skirt	falda	*'fahl-dah*
slip	combinación (*f*)	*kohm-bee-nah-see·'ohn*
suit	traje (*m*)	*'trah-heh*
sweater	suéter (*m*)	*'sweh-tehr*
sweatshirt	sudadera	*soo-dah-'deh-rah*
T-shirt	camiseta	*kah-mee-'seh-tah*
tie	corbata	*kohr-'bah-tah*
underwear	ropa interior	*'roh-pah een-teh-ree·'ohr*

l. DESCRIBING CLOTHING

> For colors, see Section 7.

beautiful	precioso (*adj*)	*preh-see-'oh-soh*
	hermoso (*adj*)	*ehr-'moh-soh*
big	grande (*adj*)	*'grahn-deh*
brocade	brocado	*broh-'kah-doh*
corduroy	pana	*'pah-nah*
cotton	algodón (*m*)	*ahl-goh-'dohn*
elegant	elegante (*adj*)	*eh-leh-'gahn-teh*
fabric	tela	*'teh-lah*
	paño	*'pah-nyoh*
felt	fieltro	*fee-'ehl-troh*
flannel	franela	*frah-'neh-lah*
in the latest style	de la última moda	*deh lah 'ool-tee-mah 'moh-dah*
lace	encaje (*m*)	*ehn-'kah-heh*
leather	cuero	*'kweh-roh*
loose	suelto (*adj*)	*'swehl-toh*
nylon	nailon, nilón (*m*)	*'nah-ee-lohn, nee-'lohn*
permanent press	inarrugable (*adj*)	*een-ah-rroo-'gah-bleh*
plaid	cuadros	*'kwah-drohs*
polka dots	lunares (*m*)	*loo-'nah-rehs*
polyester	poliéster (*m*)	*poh-lee-'ehs-tehr*
silk	seda	*'seh-dah*
small	pequeño (*adj*)	*peh-'keh-nyoh*
striped	rayado (*adj*)	*rrah-'yah-doh*
suede	gamuza	*gah-'moo-sah*
This looks bad on you.	Esto te queda mal.	*'ehs-toh teh 'keh-dah mahl*
This looks good on you.	Esto te queda bien.	*'ehs-toh teh 'keh-dah bee-'ehn*
tight	ceñido (*adj*)	*seh-'nyee-doh*
ugly	feo (*adj*)	*'feh-oh*
velvet	terciopelo	*tehr-see-oh-'peh-loh*
wool	lana	*'lah-nah*

m. CLOTHING: ACTIVITIES

enlarge	agrandar (*v*)	*ah-grahn-'dahr*
	ampliar (*v*)	*ahm-plee-'ahr*
get dressed	vestirse*	*behs-'teer-seh*
lengthen	alargar (*v*)	*ah-lahr-'gahr*

put on	ponerse*	*poh-'nehr-seh*
shorten	acortar (v)	*ah-kohr-'tahr*
take off	quitarse (v)	*kee-'tahr-seh*
tighten	apretar*	*ah-preh-'tahr*
try on	probar*	*proh-'bahr*
undress	desnudarse (v)	*dehs-noo-'dahr-seh*
wear	llevar (v)	*yeh-'bahr*

n. SHOES

boot	bota	*'boh-tah*
pair	par (m)	*pahr*
purse	bolsa	*'bohl-sah*
shoe	zapato	*sah-'pah-toh*
shoe store	zapatería	*sah-pah-tah-'ree-ah*
shoelace	cordón (m) de zapato	*kohr-'dohn deh sah-'pah-toh*
size (of shoe)	número	*'noo-meh-roh*
slipper	zapatilla	*sah-pah-'tee-yah*
sock	calcetín (m)	*kahl-seh-'teen*
stockings	medias	*'meh-dee·ahs*

o. BOOKS

adventure book	libro de aventura	*'lee-broh deh ah-behn-'too-rah*
book	libro	*'lee-broh*
• best-seller	éxito de librería	*'ehks-ee-toh deh lee-breh-'ree·ah*
bookstore	librería	*lee-breh-'ree-·ah*
comics	historieta	*ees-toh-ree-·'eh-tah*
dictionary	diccionario	*deek-see-oh-'nah-ree·oh*
encyclopedia	enciclopedia	*ehn-see-kloh-'peh-dee·ah*
guidebook	guía del viajero (f)	*'gee-ah dehl bee·ah-'heh-roh*
magazine	revista	*reh-'bees-tah*
mystery novel	novela policíaca	*noh-'beh-lah poh-lee-'see-ah-kah*
newspaper	periódico	*peh-ree-'oh-dee-koh*
novel	novela	*noh-'beh-lah*
paperback book	libro en rústica	*'lee-broh ehn 'roos-tee-kah*
poetry	poesía	*poh-eh-'see·ah*
reference book	libro de consulta	*'lee-broh deh kohn-'sool-tah*

romance book	novela romántica	*noh-'beh-lah roh-'mahn-tee-kah*
science fiction book	libro de ciencia ficción	*'lee-broh deh 'see·ehn-see·ah feek-see·'ohn*
technical book	libro técnico	*'lee-broh 'tehk-nee-koh*
textbook	libro de texto	*'lee-broh deh 'tehks-toh*
theater	teatro	*teh-'ah-troh*

26. BANKING AND COMMERCE

> For numerical concepts, see Section 1.

account	cuenta	*'kwehn-tah*
• **close an account**	liquidar una cuenta	*lee-kee-'dahr 'oo-nah 'kwehn-tah*
• **open an account**	abrir una cuenta	*ah-'breer 'oo-nah 'kwehn-tah*
bank	banco	*'bahn-koh*
• **head office**	oficina central	*oh-fee-'see·nah sehn-'trahl*
bank book	libreta de depósitos	*lee-'breh-tah deh de-'poh-see-tohs*
bank rate	tipo de descuento bancario	*'tee-poh deh des-'kwehn-toh bahn-'kah-ree·oh*
• **fixed**	fijo	*'fee-hoh*
• **variable**	variable (*adj*)	*bah-ree-'ah-bleh*
bill, banknote	billete (*m*)	*bee-'yeh-teh*
• **dollar**	dólar (*m*)	*'doh-lahr*
• **large bill**	billete grande	*bee-'yeh-teh 'grahn-deh*
• **small bill**	billete pequeño	*bee-'yeh-teh peh-'keh-nyoh*
bond	bono	*'boh-noh*
budget	presupuesto	*preh-soo-'pwehs-toh*
cash	dinero en efectivo	*dee-'neh-roh ehn eh-fehk-'tee-boh*
• **cash**	cobrar (*v*)	*koh-'brahr*
	cambiar (*v*)	*kahm-bee-'ahr*
• **cash account**	cuenta de caja	*'kwehn-tah deh 'kah-hah*
• **cash payment**	pago al contado	*'pah-goh ahl kohn-'tah-doh*
cashier, teller	cajero (a)	*kah-'heh-roh (rah)*

check	cheque (m)	'cheh-keh
• checkbook	libreta de cheques	lee-'breh-tah deh 'cheh-kehs
• checking account	cuenta corriente	'kwehn-tah koh-rree·'ehn-teh
coin	moneda	moh-'neh-dah
compound interest	interés compuesto	een-teh-'rehs kohm-'pwehs-toh
cost of living	coste (m) de vida	'kohs-teh deh 'bee-dah
credit	crédito	'kreh-dee-toh
• credit card	tarjeta de crédito	tahr-'heh-tah deh 'kreh-dee-toh
current account	cuenta corriente	'kwehn-tah koh-rree·'ehn-teh
currency	dinero en circulación	dee-'neh-roh ehn seer-koo-lah-see·'ohn
customer	cliente (m/f)	klee-'ehn-teh
debt	deuda	'deh·oo-dah
deposit	depósito	deh-'poh-see-toh
• deposit	depositar (v)	deh-poh-see-'tahr
• deposit slip	hoja de depósito	'oh-hah deh deh-'poh-see-toh
discount	descuento	dehs-'kwehn-toh
draft	letra de cambio	'leh-trah deh 'kahm-bee·oh
employee	empleado (a)	ehm-pleh-'ah-doh (-dah)
endorse	endosar (v)	ehn-doh-'sahr
• endorsement	endoso	ehn-'doh-soh
exchange	cambiar (v)	kahm-bee-'ahr
• exchange	cambio	'kahm-bee·oh
• rate of exchange	tipo de cambio	'tee-poh deh 'kahm-bee·oh
expiration date	fecha de vencimiento	'feh-chah deh behn-see-mee·'ehn-toh
foreign exchange	divisas	dee-'bee-sahs
income	ingresos	een-'greh-sohs
insurance	seguro	seh-'goo-roh
• insurance policy	póliza de seguros	'poh-lee-sah deh seh-'goo-rohs
• insurance premium	prima de seguros	'pree-mah deh seh-'goo-rohs
interest	interés (m)	een-teh-'rehs
• interest rate	tasa de interés	'tah-sah deh een-teh-'rehs
invest	invertir*	een-behr-'teer
• investment	inversión (f)	een-behr-see·'ohn
line up	hacer* cola	ah-'sehr 'koh-lah
• line	cola	'koh-lah

loan	préstamo	*'prehs-tah-moh*
• get a loan	obtener* un préstamo	*ohb-teh-'nehr oon 'prehs-tah-moh*
• loan officer	oficial de préstamos (*m/f*)	*oh-fee-see·'ahl deh 'prehs-tah-mohs*
loss	pérdida	*'pehr-dee-dah*
manager	gerente (*m/f*)	*heh-'rehn-teh*
money	dinero	*dee-'neh-roh*
money order	giro postal	*'hee-roh pohs-'tahl*
mortgage	hipoteca	*ee-poh-'teh-kah*
pay	pagar (*v*)	*pah-'gahr*
• pay off debts	saldar (*v*) las deudas	*sahl-'dahr lahs dee·'oo-dahs*
• payment	pago	*'pah-goh*
postdate	posfechar (*v*)	*pohs-feh-'chahr*
• postdate	posfecha	*pohs-'feh-chah*
profit	ganancia	*gah-'nahn-see·ah*
real estate	bienes raíces (*m*)	*bee·'eh-nehs rah-'ee-sehs*
receipt	recibo	*reh-'see-boh*
retail	venta al por menor	*'behn-tah ahl pohr meh-'nohr*
safe	caja fuerte	*'kah-hah 'fwehr-teh*
• safe deposit box	caja de seguridad	*'kah-hah deh seh-goo-ree-'dahd*
salary	salario	*sah-'lah-ree·oh*
	sueldo	*'soo·ehl-doh*
save	ahorrar (*v*)	*ah-oh-'rrahr*
• savings	ahorros	*ah-'oh-rrohs*
• savings account	cuenta de ahorros	*'kwehn-tah deh ah-'oh-rrohs*
• savings bank	caja de ahorros	*'kah-hah deh ah-'oh-rrohs*
securities (*stocks and bonds*)	valores (*m*)	*bah-'loh-rehs*
sign	firmar (*v*)	*feer-'mahr*
• signature	firma	*'feer-mah*
stock market	bolsa de valores	*'bohl-sah deh bah-'loh-rehs*
stock, share	acción (*f*)	*ahk-see·'ohn*
tax	impuesto	*eem-'pwehs-toh*
• tax exemption	exención (*f*) del impuesto	*ehks-ehn-see·'ohn dehl eem-'pwehs-toh*
teller's window	ventanilla	*behn-tah-'nee-yah*
traveler's check	cheque de viajero	*'cheh-keh deh bee·ah-'heh-roh*
wholesale	venta al por mayor	*'behn-tah ahl pohr mah-'yohr*

withdraw	retirar (v)	reh-tee-'rahr
• withdrawal	retiro	reh-'tee-roh
• withdrawal slip	hoja de retiro	'oh-hah deh reh-'tee-roh

27. GAMES AND SPORTS

a. GAMES, HOBBIES, AND PHYSICAL FITNESS

billiards	billar (m)	bee-'yahr
• billiard ball	bola de billar	'boh-lah deh bee-'yahr
• billiard table	mesa de billar	'meh-sah deh bee-'yahr
• billiard cloth	paño	'pah-nyoh
• cue	taco	'tah-koh
• pocket	bolsillo	bohl-'see-yoh
bingo	bingo	'been-goh
• bingo card	tarjeta de bingo	tahr-'heh-tah deh 'been-goh
body build	desarrollar (v) la musculatura	dehs-ah-rroh-'yahr lah moos-koo-lah-'too-rah
• weightlift	levantar (v) pesas	leh-bahn-'tahr 'peh-sahs
bowling	bolo	'boh-loh
	boliche	boh-'lee-cheh
• bowl	jugar* a los bolos (al boliche)	hoo-'gahr ah lohs 'boh-lohs (ahl boh-'lee-cheh)
• bowling alley	bolera	boh-'leh-rah
• bowling ball	bola	'boh-lah
checkers	damas	'dah-mahs
• checkerboard	tablero de damas	tah-'bleh-roh deh 'dah-mahs
chess	ajedrez (m)	ah-heh-'drehs
• bishop	alfil (m)	ahl-'feel
• checkmate	jaque mate (m)	'hah-keh 'mah-teh
• chessboard	tablero de ajedrez	tah-'bleh-roh deh ah-heh-'drehs
• king	rey (m)	'reh-ee
• knight	caballo	kah-'bah-yoh
• pawn	peón (m)	peh-'ohn
• queen	reina	'reh-ee-nah
• rook	torre (f)	'toh-rreh
coin	moneda	moh-'neh-dah
• coin collecting	numismática	noo-mess-'mah-tee-kah
darts	dardos	'dahr-dohs
dice	dados	'dah-dohs
game	juego	'hweh-goh
gymnasium	gimnasio	heem-'nah-see-oh
• work out	hacer* gimnasia	ah-'sehr geem-'nah-see·ah

hobby	pasatiempo	*pah-sah-tee-'ehm-poh*
instrument	instrumento	*eens-troo-'mehn-toh*
• play an instrument	tocar (*v*) un instrumento	*toh-'kahr oon eens-troo-'mehn-toh*
jog	correr (*v*) a trote corto	*koh-'rrehr ah 'troh-teh 'kohr-toh*
mountain climbing	alpinismo	*ahl-pee-'nees-moh*
• knapsack	mochila	*moh-'chee-lah*
• rope	cuerda	*'kwehr-dah*
play (*a game*)	jugar*	*hoo-'gahr*
playing cards	cartas	*'kahr-tahs*
	naipes (*m*)	*'nah·ee-pehs*
• clubs	bastos	*'bahs-tohs*
• diamonds	diamantes (*m*)	*dee·ah-'mahn-tehs*
• hearts	corazones (*m*)	*koh-rah-'soh-nehs*
• spades	picos	*'pee-kohs*
	espadas	*ehs-'pah-dahs*
• shuffle	barajar (*v*)	*bah-rah-'hahr*
run	correr (*v*)	*koh-'rrehr*
skate	patinar (*v*)	*pah-tee-'nahr*
• skating	patinaje (*m*)	*pah-tee-'nah-heh*
• roller skating	patinaje sobre ruedas	*pah-tee-'nah-heh 'soh-breh 'rweh-dahs*
stamp	estampilla	*ehs-tahm-'pee-yah*
	sello	*'seh-yoh*
• stamp collecting	filatelia	*fee-lah-'teh-lee·ah*
swim	nadar (*v*)	*nah-'dahr*
• swimming	natación (*f*)	*nah-tah-see-'ohn*

b. SPORTS

amateur	aficionado (*adj*)	*ah-fee-see·oh-'nah-doh*
athlete	atleta (*m/f*)	*aht-'leh-tah*
ball	pelota	*peh-'loh-tah*
• catch (*ball*)	agarrar (coger*) (*v*)	*ah-gah-'rrahr (koh-'hehr)*
• hit (*ball*)	pegar (le) (*v*) a	*peh-'gahr (-leh) ah*
• kick (*ball*)	pastear (*v*)	*pah-teh-'ahr*
• pass (*ball*)	pasar (*v*)	*pah-'sahr*
• throw (*ball*)	lanzar (*v*)	*lahn-'sahr*
baseball	béisbol (*m*)	*'beh·ees-bohl*
• ball	pelota de béisbol	*peh-'loh-tah deh 'beh·ees-bohl*
• base	base	*'bah-seh*
• bat	bate (*m*)	*'bah-teh*
• batter	bateador (*m*)	*bah-teh-ah-'dohr*
• glove	guante (*m*)	*'gwahn-teh*

• **home base**	base meta	*'bah-seh 'meh-tah*
• **home run**	jonrón *(m)*	*hohn-'rohn*
basketball	básquetbol *(m)*	*'bahs-keht-bohl*
	baloncesto	*bah-lohn-'sehs-toh*
• **basket**	canasta	*kah-'nahs-tah*
• **basketball**	balón de básquetbol	*bah-'lohn deh 'bahs-keht-bohl*
• **basketball court**	cancha	*'kahn-chah*
bicycle racing	ciclismo	*see-'klees-moh*
boxing	boxeo	*boh-'kseh-oh*
• **boxing gloves**	guantes de boxeo	*'gwahn-tehs deh boh-'kseh-oh*
• **boxing ring**	ring *(m)*	*reengh*
car racing	carreras de coches	*kah-'rreh-rahs deh 'koh-chehs*
coach	entrenador (a)	*ehn-treh-nah-'dohr (-rah)*
competition	competencia	*kohm-peh-'tehn-see·ah*
fencing	esgrima	*ehs-'gree-mah*
• **fencing bout**	encuentro de esgrima	*ehn-'kwehn-troh deh ehs-'gree-mah*
field	campo	*'kahm-poh*
football	fútbol americano	*'foot-bohl ah-meh-ree-'kah-noh*
game, match	partido	*pahr-'tee-doh*
goal	gol *(m)*	*gohl*
golf	golf *(m)*	*gohlf*
helmet	casco	*'kahs-koh*
hockey	hockey *(m)*	*'hoh-kee*
• **field hockey**	hockey sobre hierba	*'hoh-kee 'soh-breh ee-'ehr-bah*
• **ice hockey**	hockey sobre hielo	*'hoh-kee soh-breh ee-'eh-loh*
• **puck**	disco	*'dees-koh*
• **skate**	patinar *(v)*	*pah-tee-'nahr*
net	red *(f)*	*rehd*
pass	pase *(m)*	*'pah-seh*
penalty	tiro penal	*'tee-roh peh-'nahl*
play	jugada	*hoo-'gah-dah*
• **player**	jugador (a)	*hoo-gah-'dohr (-rah)*
• **playoffs**	partido de desempate	*pahr-'tee-doh deh dehs-ehm-'pah-teh*
point	punto	*'poon-toh*
	tanto	*'tahn-toh*
professional	profesional *(adj)*	*proh-feh-see·oh-'nahl*
race	carrera	*kah-'rreh-rah*
• **horse racing**	carreras de caballo	*kah-'rreh-rahs deh kah-'bah-yoh*

• racetrack	hipódromo	ee-'poh-droh-moh
referee	árbitro	'ahr-bee-troh
score	marcar (v)	mahr-'kahr
• draw, tie	empate (m)	ehm-'pah-teh
• tie	empatar (v)	ehm-pah-'tahr
• lose	perder*	pehr-'dehr
• loss	pérdida	'pehr-dee-dah
• win	victoria	beek-'toh-ree-ah
• win	ganar (v)	gah-'nahr
ski	esquiar*	ehs-kee-'ahr
• ski	esquí (m)	ehs-'kee
• water ski	esquiar (v) en el agua	ehs-kee-'ahr ehn ehl 'ah-gwah
• water skiing	esquí acuático	ehs-'kee ah-'kwah-tee-koh
soccer	fútbol (m)	'foot-bohl
• soccer ball	balón de fútbol (m)	bah-'lohn deh 'foot-bohl
• soccer player	futbolista (m/f)	foot-boh-'lees-tah
• goalie	portero	pohr-'teh-roh
sport	deporte (m)	deh-'pohr-teh
• practice a sport	practicar (v) un deporte	prahk-tee-'kahr oon deh-'pohr-teh
• sports event	encuentro deportivo	ehn-'kwehn-troh deh-pohr-'tee-boh
• sports fan	aficionado deportivo	ah-fee-see-oh-'nah-doh deh-pohr-'tee-boh
stadium	estadio	ehs-'tah-dee-oh
team	equipo	eh-'kee-poh
tennis	tenis (m)	'teh-nees
• racket	raqueta	rah-'keh-tah
ticket	boleto	boh-'leh-toh
	billete	bee-'yeh-teh
track	pista	'pees-tah
track and field	atletismo en pista	aht-leh-'tees-moh ehn 'pees-tah
volleyball	volibol (m)	boh-lee-'bohl
water polo	polo acuático	'poh-loh ah-'kwah-tee-koh
wrestling	lucha libre	'loo-chah 'lee-breh

28. THE ARTS

a. CINEMA

actor	actor	ahk-'tohr
actress	actriz	ahk-'trees
aisle	pasillo	pah-'see-yoh

box office	taquilla	*tah-'kee-yah*
lobby	vestíbulo	*beh-'stee-boo-loh*
movie, film	película	*peh-'lee-koo-lah*
• make a movie	filmar (v) una película	*feel-'mahr 'oo-nah peh-'lee-koo-lah*
• premiere showing	estreno	*ehs-'treh-noh*
movie director	director cinematográfico	*dee-rehk-'tohr see-neh-mah-toh-'grah-fee-koh*
movie star	estrella de cine	*ehs-'treh-yah deh 'see-neh*
movies	películas	*peh-'lee-koo-lahs*
row	fila	*'fee-lah*
screen	pantalla	*pahn-'tah-yah*
seat	asiento	*ah-'see·ehn-toh*
soundtrack	banda sonora	*'bahn-dah soh-'noh-rah*

FOCUS: Some Hispanic Movie Directors

Luis Buñuel (Spaniard) (1900–1983)	*Tristana, Viridiana, Los olvidados*
Carlos Saura (Spaniard) (1932–)	*Carmen, Bodas de sangre*
Eliseo Subiela (Argentinian)	*Hombre mirando al sudeste*
Luis Puenzo (Argentinian)	*La historia oficial*

b. ART/SCULPTURE/ARCHITECTURE

architecture	arquitectura	*ahr-kee-tehk-'too-rah*
• blueprint	cianotipo	*see-ah-noh-'tee-poh*
art	arte (m/f)	*'ahr-teh*
artist	artista (m/f)	*ahr-'tees-tah*
brush	pincel (m)	*peen-'sehl*
canvas	lienzo	*lee-'ehn-soh*
drawing	dibujo	*dee-'boo-hoh*
easel	caballete (m)	*kah-bah-'yeh-teh*
etching	aguafuerte (m)	*ah-gwah-'fwehr-teh*
exhibition	exhibicion (f)	*enk-see-bee-see-'ohn*
fresco painting	fresco	*'frehs-koh*
masterpiece	obra maestra	*'oh-brah mah-'ehs-trah*

paint	pintar (*v*)	*peen-'tahr*
• **paint**	pintura	*peen-'too-rah*
• **painter**	pintor (a)	*peehn-'tohr ('toh-rah)*
• **painting**	pintura	*peen-'too-rah*
	cuadro	*kwah-droh*
palette	paleta	*pah-'leh-tah*
pastel	pastel (*m*)	*pahs-'tehl*
portrait	retrato	*reh-'trah-toh*
sculpt	esculpir (*v*)	*ehs-kool-'peer*
• **sculptor**	escultor	*ehs-'kool-'tohr*
• **sculptress**	escultora	*ehs-kool-'toh-rah*
• **sculpture**	escultura	*ehs-kool-'too-rah*
tapestry	tapicería	*tah-pee-seh-'ree-ah*
watercolor	acuarela	*ah-kwah-'reh-lah*

FOCUS: Some Hispanic Artists

El Greco (Spaniard) (1544–1614)	*El entierro del Conde de Orgaz*
Diego Velásquez (Spaniard) (1599–1660)	*Las meninas, La rendición de Breda (Las lanzas)*
Francisco de Goya (Spaniard) (1746–1828)	portraits of *Carlos III, Carlos IV y su familia, Los caprichos, Las majas*
Diego Rivera (Mexican) (1886–1957)	noted for his murals depicting the history and social problems of Mexico
José Clemente Orozco (Mexican) (1883–1949)	noted for his murals depicting revolutionary themes, among others *El grito de Hidalgo*
Pablo Picasso (Spaniard) (1881–1973)	noted for his cubist paintings and *Guernica*, his portrayal of the horrors of the Spanish Civil War

c. MUSIC/DANCE

accordion	acordeón (*m*)	*ah-kohr-deh-'ohn*
ballet	ballet (*m*)	*bah-'leht*

brass instruments	cobres (*m*)	*'koh-brehs*
• **horn**	corneta	*kohr-'neh-tah*
• **trombone**	trombón (*m*)	*trohm-'bohn*
• **trumpet**	trompeta	*trohm-'peh-tah*
• **tuba**	tuba	*'too-bah*
classical music	música clásica	*'moo-see-kah 'klah-see-kah*
composer	compositor (a)	*kom-poh-see-'tohr (-rah)*
• **composition**	composición	*kohm-poh-see-see-'ohn*
concert	concierto	*kohn-see-'ehr-toh*
dance	baile (*m*)	*'bah·ee-leh*
• **dance**	bailar (*v*)	*bah·ee-'lahr*
• **dancer**	bailarín, bailarina	*bah·ee-lah-'reen, bah·ee-la-'ree-nah*
folk music	música folklórica	*'moo-see-kah fohl-'kloh-ree-kah*
guitar	guitarra	*gee-'tah-rrah*
• **guitarist**	guitarrista (*m/f*)	*gee-tah-'rrees-tah*
harmony	armonía	*ahr-moh-'nee·ah*
harp	arpa (*f*)	*'ahr-pah*
instrument	instrumento	*eens-troo-'mehn-toh*
• **play an instrument**	tocar (*v*) un instrumento	*toh-'kahr oon eens-troo-'mehn-toh*
jazz	jazz (*m*)	*yahs*
keyboard instruments	instrumentos de teclado	*eens-troo-'mehn-tohs de teh-'klah-doh*
• **grand piano**	piano de cola	*pee-'ah-noh deh 'koh-lah*
• **harpsichord**	clavicordio	*klah-bee-'kohr-dee·oh*
• **organ**	órgano	*'ohr-gah-noh*
• **piano**	piano	*pee-'ah-noh*
• **synthesizer**	sintetizador (*m*)	*seen-teh-tee-sah-'dohr*
• **upright piano**	piano vertical	*pee-'ah-noh behr-tee-'kahl*
light music	música ligera	*'moo-see-kah lee-'heh-rah*
mandolin	mandolina	*mahn-doh-'lee-nah*
music	música	*'moo-see-kah*
• **musician**	músico (a)	*'moo-see-koh (-kah)*
note	nota	*'noh-tah*
opera	ópera	*'oh-peh-rah*
orchestra	orquesta	*ohr-'kehs-tah*
orchestra conductor	director de orquesta	*dee-rehk-'tohr deh ohr-'kehs-tah*
percussion instruments	instrumentos de percusión	*eens-troo-'mehn-tohs deh pehr-koo-see-'ohn*
• **bass drum**	bombo	*'bohm-boh*

• cymbals	címbalos	*'seem-bah-lohs*
• drum	tambor (*m*)	*tahm-'bohr*
• set of drums	tambores (*m*)	*tahm-'boh-rehs*
• timpani	timbales (*m*)	*teem-'bah-lehs*
pianist	pianista (m, f)	*pee·ah-'nees-tah*
player	músico (a)	*'moo-see-koh (-kah)*
prelude	preludio	*preh-'loo-dee·oh*
rhythm	ritmo	*'reet-moh*
rock music	música rock	*'moo-see-kah rohk*
• rock group	grupo de rock	*'groo-poh deh rohk*
show	espéctaculo	*ehs-pehk-'tah-koo-loh*
song	canción (*f*)	*kahn-see-'ohn*
• sing	cantar (*v*)	*kahn-'tahr*
• singer	cantante (*m/f*)	*kahn-'tahn-teh*
string instruments	instrumentos de cuerda	*eens-troo-'mehn-tohs deh 'kwehr-dah*
• bow	arco	*'ahr-koh*
• cello	violoncelo	*bee·oh-lohn-'seh-loh*
• double bass	contrabajo	*kohn-trah-'bah-hoh*
• string	cuerda	*'kwehr-dah*
• viola	viola	*bee-'oh-lah*
• violin	violín	*bee·oh-'leen*
• violinist	violinista (*m/f*)	*bee·oh-lee-'nees-tah*
symphony	sinfonía	*seen-foh-'nee·ah*
wind instruments	instrumentos de viento	*eens-troo-'mehn-tohs deh vee·'ehn-toh*
• bagpipes	gaita	*'ga·ee-tah*
• bassoon	bajón (*m*)	*bah-'hohn*
• clarinet	clarinete (*m*)	*klah-ree-'neh-teh*
• flute	flauta	*'flow-tah*
• oboe	oboe (*m*)	*oh-'boh-eh*
• saxophone	saxofón	*sah-ksoh-'fohn*

FOCUS: Some Hispanic Composers and Musicians

Isaac Albéniz (Spaniard) (1860–1909)	*Iberia*
Enrique Granados (Spaniard) (1867–1916)	*Danzas españolas, Goyescas*
Ernesto Lecuona (Cuban) (1896–1963)	*Malagueña*
Andrés Segovia (Spaniard) (1893–1987)	classical guitarist
Pablo Casals (Spaniard) (1876–1973)	cellist

d. LITERATURE

analogy	analogía	*ah-nah-loh-'hee-ah*
antithesis	antítesis (*f*)	*ahn-'tee-teh-sees*
appendix	apéndice (*m*)	*ah-'pehn-dee-seh*
autobiography	autobiografía	*ow-toh-bee-oh-grah-'fee·ah*
ballad	romance (*m*)	*roh-'mahn-seh*
baroque	barroco (*n, adj*)	*bah-'rroh-koh*
bible	biblia	*bee-'blee·ah*
biography	biografía	*bee·oh-grah-'fee·ah*
chapter	capítulo	*kah-'pee-too-loh*
character (*in a book, play, etc.*)	personaje (*m*)	*pehr-soh-'nah-heh*
conflict	conflicto	*kohn-'fleek-toh*
criticism	crítica	*'kree-tee-kah*
dialogue	diálogo	*dee-'ah-loh-goh*
essay	ensayo	*ehn-'sah-yoh*
euphemism	eufemismo	*eh·oo-feh-'mees-moh*
fable	fábula	*'fah-boo-lah*
fairy tale	cuento de hadas	*'kwehn-toh deh 'ah-dahs*
fiction	ficción (*f*)	*feek-see-'ohn*
folklore	folklore (*m*)	*fohl-'klohr-eh*
genre	género	*'heh-neh-roh*
hyperbole	hipérbole (*f*)	*ee-'pehr-boh-leh*
idiom	modismo	*moh-'dees-moh*
irony	ironía	*ee-roh-'nee·ah*
legend	leyenda	*leh-'yehn-dah*
literature	literatura	*lee-teh-rah-'too-rah*
main character	protagonista (*m/f*)	*proh-tah-goh-'nees-tah*
metaphor	metáfora	*meh-'tah-foh-rah*
monologue	monólogo	*moh-'noh-loh-goh*
myth	mito	*'mee-toh*
mythology	mitología	*mee-toh-loh-'hee-ah*
novel	novela	*noh-'beh-lah*
onomatopoeia	onomatopeya	*oh-noh-mah-toh-'peh-yah*
parable	parábola	*pah-'rah-boh-lah*
paradox	paradoja	*pah-rah-'doh-hah*
pen name	seudónimo	*seh·oo-'doh-nee-moh*
personification	personificación (*f*)	*pehr-soh-nee-fee-kah-see-'ohn*
• personify	personificar (*v*)	*pehr-soh-nee-fee-'kahr*
plagiarism	plagio	*'plah-gee·oh*
plot	trama (*f*)	*'trah-mah*
poet	poeta	*poh-'eh-tah*
	poetisa	*poh·eh-'tee-sah*
point of view	punto de vista	*'poon-toh deh 'bees-tah*

preface	prefacio	*preh-'fah-see·oh*
prologue	prólogo	*'proh-loh-goh*
proverb	proverbio	*proh-'behr-bee·oh*
pun	retruécano	*reh-'trweh-kah-noh*
rhetoric	retórica	*reh-'toh-ree-kah*
rhyme	rima	*'ree-mah*
satire	sátira	*'sah-tee-rah*
short story	cuento	*'kwehn-toh*
simile	símil *(m)*	*'see-meel*
soliloquy	soliloquio	*soh-lee-'loh-kee·oh*
sonnet	soneto	*soh-'neh-toh*
symbol	símbolo	*'seem-boh-loh*
style	estilo	*eh-'stee-loh*
theme	tema *(m)*	*'teh-mah*
verse	verso	*'behr-soh*
work	obra	*'oh-brah*
writer	escritor (a)	*ehs-kree-'tohr (-'toh-rah)*

FOCUS: Some Hispanic Writers

Garcilaso de la Vega (Spaniard) (1501–1536)	*Sonetos*
Miguel de Cervantes (Spaniard) (1547–1616)	*Avenuturas del ingenioso hidalgo don Quijote de la Mancha*
Sor Juana Inés de la Cruz (Mexican) (1651–1695)	*Respuesta a Sor Filotea de la Cruz*
Rubén Darío (Nicaraguan) (1867–1916)	*Prosas profanas*
Pablo Neruda (Chilean) (1904–1973)	*Residencia en la tierra, Odas elementales*
Carlos Fuentes (Mexican) (1928–)	*La muerte de Artemio Cruz*
Gabriel García Márquez (Colombian) (1928–)	*Cien años de soledad*

FOCUS: Some Hispanic Playwrights

Félix Lope de Vega y Carpio (Spaniard) (1562–1635)	*Fuenteovejuna*
Pedro Calderón de la Barca (Spaniard) (1600–1681)	*La vida es sueño*
José Zorrilla (Spaniard) (1817–1893)	*Don Juan Tenorio*
Federico García Lorca (Spaniard) (1898–1936)	*Bodas de sangre*
Antonio Buero Vallejo (Spaniard) (1916–)	*El sueño de la razón*

e. THEATER

act	acto	*'ahk-toh*
• act	actuar (*v*)	*ahk-'twahr*
applause	aplauso	*ah-'plow-soh*
• applaud	aplaudir (*v*)	*ah-plow-'deer*
audience	público	*'poo-blee-koh*
cast	reparto	*reh-'pahr-toh*
character	personaje (*m*)	*pehr-soh-'nah-heh*
comedian	comediante (*m/f*)	*koh-meh-dee-'ahn-teh*
comedy	comedia	*koh-'meh-dee·ah*
curtain	telón (*m*)	*teh-'lohn*
drama	drama (*m*)	*'drah-mah*
hero	héroe (*m*)	*'eh-roh-eh*
heroine	heroína (*f*)	*eh-roh-'ee-nah*
intermission	entreacto	*ehn-treh-'ahk-toh*
open (*play*)	estrenar (*v*)	*ehs-treh-'nahr*
opening night	estreno	*ehs-'treh-noh*
perform	representar (*v*)	*reh-preh-sehn-'tahr*
• performance	representación (*f*)	*reh-preh-sehn-tah-see·'ohn*
play the role of	hacer* el papel de	*ah-'sehr ehl pah-'pehl deh*
playwright	dramaturgo	*drah-mah-'toor-goh*
plot	argumento	*ahr-goo-'mehn-toh*
	trama	*'trah-mah*
program	programa (*m*)	*proh-'grah-mah*
rehearse	ensayar (*v*)	*ehn-sah-'yahr*

role	papel (m)	pah-'pehl
scene	escena	ehs-'seh-nah
scenery	decorado	deh-koh-'rah-doh
stage	escenario	ehs-seh-'nah-ree·oh
theater	teatro	teh-'ah-troh
tragedy	tragedia	trah-'heh-dee·ah
usher	acomodador (m)	ah-koh-moh-dah-'dohr
wings (of stage)	bastidores (m)	bahs-tee-'doh-rehs

29. HOLIDAYS AND GOING OUT

a. HOLIDAYS/SPECIAL OCCASIONS

anniversary	aniversario	ah-nee-behr-'sah-ree·oh
birthday	cumpleaños (m)	koom-pleh-'ah-nyohs
Christmas	Navidad (f)	Nah-bee-'dahd
engagement	noviazgo	noh-bee-'ahs-goh
holiday (official)	día de fiesta	'dee·ah deh fee·'ehs-tah
holidays	días de fiesta	'dee·ahs deh fee·'ehs-tah
New Year's Day	día del Año Nuevo	'dee·ah dehl 'ah-nyoh 'nweh-boh
New Year's Eve	Nochevieja	noh-cheh-vee·'eh-hah
picnic	picnic (m)	'peek-neek
vacation	vacaciones (f)	bah-kah-see·'oh-nehs
• go on vacation	ir* de vacaciones	eer deh bah-kah-see·'oh-nes
wedding	boda	'boh-dah

b. GOING OUT

dance	bailar (v)	bah·ee-'lahr
• dance	baile (m)	'bah·ee-leh
discothèque	discoteca	dees-koh-'teh-kah
go out	salir*	sah-'leer
have fun	divertirse*	dee-behr-'teer-seh
party	fiesta	fee·'ehs-tah
• invitation	invitación (f)	een-bee-tah-see·'ohn
remain, stay	quedarse (v)	keh-'dahr-seh
return	volver*	bohl-'behr
	regresar (v)	reh-greh-'sahr
visit	visitar (v)	bee-see-'tahr

c. SPECIAL GREETINGS

Best wishes	Vaya con Dios.	*'bah-yah kohn dee-'ohs*
Congratulations!	¡Felicitaciones! ¡Enhorabuena!	*feh-lee-see-tah-see-'oh-nehs, ehn-oh-rah-'bweh-nah*
Happy Birthday.	Feliz cumpleaños.	*feh-'lees koom-pleh-'ah-nyohs*
Happy New Year.	Feliz Año Nuevo.	*feh-'lees 'ah-nyoh 'nweh-boh*
Have a good holiday!	¡Qué pasen buenas vacaciones!	*keh 'pah-sehn 'bweh-nahs bah-kah-see-'oh-nehs*
Have fun.	Diviértase.	*dee-bee-'ehr-tah-seh*
Merry Christmas.	Feliz Navidad.	*feh-'lees nah-bee-'dahd*

TRAVEL

30. CHOOSING A DESTINATION

a. AT THE TRAVEL AGENCY

abroad	al extranjero	*ahl ehks-trahn-'heh-roh*
brochure	folleto	*foh-'yeh-toh*
charter flight	vuelo fletado	*'bweh-loh fleh-'tah-doh*
city	ciudad (*f*)	*see·oo-'dahd*
• capital city	ciudad capital	*see·oo-'dahd kah-pee-'tahl*
class	clase (*f*)	*'klah-seh*
• economy class	clase turista (*f*)	*'klah-seh too-'rees-tah*
• first class	primera clase	*pree-'meh-rah 'klah-seh*
continent	continente (*m*)	*kohn-'tee-'nehn-teh*
country	país (*m*)	*pah-'ees*
downtown	centro	*'sehn-troh*
insurance	seguros	*seh-'goo-rohs*
nation	nación (*f*)	*nah-see-'ohn*
outskirts, suburbs	afueras	*ah-'fweh-rahs*
see	ver (*v*)	*behr*
ticket	boleto	*boh-'leh-toh*
	billete	*bee-'yeh-teh*
• buy a ticket	comprar un boleto (billete)	*kohm-'prahr oon boh'leh-toh (bee-'yeh-teh)*
• return (*ticket*)	de regreso	*deh reh-'greh-soh*
• round-trip (*ticket*)	de ida y vuelta	*deh 'ee-dah ee 'bwehl-tah*
tour, excursion	gira	*'hee-rah*
	excursión (*f*)	*ehks-koor-see-'ohn*
• tour guide	guía (*m/f*) de turismo	*'gee-ah deh too-'rees-moh*
• touring bus	autobús de turismo	*ow-toh-'boos deh too-'rees-moh*
tourist	turista (*m/f*)	*too-'rees-tah*
travel	viajar (*v*)	*bee·ah-'hahr*
• by boat	en barco	*ehn 'bahr-koh*
• by plane	en avión	*ehn ah-bee-'ohn*
• by train	en tren	*ehn trehn*
• travel agency	agencia de viajes	*ah-'hehn-see·ah deh bee-'ah-hehs*

trip	viaje (*m*)	*bee-'ah-heh*
• **Have a nice trip.**	Buen viaje.	*bwehn bee-'ah-heh*
• **take a trip**	hacer* un viaje	*ah-'sehr oon bee-'ah-heh*
world	mundo	*'moon-doh*

b. COUNTRIES AND CONTINENTS

Africa	Africa	*'ah-free-kah*
America	América	*ah-'meh-ree-kah*
• **Latin America**	Latinoamérica	*lah-tee-noh-ah-'meh-ree-kah*
• **North America**	Norteamérica	*nohr-teh-ah-'meh-ree-kah*
• **South America**	Sudamérica	*sood-ah-'meh-ree-kah*
Asia	Asia	*'ah-see-ah*
Australia	Australia	*ows-'trah-lee-ah*
Austria	Austria	*'ows-tree-ah*
Belgium	Bélgica	*'behl-hee-kah*
Brazil	Brasil (*m*)	*brah-'seel*
Canada	Canadá (*m*)	*kah-nah-'dah*
China	China	*'chee-nah*
Denmark	Dinamarca	*dee-nah-'mahr-kah*
Egypt	Egipto	*eh-'heep-toh*
England	Inglaterra	*een-glah-'teh-rrah*
Europe	Europa	*ee-oo-'roh-pah*
Finland	Finlandia	*feen-'lahn-dee-ah*
France	Francia	*'frahn-see-ah*
Germany	Alemania	*ah-leh-'mah-nee-ah*
Greece	Grecia	*'greh-see-ah*
Greenland	Groenlandia	*groh-ehn-'lahn-dee-ah*
Holland	Holanda	*oh-'lahn-dah*
Ireland	Irlanda	*'eer-'lahn-dah*
Israel	Israel	*ees-rrah-'ehl*
Italy	Italia	*ee-'tah-lee-ah*
Japan	Japón (*m*)	*hah-'pohn*
Luxembourg	Luxemburgo	*loo-ksehm-'boor-goh*
Mexico	México	*'meh-hee-koh*
Norway	Noruega	*noh-roo-'eh-gah*
Poland	Polonia	*poh-'loh-nee-ah*
Portugal	Portugal	*pohr-too-'gahl*
Russia	Rusia	*'roo-see-ah*
Scotland	Escocia	*ehs-'koh-see-ah*
Spain	España	*ehs-'pah-nyah*
Sweden	Suecia	*'sweh-see-ah*
Switzerland	Suiza	*'swee-sah*
United States	los Estados Unidos	*lohs ehs-'tah-dohs oo-'nee-dohs*

c. A FEW CITIES

Berlin	Berlín	*behr-'leen*
Lisbon	Lisboa	*lees-'boh-ah*
London	Londres	*'lohn-drehs*
Mexico City	Ciudad de México	*see·oo-dahd deh 'meh-hee-koh*
Moscow	Moscú	*mohs-'koo*
New York	Nueva York	*'nweh-bah yohrk*
Paris	París	*pah-'rees*
Rome	Roma	*'roh-mah*
Stockholm	Estocolmo	*ehs-toh-'kohl-moh*
Tokyo	Tokio	*'toh-kee·oh*

d. NATIONALITIES AND LANGUAGES

> All nationalities are given in their masculine form. Unless otherwise indicated in parentheses, the principal language name is the same as the nationality.

American	americano (inglés)	*ah-meh-ree-'kah-noh (een-'glehs)*
Arabic	árabe	*'ah-rah-beh*
Argentinian	argentino (español)	*ahr-hehn-'tee-noh*
Australian	australiano (inglés)	*ows-trah-lee-'ah-noh*
Belgian	belga (flamenco, francés)	*'behl-gah*
Bolivian	boliviano (español)	*boh-lee-bee-'ah-noh*
Brazilian	brasileño (portugués)	*brah-see-'leh-'nyoh*
Canadian	canadiense (inglés, francés)	*kah-nah-dee-'ehn-seh*
Chilean	chileno (español)	*chee-'leh-noh*
Chinese	chino	*'chee-noh*
Colombian	colombiano (español)	*koh-lohm-bee-'ah-noh*
Costa Rican	costarricense (español)	*kohs-tah-ree-'sehn-seh*
Cuban	cubano (español)	*koo-'bah-noh*
Danish	danés	*dah-'nehs*
Dominican (*Dominican Republic*)	dominicano (español)	*doh-mee-nee-'kah-noh*
Dutch	holandés	*oh-lahn-'dehs*

Ecuadorian	ecuatoriano (español)	*eh-kwah-toh-ree-'ah-noh*
English	inglés	*een-'glehs*
French	francés	*frahn-'sehs*
German	alemán	*ah-leh-'mahn*
Greek	griego	*gree-'eh-goh*
Guatemalan	guatemalteco (español)	*gwah-teh-mahl-'teh-koh*
Honduran	hondureño (español)	*ohn-doo-'reh-nyoh*
Irish	irlandés (inglés)	*eer-lahn-'dehs*
Italian	italiano	*ee-tah-lee-'ah-noh*
Japanese	japonés	*hah-poh-'nehs*
Nicaraguan	nicaragüense (español)	*nee-kah-rah-'gwehn-seh*
Norwegian	noruego	*noh-'rweh-goh*
Panamanian	panameño (español)	*pah-nah-'meh-nyoh*
Paraguayan	paraguayo (español)	*pah-rah-'gwah-yoh*
Peruvian	peruano (español)	*peh-'rwah-noh*
Polish	polaco	*poh-'lah-koh*
Portuguese	portugués	*pohr-too-'gehs*
Puerto Rican	puertorriqueño (español)	*pwehr-toh-rree-'keh-nyoh*
Russian	ruso	*'rroo-soh*
Salvadoran	salvadoreño (español)	*sahl-bah-doh-'reh-nyoh*
Spanish	español	*ehs-pah-'nyohl*
Swedish	sueco	*'sweh-koh*
Swiss	suizo (alemán, italiano, francés)	*'swee-soh*
Uruguayan	uruguayo (español)	*oo-roo-'gwah-yoh*
Venezuelan	venezolano (español)	*beh-neh-soh-'lah-noh*

31. PACKING AND GOING THROUGH CUSTOMS

baggage, luggage	equipaje (*m*)	*eh-kee-'pah-heh*
• hand luggage	equipaje de mano	*eh-kee-'pah-heh deh 'mah-noh*
border	frontera	*frohn-'teh-rah*
carry	llevar (*v*)	*yeh-'bahr*
customs	aduana	*ah-'dwah-nah*
• customs officer	aduanero	*ah-dwah-'neh-roh*
declare	declarar (*v*)	*deh-klah-'rahr*
• nothing to declare	nada que declarar	*'nah-dah keh deh-klah-'rahr*
• something to declare	algo que declarar	*'ahl-goh keh deh-klah-'rahr*

documents	documentos	*doh-koo-'mehn-tohs*
duty tax	derechos de aduana	*deh-'reh-chohs deh ah-'dwah-nah*
• **pay duty**	pagar (*v*) los derechos de aduana	*pah-'gahr lohs deh-'reh-chohs de ah-'dwah-nah*
foreign currency	moneda extranjera	*moh-'neh-dah ehks-trahn-'heh-rah*
foreigner	extranjero (a)	*ehks-trahn-'heh-roh (rah)*
form (*to fill out*)	formulario	*fohr-moo-'lah-ree·oh*
• **fill out**	llenar (*v*)	*yeh-'nahr*
identification card	tarjeta de identificación	*tahr-'heh-tah deh ee-dehn-tee-fee-kah-see-'ohn*
import	importar (*v*)	*eem-pohr-'tahr*
knapsack	mochila	*moh-'chee-lah*
passport	pasaporte (*m*)	*pah-sah-'pohr-teh*
suitcase	maleta	*mah-'leh-tah*
tariff	tarifa	*tah-'ree-fah*
visa	visado	*bee-'sah-doh*
	visa	*'bee-sah*
weight	peso	*'peh-soh*
• **heavy**	pesado (*adj*)	*peh-'sah-doh*
• **light**	ligero (*adj*)	*lee-'heh-roh*
• **maximum**	máximo (*adj*)	*'mah-ksee-moh*

32. TRAVELING BY AIR

a. IN THE TERMINAL

airline	línea aérea	*'lee-neh-ah ah-'eh-reh-ah*
airport	aeropuerto	*ah-eh-roh-'pwehr-toh*
arrival	llegada	*yeh-'gah-dah*
board	subir (*v*) a	*soo-'beer ah*
• **boarding**	embarque (*m*)	*ehm-'bahr-keh*
• **boarding pass**	tarjeta de embarque	*tahr-'heh-tah deh ehm-'bahr-keh*
check (*luggage*)	facturar (*v*)	*fahk-too-'rahr*
	depositar (*v*)	*deh-poh-see-'tahr*
connection	conexión (*f*)	*koh-neh-ksee·'ohn*
• **make a connection**	hacer* conexión	*ah-'sehr koh-neh-ksee·'ohn*
departure	salida	*sah-'lee-dah*
economy class	clase turista	*'klah-seh too-'rees-tah*
first class	primera clase	*pree-'meh-rah 'klah-seh*
flight	vuelo	*'bweh-loh*

gate	puerta	*'pwehr-tah*
lost and found	oficina de objetos perdidos	*oh-fee-'see-nah deh ohb-'heh-tohs pehr-'dee-dohs*
no smoking	no fumar	*noh foo-'mahr*
• no smoking section	sección de no fumar	*sehk-see-'ohn deh noh foo-'mahr*
• smoking section	sección de fumar	*sehk-see-'ohn deh foo-'mahr*
porter	maletero, mozo	*mah-leh-'teh-roh, 'moh-soh*
reservation	reservación (*f*)	*reh-sehr-bah-see-'ohn*
	reserva	*reh-'sehr-bah*
terminal	terminal (*f*)	*tehr-mee-'nahl*
ticket	boleto	*boh-'leh-toh*
	billete (*m*)	*bee-'yeh-teh*
ticket agent	vendedor de boletos (billetes)	*behn-deh-'dohr deh boh-'leh-tohs (bee-'yeh-tehs)*
waiting room	sala de espera	*'sah-lah deh ehs-'peh-rah*

b. FLIGHT INFORMATION

canceled	cancelado (*adj*)	*kahn-seh-'lah-doh*
direct flight	vuelo directo	*'bweh-loh dee-'rehk-toh*
early	temprano	*tehm-'prah-noh*
late	tarde	*'tahr-deh*
on time	a tiempo	*ah tee·'ehm-poh*

c. ON THE PLANE

airplane	avión (*m*)	*ah-bee-'ohn*
aisle	pasillo	*pah-'see-yoh*
altitude	altitud (*f*)	*ahl-tee-'tood*
cabin	cabina	*kah-'bee-nah*
copilot	copiloto	*koh-pee-'loh-toh*
crew	tripulación (*f*)	*tree-poo-lah-see-'ohn*
emergency procedures	procedimientos de emergencia	*proh-seh-dee-mee·'ehn-tohs deh eh-mehr-'hehn-see·ah*
flight attendant	aeromozo (a)	*ah-ee-roh-'moh-soh (-sah)*
	azafata	*ah-sah-'fah-tah*
fly	volar*	*boh-'lahr*
headphones	audífonos	*ow-'dee-foh-nohs*
	auriculares (*m*)	*ow-ree-koo-'lah-rehs*

land	aterrizar (v)	*ah-teh-rree-'sahr*
• **landing**	aterrizaje (m)	*ah-teh-ree-'sah-heh*
• **landing gear**	tren (m) de aterrizaje	*trehn deh ah-teh-ree-'sah-heh*
life jacket	chaleco salvavidas	*chah-'leh-koh sahl-bah-'bee-dahs*
liftoff	despegue (m)	*dehs-'peh-geh*
make a stop	hacer* una escala	*ah-'sehr 'oo-nah ehs-'kah-lah*
oxygen	oxígeno	*ohks-'ee-heh-noh*
passenger	pasajero	*pah-sah-'heh-roh*
runway	pista	*'pees-tah*
seat	asiento	*ah-see-'ehn-toh*
• **aisle seat**	asiento de pasillo	*ah-see-'ehn-toh deh pah-'see-yoh*
• **window seat**	asiento de ventanilla	*ah-see-'ehn-toh deh behn-tah-'nee-yah*
seat belt	cinturón (m) de seguridad	*seen-too-'rohn deh seh-goo-ree-'dahd*
• **buckle up**	abrocharse (v)	*ah-broh-'chahr-seh*
• **fasten**	asegurar (v)	*ah-seh-goo-'rahr*
• **unbuckle**	desabrocharse (v)	*dehs-ah-broh-'chahr-seh*
sit down	sentarse*	*sehn-'tahr-seh*
take off	despegar (v)	*dehs-peh-'gahr*
• **take off**	despegue (m)	*dehs-'peh-geh*
toilet	retrete (m)	*reh-'treh-teh*
tray	bandeja	*bahn-'deh-hah*
turbulence	turbulencia	*toor-boo-'lehn-see·ah*
wheel	rueda	*'rweh-dah*
wing	ala (f)	*'ah-lah*

33. ON THE ROAD

a. VEHICLES

ambulance	ambulancia	*ahm-boo-'lahn-see·ah*
automobile	automóvil	*ow-toh-'moh-beel*
bicycle	bicicleta	*bee-see-'kleh-tah*
• **brake**	freno	*'freh-noh*
• **chain**	cadena	*kah-'deh-nah*
• **chain guard**	cárter (m)	*'kahr-tehr*
• **handlebar**	manillar (m)	*mah-nee-'yahr*
• **pedal**	pedal (m)	*peh-'dahl*
• **seat**	sillín (m)	*see-'yeen*
• **spoke**	radio	*'rah-dee·oh*
• **tire**	llanta	*'yahn-tah*

bus	autobús (*m*)	*ow-toh-'boos*
	camión (*Mexico*)	*kah-mee·'ohn*
• streetcar	tranvía (*m*)	*trahn-'bee·ah*
car	carro	*'kah-rroh*
	coche (*m*)	*'koh-cheh*
• rented car	coche alquilado	*'koh-cheh ahl-kee-'lah-doh*
• sports car	coche deportivo	*'koh-cheh deh-pohr-'tee-boh*
compact car	coche pequeño	*'koh-cheh peh-'keh-nyoh*
motorcycle	moto	*'moh-toh*
	motocicleta	*moh-toh-see-'kleh-tah*
taxi	taxi (*m*)	*'tah-ksee*
• taxi driver	taxista (*m/f*)	*tah-'ksees-tah*
tow truck	grúa de remolque	*'groo-ah deh reh-'mohl-keh*
trailer	remolque (*m*)	*reh-'mohl-keh*
truck	camión (*m*)	*kah-mee·'ohn*
• truck driver	camionero	*kah-mee·oh-'neh-roh*
van	furgón (*m*)	*foor-'gohn*
vehicle	vehículo	*beh-'ee-koo-loh*

b. DRIVING: PEOPLE AND DOCUMENTS

driver	conductor (a)	*kohn-dook-'tohr (-'toh-rah)*
driver's license	licencia para conducir*	*lee-'sehn-see·ah 'pah-rah kohn-doo-'seer*
insurance card	tarjeta de seguro	*tahr-'heh tah deh seh-'goo-roh*
passenger	pasajero	*pah-sah-'heh-roh*
pedestrian	peatón (*m*)	*peh-ah-'tohn*
police	policía (*f*)	*poh-lee-'see·ah*
• policeman	policía (*m*)	*poh-lee-'see·ah*
• policewoman	policía (*f*)	*poh-lee-'see·ah*
• traffic policeman	guardia (*m*)	*'gwahr-dee·ah*
• traffic policewoman	guardia (*f*)	*'gwahr-dee·ah*
road map	mapa (*m*) de carreteras	*'mah-pah deh kah-rreh-teh-rahs*
title of ownership	título	*'tee-too-loh*

c. DRIVING: ADDITIONAL VOCABULARY

| accident | accidente (*m*) | *ahk-see-'dehn-teh* |
| back up | retroceder (*v*) | *reh-troh-seh-'dehr* |

block (*city*)	cuadra	'kwah-drah
	manzana	mahn-'sah-nah
brake	frenar (*v*)	freh-'nahr
bridge	puente (*m*)	'pwehn-teh
change gears	cambiar (*v*) de	kahm-bee-'ahr deh beh-
	velocidad	loh-see-'dahd
corner (*street*)	esquina	ehs-'kee-nah
curve	curva	'koor-bah
distance	distancia	dees-'tahn-see-ah
drive	conducir*	kohn-doo-'seer
	manejar (*v*)	mah-neh-'hahr
fine, ticket	multa	'mool-tah
gas station	gasolinera	gah-soh-lee-'neh-rah
• check the oil	mirar (*v*) el nivel del	mee-'rahr ehl nee-'behl
	aceite	dehl ah-'seh·ee-teh
• diesel	diesel (*m*)	dee-eh-'sehl
• fill up	llenar (*v*)	yeh-'nahr
• fix	reparar (*v*)	reh-pah-'rahr
• gasoline	gasolina	gah-soh-'lee-nah
• leaded gas	gasolina con plomo	gah-soh-'lee-nah kohn 'ploh-moh
• mechanic	mecánico	meh-'kah-nee-koh
• self-service	autoservicio	ow-toh-sehr-'bee-see·oh
• tools	herramientas	eh-rrah-mee-'ehn-tahs
• unleaded gas	gasolina sin plomo	gah-soh-'lee-nah seen 'ploh-moh
go forward	adelantarse (*v*)	ah-deh-lahn-'tahr-seh
go through a red light	pasar (*v*) por una luz roja	pah-'sahr pohr 'oo-nah loos 'rroh-hah
highway	carretera	kah-rreh-'teh-rah
intersection	bocacalle (*f*)	boh-kah-'kah-yeh
	cruce (*m*)	'kroo-seh
lane (*traffic*)	carril (*m*)	kah-'rreel
park	estacionar (*v*)	ehs-tah-see·oh-'nahr
• parking	estacionamiento	ehs-tah-see·oh-nah-mee·'ehn-toh
• public parking	estacionamiento público	ehs-tah-see·oh-nah-mee·'ehn-toh 'poo-blee-koh
pass	pasar (*v*)	pah-'sahr
	adelantar (*v*)	ad-deh-lahn-'tahr
pedestrian crossing	paso de peatones (*m*)	pah-soh deh peh-ah-'toh-nehs
ramp	rampa	'rahm-pah
road	camino	kah-'mee-noh
rush hour	hora de punta	'oh-rah deh 'poon-tah
signal	señal (*f*)	seh-'nyahl
speed	velocidad (*f*)	beh-loh-see-'dahd

• **slow down**	ir* más despacio	*eer mahs dehs-'pah-see·oh*
• **speed up**	acelerar (v)	*ah-seh-leh-'rahr*
start (*the car*)	arrancar (v)	*ah-rrahn-'kahr*
toll	peaje (m)	*peh-'ah-heh*
• **toll booth**	barrera de peaje	*bah-'rreh-rah deh peh-'ah-heh*
traffic	tráfico	*'trah-fee-koh*
traffic light	semáforo	*seh-'mah-foh-roh*
tunnel	túnel (m)	*'too-nehl*
turn	dar* la vuelta	*dahr lah 'bwehl-tah*
• **to the left**	a la izquierda	*ah lah ees-kee-'ehr-dah*
• **to the right**	a la derecha	*ah lah deh-'reh-chah*

d. ROAD SIGNS

caution	cuidado	*kwee-'dah-doh*
danger	peligro	*peh-'lee-groh*
dangerous crossing	cruce (m) peligroso	*'kroo-seh peh-lee-'groh-soh*
detour	desvío	*dehs·'bee·oh*
emergency lane	carril (m) de emergencia	*kah-'rreel deh eh-mehr-'hehn-see·ah*
intersection	intersección (f)	*een-tehr-sehk-see·'ohn*
	cruce (m)	*'kroo-seh*
keep to the right	conserve su derecha	*kohn-'sehr-beh soo deh-'reh-chah*
level crossing	paso a nivel	*'pah-soh ah nee-'behl*
merge	empalme (m)	*ehm-'pahl-meh*
narrow bridge	puente angosto	*'pwehn-teh ahn-'gohs-toh*
no entry	dirección prohibida	*dee-rehk-see·'ohn proh-ee'bee-dah*
no left turn	prohibido girar a la izquierda	*proh-ee-'bee-doh hee-'rahr ah lah ees-kee·'ehr-dah*
no parking	prohibido estacionar	*proh-ee-'bee-doh ehs-tah-see-oh-'nahr*
no passing	prohibido adelantar	*proh-ee-'bee-doh ah-deh-lahn-'tahr*
no right turn	prohibido girar a la derecha	*proh-ee-'bee-doh hee-'rahr ah lah deh-'reh-chah*
no U-turn	prohibido dar la vuelta	*proh-ee-'bee-doh dahr lah 'bwehl-tah*
no stopping	prohibido parar	*proh-ee-'bee-doh pah-'rahr*

one way	dirección única	dee-rehk-see·'ohn 'oo-nee-kah
pedestrian crosswalk	paso de peatones	'pah-soh deh peh-ah-'toh-nehs
slippery when wet	resbaladizo cuando mojado	rehs-bah-lah-'dee-soh 'kwahn-doh moh-'hah-doh
slow	despacio	dehs-'pah-see·oh
speed limit	velocidad máxima	beh-loh-see-'dahd 'mah-ksee-mah
stop	alto	'ahl-toh
	parada	pah-'rah-dah
toll	peaje (m)	peh-'ah-heh
tow-away zone	zona de remolque	'soh-nah deh reh-'mohl-keh
underpass	paso subterráneo	'pah-soh soob-teh-'rrah-neh-oh
wind gusts	vientos fuertes	bee·'ehn-tohs 'fwehr-tehs
work in progress	obras	'oh-brahs
yield	ceder (v) el paso	seh-'dehr ehl 'pah-soh

e. THE CAR

air conditioning	aire acondicionado	'ah·ee-reh ah-kohn-dee-see·oh-'nah-doh
battery	batería	bah-teh-'ree-ah
brake	freno	'freh-noh
bumper	parachoques (m)	pah-rah-'choh-kehs
car body	carrocería	kah-rroh-seh-'ree-ah
car window	ventanilla	behn-tah-'nee-yah
carburetor	carburador (m)	kahr-boo-rah-'dohr
clutch	embrague (m)	ehm-'brah-geh
dashboard	tablero de instrumentos	tah-'bleh-roh deh eens-troo-'mehn-tohs
door	puerta	'pwehr-tah
electrical system	sistema eléctrico	sees-'teh-mah eh-'lehk-tree-koh
fan	ventilador (m)	behn-tee-lah-'dohr
• fan belt	correa de ventilador	koh-'rreh-ah deh behn-tee-lah-'dohr
filter	filtro	'feel-troh
gas pedal	acelerador (m)	ah-seh-leh-rah-'dohr
gas tank	tanque (m)	'tahn-keh
gearshift	cambio de velocidad	'kahm-bee·oh deh beh-loh-see-'dahd

No U-turn

No passing

Border crossing

Traffic signal ahead

Speed limit

Traffic circle (roundabout) ahead

Minimum speed limit

All traffic turns left

End of no passing zone

DIRECCIÓN ÚNICA

One-way street

DESVÍO

Detour

Danger ahead

Entrance to expressway

Expressway ends

Guarded railroad crossing

Yield

Stop

Right of way

Dangerous intersection ahead

Gasoline (petrol) ahead

Parking

No vehicles allowed

Dangerous curve

Pedestrian crossing

Oncoming traffic has right of way

No bicycles allowed

No parking allowed

No entry

No left turn

generator	generador (*m*)	*heh-neh-rah-'dohr*
glove compartment	guantera	*gwahn-'teh-rah*
handle	manija	*mah-'nee-hah*
hazard flash	luces de emergencia	*'loo-sehs deh eh-mehr-'gehn-see·ah*
headlight	faro delantero	*'fah-roh deh-lahn-'teh-roh*
heater	calefacción (*f*)	*kah-leh-fahk-see-'ohn*
hood	capó (*m*)	*kah-'poh*
horn	claxon (*m*), bocina	*'klah-ksohn, boh-'see-nah*
horsepower	caballo de fuerza	*kah-'bah-yoh deh 'fwehr-sah*
ignition	encendido	*ehn-sehn-'dee-doh*
jack	gato	*'gah-toh*
license plate	placa	*'plah-kah*
lights	luces (*f*)	*'loo-sehs*
mileage	kilometraje (*m*)	*kee-loh-meh-'trah-heh*
motor, engine	motor (*m*)	*moh-'tohr*
muffler	mofle (*m*)	*'moh-fleh*
spark plug	bujía	*boo-'hee·ah*
starter	arranque (*m*)	*ah-'rrahn-keh*
steering wheel	volante (*m*)	*boh-'lahn-teh*
tire	llanta	*'yahn-tah*
• flat tire	pinchazo	*peen-'chah-soh*
	llanta desinflada	*'yahn-tah dehs-een-'flah-dah*
transmission	transmisión (*f*)	*trahs-mee-see-'ohn*
trunk	baúl (*m*)	*bah-'ool*
	valija	*bah-'lee-hah*
turn signal	indicador (*m*) de direccción	*een-dee-kah-'dohr deh dee-rehk-see-'ohn*
wheel	la rueda	*lah 'rweh-dah*
windshield	parabrisas (*m*)	*pah-rah-'bree-sahs*
• windshield washer	limpiaparabrisas (*m*)	*leem-pee·ah-pah-rah-'bree-sahs*

34. TRAIN, BUS, AND SUBWAY

bus	autobus (*m*)	*ow-toh-'boos*
bus driver	conductor (a)	*kohn-dok-'tohr (-rah)*
bus station	estación (*f*) de autobuses	*ehs-tah-see-'ohn deh ow-toh-'boo-sehs*
conductor (*train*)	revisor (*m*)	*reh-bee-'sohr*
conductor (*bus*)	conductor (*m*)	*kohn-dook-'tohr*

compartment	compartimiento	*kohm-pahr-tee-mee-'ehn-toh*
• no smoking	de no fumar	*deh noh foo-'mahr*
• smoking	de fumar	*deh foo-'mahr*
connection	enlace (m)	*ehn-'lah-seh*
	conexión (f)	*koh-neh-ksee-'ohn*
direct train	tren (m) directo	*trehn dee-'rehk-toh*
express (bus/train)	expreso	*ehks-'preh-soh*
leave, depart	salir*	*sah-'leer*
	partir (v)	*pahr-'teer*
miss (the train, etc.)	perder* (el tren)	*pehr-'dehr (ehl trehn)*
local train	tren de cercanías	*trehn deh sehr-kah-'nee·ahs*
newsstand	kiosko	*kee-'ohs-koh*
platform	andén (m)	*ahn-'dehn*
porter	maletero	*mah-leh-'teh-roh*
railroad	ferrocarril (m)	*feh-rroh-kah-'rreel*
• railroad station	estación (f) de ferrocarril	*ehs-tah-see-'ohn deh feh-rroh-kah-'rreel*
schedule	horario	*oh-'rah-ree·oh*
• early	temprano	*tehm-'prah-noh*
• late	tarde	*'tahr-deh*
• on time	a tiempo	*ah tee-'ehm-poh*
seat	asiento	*ah-see-'ehn-toh*
• economy	clase turista	*'klah-seh too-'rees-tah*
• first class	primera clase	*pree-'meh-rah 'klah-seh*
stop	parada	*pah-'rah-dah*
subway	metro	*'meh-tro*
	subterráneo	*soob-teh-'rrah-neh-oh*
• subway station	estación del metro	*ehs-tah-see-'ohn del 'meh-troh*
take (the train, etc.)	tomar (v) el tren	*toh-'mahr ehl trehn*
ticket	boleto	*boh-'leh-toh*
	billete (m)	*bee-'yeh-teh*
• buy a ticket	comprar (v) un boleto	*kohm-'prahr oon boh-'leh-toh*
• ticket agent	vendedor (m) de boletos	*behn-deh-'dohr deh boh-'leh-tohs*
• ticket counter	taquilla	*tah-'kee-yah*
	boletería	*boh-leh-teh-'ree·ah*
track	vía	*bee-ah*
train	tren (m)	*trehn*
• All aboard!	¡Todos a bordo!	*'toh-dohs ah 'bohr-doh*
• coach	vagón (m)	*bah-'gohn*
• coach class	segunda clase	*seh-'goon-dah 'klah-seh*
• train station	estación de trenes	*ehs-tah-see-'ohn deh 'treh-nehs*
wait for	esperar (v)	*ehs-peh-'rahr*

35. HOTELS

a. LODGING

boarding house	casa de huéspedes	'kah-sah deh 'wehs-peh-dehs
hotel	hotel (m)	oh-'tehl
• luxury hotel	hotel de primera categoría	oh-'tehl deh pree-'meh-rah kah-teh-goh-'ree·ah
motel	motel (m)	moh-'tehl
youth hostel	albergue juvenil (m)	ahl-'behr-geh hoo-beh-'neel

b. STAYING IN HOTELS

bellboy	botones (m)	boh-'toh-nehs
bill	cuenta	'kwehn-tah
• ask for the bill	pedir* la cuenta	peh-'deer lah 'kwehn-tah
breakfast	desayuno	dehs-ah-'yoo-noh
• breakfast included	desayuno incluido	dehs-ah-'yoo-noh een-'klwee-doh
call for a taxi	pedir* un taxi	peh-'deer oon 'tah-ksee
complain	quejarse (v)	keh-'dahr-seh
• complaint	queja	'keh-hah
doorman	portero	pohr-'teh-roh
electric adaptor	adaptador eléctrico (m)	ah-dahp-tah-'dohr eh-'lehk-tree-koh
elevator	ascensor (m)	ahs-sehn-'sohr
entrance	entrada	ehn-'trah-dah
exit	salida	sah-'lee-dah
floor	piso	'pee-soh
garage	garaje (m)	gah-'rah-heh
hotel clerk	dependiente (a)	deh-pehn-dee·'ehn-teh (-tah)
ice cubes	cubitos de hielo	koo-'bee-tohs deh ee·'eh-loh
identification card	tarjeta de identificación	tahr-'heh-tah deh ee-dehn-tee-fee-kah-see·'ohn
key	llave (f)	'yah-beh
• return the key before leaving	devolver* la llave antes de salir	deh-bohl-'behr lah 'llah-beh 'ahn-tehs deh sah-'leer

lobby	vestíbulo	behs-'tee-boo-loh
• main door	puerta principal	'pwehr-tah preen-see-'pahl
• main floor	planta baja	'plahn-tah 'bah-hah
luggage	equipaje (m)	eh-kee-'pah-heh
• luggage rack	portaequipajes (m)	pohr-tah-eh-kee-'pah-hehs
maid	criada	kree·'ah-dah
manager	gerente (m/f)	heh-'rehn-teh
message	mensaje (m)	mehn-'sah-heh
passport	pasaporte (m)	pah-sah-'pohr-teh
pay	pagar (v)	pah-'gahr
• by check	con cheque	kohn 'cheh-keh
• cash	en efectivo	ehn eh-fehk-'tee-boh
• credit card	con tarjeta de crédito	kohn tahr-'heh-tah deh 'kreh-dee-toh
• traveler's check	con cheque de viajeros	kohn 'cheh-keh deh bee·ah-heh-rohs
pool	alberca	ahl-'behr-kah
	piscina	pees-'see-nah
porter	maletero	mah-leh-'teh-roh
price	precio	'preh-see·oh
• high season	temporada de mucha actividad	tehm-poh-'rah-dah deh 'moo-chah ahk-tee-bee-'dahd
• low season	temporada de menos actividad	tehm-poh-'rah-dah deh 'meh-nohs akh-tee-bee-'dahd
receipt	recibo	reh-'see-boh
reception desk	recepción (f)	reh-sehp-see·'ohn
reservation	reservación (f)	reh-sehr-bah-see·'ohn
room	cuarto	'kwahr-toh
	habitación (f)	ah-bee-tah-see·'ohn
• Do you have a vacant room?	¿Tiene Ud. un cuarto libre?	tee·'eh-neh oos-'tehd oon 'kwahr-toh 'lee-breh
• double room	cuarto doble	'kwahr-toh 'doh-bleh
• double bed	cama matrimonial	'kah-mah mah-tree-moh-nee·'ahl
• single bed	cama sencilla	'kah-mah sehn-'see-yah
• room with two beds	cuarto con dos camas	'kwahr-toh kohn dohs 'kah-mahs
• single room	cuarto sencillo	'kwahr-toh sehn-'see-yoh
services	servicios	sehr-'bee-see·ohs
stairs	escalera	ehs-kah-'leh-rah
view	vista	'bee-stah

c. THE HOTEL ROOM

> See also Section 23.

armchair	sillón (*m*)	*see-'yohn*
balcony	balcón (*m*)	*bahl-'kohn*
• sliding door	puerta corrediza	*poo-'ehr-tah koh-rreh-'dee-sah*
bathroom	baño	*'bah-nyoh*
bathtub	bañera	*bah-'nyeh-rah*
bed	cama	*'kah-mah*
• double bed	cama matrimonial	*'kah-mah mah-tree-moh-nee-'ahl*
bedside table	mesilla de noche	*meh-'see-yah deh 'noh-cheh*
bedspread	cubrecama (*m*)	*koo-breh-'kah-mah*
blanket	manta	*'mahn-tah*
chest of drawers	cómoda	*'koh-moh-dah*
closet	armario	*ahr-mah-ree-'oh*
clothes hanger	percha	*'pehr-chah*
	gancho	*'gahn-choh*
curtains	cortinas	*kohr-'tee-nahs*
dresser	tocador (*m*)	*toh-kah-'dohr*
faucet	grifo	*'gree-foh*
lamp	lámpara	*'lahm-pah-rah*
lights	luces (*f*)	*'loo-sehs*
• current	corriente (*m*)	*koh-rree-'ehn-teh*
• light switch	interruptor (*m*)	*een-teh-rroop-'tohr*
• turn off	apagar (*v*)	*ah-pah-'gahr*
• turn on	encender*	*ehn-sehn-'dehr*
mirror	espejo	*ehs-'peh-hoh*
pillow	almohada	*ahl-moh-'ah-dah*
radio	radio	*'rah-dee-oh*
reading lamp	lámpara para leer	*'lahm-pah-rah 'pah-rah leh-'ehr*
soap bar	pastilla de jabón	*pahs-'tee-yah deh hah-'bohn*
shampoo	champú (*m*)	*chahm-'poo*
sheets	sábanas	*'sah-bah-nahs*
shower	ducha	*'doo-chah*
sink, wash basin	lavabo	*lah-'bah-boh*
• cold water	agua fría	*'ah-gwah 'free-ah*
• hot water	agua caliente	*'ah-gwah cah-lee-'ehn-teh*
table	mesa	*'meh-sah*

telephone	teléfono	*teh-'leh-foh-noh*
television set	televisor (*m*)	*teh-leh-bee-'sohr*
thermostat	termostato	*tehr-mohs-'tah-toh*
toilet	inodoro	*een-oh-'doh-roh*
• **toilet paper**	papel higiénico	*pah-'pehl ee-hee-'ehn-nee-koh*
towel	toalla	*toh-'ah-yah*

36. ON VACATION

a. SIGHTSEEING

amphitheater	anfiteatro	*ahn-fee-teh-'ah-troh*
avenue	avenida	*ah-beh-'nee-dah*
basilica	basílica	*bah-'see-lee-kah*
bell tower	campanario	*kahn-pah-'nah-ree·oh*
bridge	puente (*m*)	*'pwehn-teh*
bullring	plaza de toros	*'plah-sah deh 'toh-rohs*
castle	castillo	*kahs-'tee-yoh*
cathedral	catedral (*f*)	*kah-teh-'drahl*
church	iglesia	*ee-'gleh-see·ah*
city	ciudad (*f*)	*see·oo-'dahd*
city map	plano de la ciudad	*'plah-noh deh lah see·oh-'dahd*
corner	esquina	*ehs-'kee-nah*
downtown	centro	*'sehn-troh*
guide	guía (*m/f*)	*'gee·ah*
• **guidebook**	guía (*f*) del viajero	*'gee·ah dehl bee·ah-'heh-roh*
intersection	bocacalle (*f*)	*boh-kah-'kah-yeh*
kiosk	kiosko	*kee-'ohs-koh*
monument	monumento	*moh-noo-'mehn-toh*
museum	museo	*moo-'seh-oh*
• **art museum**	museo de arte (*m*)	*moo-'seh-oh deh 'ahr-teh*
park	parque (*m*)	*'pahr-keh*
park bench	banco	*'bahn-koh*
parking meter	parquímetro	*pahr-'kee-meh-troh*
pedestrian crosswalk	paso de peatones	*'pah-soh deh peh-ah-'toh-nehs*
public garden	jardín público	*hahr-'deen 'poo-blee-koh*
public notices	avisos públicos	*ah-'bee-sohs 'poo-blee-kohs*
public telephone	teléfono público	*teh-'leh-foh-noh 'poo-blee-koh*
public washroom	servicio público	*sehr-'bee-see·oh 'poo-blee-koh*

railway crossing	cruce (*m*) de vías	*'kroo-seh deh 'bee·ahs*
sidewalk	acera	*ah-'seh-rah*
square	plaza	*'plah-sah*
street	calle (*f*)	*'kah-yeh*
• **street sign**	letrero	*leh-'treh-roh*
take an excursion	hacer* una gira	*ah-'sehr 'oo-nah 'hee-rah*
temple	templo	*'tehm-ploh*
tower	torre (*f*)	*'toh-rreh*
traffic light	semáforo	*seh-'mah-foh-roh*
water fountain	fuente (*f*)	*'fwehn-teh*

b. GETTING OUT OF THE CITY

beach	playa	*'plah-yah*
• **get a suntan**	broncearse (*v*)	*brohn-seh-'ahr-seh*
boat	barco	*'bahr-koh*
brook	arroyo	*ah-'rroh-yoh*
campground	campamento	*kahm-pah-'mehn-toh*
canoe	canoa	*kah-'noh-ah*
canteen	cantimplora	*kahn-teem-'ploh-rah*
cap	gorra	*'goh-rrah*
cruise	crucero	*kroo-'seh-roh*
fish	pescar (*v*)	*pehs-'kahr*
• **go fishing**	ir* de pesca	*eer deh 'pehs-kah*
in the country	en el campo	*ehn ehl 'kahm-poh*
in the mountains	en las montañas	*ehn lahs mohn-'tah-nyahs*
lake	lago	*'lah-goh*
mountain climbing	alpinismo	*ahl-pee-'nees-moh*
river	río	*'ree-oh*
rope	cuerda	*'kwehr-dah*
sea	mar (*m*)	*mahr*
skiing	esquí (*m*)	*ehs-'kee*
• **ski resort**	lugar (*m*) para esquiar	*loo-'gahr 'pah-rah ehs-kee-'ahr*
sleeping bag	saco de dormir	*'sah-koh deh dohr-'meer*
tent	tienda	*tee-'ehn-dah*
trip	viaje (*m*)	*bee-'ah-heh*
vacation	vacaciones (*f*)	*bah-kah-see-'oh-nehs*
• **on vacation**	de vacaciones	*deh bah-kah-see-'oh-nehs*

c. ASKING FOR DIRECTIONS

across	a través de	*ah trah-'behs deh*
ahead	adelante	*ah-deh-'lahn-teh*

at the end of	al final de	*ahl fee-'nahl deh*
at the top of	a la cumbre de	*ah lah 'koom-breh deh*
behind	detrás de	*deh-'trahs deh*
cross (*over*)	cruzar (*v*)	*kroo-'sahr*
• cross the street	cruzar (*v*) la calle	*kroo-'sahr lah 'kah-yeh*
down	abajo (*adv*)	*ah-'bah-hoh*
enter	entrar (*v*) a (en)	*ehn-'trahr ah (ehn)*
• entrance	entrada	*ehn-'trah-dah*
everywhere	en todas partes	*ehn 'toh-dahs 'pahr-tehs*
exit, go out	salir*	*sah-leer*
• exit	salida	*sah-'lee-dah*
far (from)	lejos (de)	*'leh-hohs (deh)*
follow	seguir*	*seh-'geer*
go	ir*	*eer*
go down	bajar (*v*)	*bah-'hahr*
go up	subir (*v*)	*soo-'beer*
here	aquí	*ah-'kee*
	acá	*ah-'kah*
in front of	delante de	*deh-'lahn-teh deh*
in front of (*facing*)	en frente de	*ehn 'frehn-teh deh*
inside	dentro (*adv*)	*'dehn-troh*
	adentro (*adv*)	*ah-'dehn-troh*
• inside of	dentro de (*prep*)	*'dehn-troh deh*
near	cerca de (*prep*)	*'sehr-kah deh*
• nearby	cerca (*adv*)	*'sehr-kah*
outside	afuera (*adv*)	*ah-'fweh-rah*
straight ahead	derecho (*adv*)	*deh-'reh-choh*
there	allí	*ah-'yee*
	allá	*ah-'yah*
through	por (*prep*)	*pohr*
	a través de (*prep*)	*ah trah-'behs deh*
to the east	al este	*ahl 'ehs-teh*
to the left	a la izquierda	*ah lah ees-kee-'ehr-dah*
to the north	al norte	*ahl 'nohr-teh*
to the right	a la derecha	*ah lah deh-'reh-chah*
to the south	al sur	*ahl soor*
to the west	al oeste	*ahl oh-ehs-teh*
towards	hacia (*prep*)	*'ah-see-ah*
turn	dar* la vuelta	*dahr lah 'bwehl-tah*

Can you tell me where . . . ? = ¿Me puede Ud. decir dónde . . . ?

Where is . . .? = ¿Dónde está . . . ?

How do you get to? = ¿Cómo se llega a . . . ?

SCHOOL AND WORK

37. SCHOOL

a. TYPES OF SCHOOLS AND GRADES

coed school	colegio mixto	*koh-'leh-gee·oh 'meeks-toh*
conservatory	conservatorio	*kohn-sehr-bah-'toh-ree·oh*
day-care center	guardería	*gwahr-deh-'ree·ah*
elementary school	escuela primaria	*ehs-'kweh-lah pree-'mah-ree·ah*
evening school	escuela nocturna	*ehs-'kweh-lah nohk-'toor-nah*
grade	clase (*f*)	*'klah-seh*
• **first grade**	primer grado	*pree-'mehr 'grah-doh*
high school	escuela secundaria	*ehs-'kweh-lah seh-koon-'dah-ree·ah*
junior high school	instituto de bachillerato elemental	*eens-tee-'too-toh deh bah-chee-yeh-'rah-toh eh-leh-mehn-'tahl*
kindergarten	escuela de párvulos	*ehs-'kweh-lah deh 'pahr-boo-lohs*
nursery school	escuela de párvulos	*ehs-'kweh-lah deh 'pahr-boo-lohs*
private school	escuela privada	*ehs-'kweh-lah pree-'bah-dah*
technical school	instituto laboral	*eens-tee-'too-toh lah-boh-'rahl*
university	universidad (*f*)	*oo'nee-behr-see-'dahd*
• **year** (*e.g., at university*)	año escolar	*'ah-nyoh ehs-koh-'lahr*
• **first year**	primer año	*pree-'mehr 'ah-nyoh*
• **second year**	segundo año	*seh-'goon-doh 'ah-nyoh*
vocational school	escuela vocacional	*ehs-'kweh-lah boh-kah-see·oh-'nahl*

b. THE CLASSROOM

atlas	átlas (*m*)	*'aht-lahs*
ballpoint pen	bolígrafo	*boh-'lee-grah-foh*
blackboard	pizarra	*pee-'sah-rrah*
blackboard eraser	borrador (*m*)	*boh-rrah-'dohr*

book	libro	*'lee-broh*
bookcase	estante (*m*)	*ehs-'tahn-teh*
chalk	tiza	*'tee-sah*
compass	compás (*m*)	*kohm-'pahs*
date book	diario	*dee·'ah-ree·oh*
desk (*classroom*)	pupitre (*m*)	*poo-'pee-treh*
desk (*office*)	escritorio	*ehs-kree-'toh-ree·oh*
	despacho	*dehs-'pah-choh*
dictionary	diccionario	*deek-see-oh-'nah-ree·oh*
encyclopedia	enciclopedia	*ehn-see-kloh-'peh-dee·ah*
eraser (*pencil*)	goma	*'goh-mah*
	borrador (*m*)	*boh-rrah-'dohr*
eyeglasses	gafas	*'gah-fahs*
	anteojos	*ahn-teh-'oh-hohs*
film projector	proyector (*m*)	*proh-yehk-'tohr*
ink	tinta	*'teen-tah*
magazine	revista	*reh-'bees-tah*
map	mapa (*m*)	*'mah-pah*
notebook	cuaderno	*kwah-'dehr-noh*
paper	papel (*m*)	*pah-'pehl*
pen	pluma	*'ploo-mah*
pencil	lápiz (*m*)	*'lah-pees*
record player	tocadiscos (*m*)	*toh-kah-'dees-kohs*
ruler	regla	*'reh-glah*
school bag	mochila	*moh-'chee-lah*
slide projector	proyector de diapositivas	*proh-yehk-'tohr deh dee·ah-poh-see-'tee-bahs*
tack	tachuela	*tah-'chweh-lah*
tape recorder	grabadora	*grah-bah-'doh-rah*
textbook	libro de texto	*'lee-broh deh 'tehks-toh*
wall map	mapa mural (*m*)	*'mah-pah moo-'rahl*

c. AREAS OF A SCHOOL

campus	ciudad universitaria	*see·oo-'dahd oo-nee-behr-see-'tah-ree·ah*
	campus (*m*)	*'kahm-poos*
classroom	aula (*f*)	*'ow-lah*
gymnasium	gimnasio	*heem-'nah-see·oh*
hallway	pasillo	*pah-'see-yoh*
	corredor (*m*)	*koh-rreh-'dohr*
laboratory	laboratorio	*lah-boh-rah-'toh-ree·oh*
• chemistry lab	laboratorio de química	*lah-boh-rah-'toh-ree·oh deh 'kee-mee-kah*

• language lab	laboratorio de lenguas	*lah-boh-rah-'toh-ree·oh deh 'lehn-gwahs*
main office	oficina central	*oh-fee-'see-nah sehn-'trahl*
library	biblioteca	*bee-blee·oh-'teh-kah*
professor's office	oficina (del profesor, de la profesora)	*oh-fee-'see-nah (dehl proh-feh-'sohr, deh lah proh-feh-'soh-rah)*
school yard	patio	*'pah-tee·oh*

d. SCHOOL: PEOPLE

assistant	ayudante (*m/f*)	*ah-yoh-'dahn-teh*
class of students	clase (*f*)	*'klah-seh*
custodian	portero	*pohr-'teh-roh*
lab technician	ayudante de laboratorio	*ah-yoo-'dahn-teh deh lah-boh-rah-'toh-ree·oh*
librarian	bibliotecario(a)	*bee-blee-oh-teh-'kah-ree·oh (-ah)*
president of a university	rector (*m*)	*rehk-'tohr*
principal	director(a)	*dee-rehk-'tohr (-rah)*
schoolmate	compañero(a) de clase	*kohm-pah-'nyeh-roh (-rah) deh 'klah-seh*
secretary	secretario(a)	*seh-kre-'tah-ree·oh (-ah)*
student	alumno(a)	*ah-'loom-noh (-nah)*
	estudiante (*m/f*)	*ehs-too-dee-'ahn-teh*
teacher	profesor(a)	*proh-feh-'sohr (-rah)*
• elementary school teacher	maestro(a)	*mah-'ehs-troh (-trah)*
• high school teacher	profesor(a)	*proh-feh-'sohr (-rah)*

e. SCHOOL: SUBJECTS

accounting	contabilidad (*f*)	*kohn-tah-bee-lee-'dahd*
anatomy	anatomía	*ah-nah-toh-'mee·ah*
anthropology	antropología	*ahn-troh-poh-loh-'hee·ah*
archaeology	arqueología	*ahr-keh-oh-loh-'hee·ah*
architecture	arquitectura	*ahr-kee-tehk-'too-rah*
art	arte (*m*)	*'ahr-teh*
astronomy	astronomía	*ahs-troh-noh-'mee·ah*
biology	biología	*bee·oh-loh-'hee·ah*
botany	botánica	*boh-'tah-nee-kah*
calculus	cálculo	*'kahl-koo-loh*

chemistry	química	'kee-mee-kah
commerce	comercio	koh-'mehr-see·oh
economics	economía	eh-koh-noh-'mee·ah
engineering	ingeniería	een-heh-nee·eh-'ree·ah
fine arts	bellas artes	'beh-yahs 'ahr-tehs
geography	geografía	heh-oh-grah-'fee·ah
geometry	geometría	heh-oh-meh-'tree·ah
history	historia	ees-'toh-ree·ah
languages (foreign)	lenguas (extranjeras)	'lehn-gwahs (ehks-trahn-'heh-rahs)
law	derecho	deh-'reh-choh
	leyes (f)	'leh-yehs
literature	literatura	lee-teh-rah-'too-rah
mathematics	matemáticas	mah-teh-'mah-tee-kahs
medicine	medicina	meh-dee-'see-nah
music	música	'moo-see-kah
philosophy	filosofía	fee-loh-soh-'fee·ah
physics	física	'fee-see-kah
political science	ciencia política	see-'ehn-see·ah poh-'lee-tee-kah
psychology	psicología	see-koh-loh-'hee·ah
science	ciencia	see-'ehn-see·ah
sociology	sociología	soh-see-oh-loh-'hee·ah
statistics	estadística	ehs-tah-'dees-tee-kah
subject	asignatura	ah-seeg-nah-'too-rah
trigonometry	trigonometría	tree-goh-noh-meh-'tree·ah
zoology	zoología	soh-oh-loh-'hee·ah

f. ADDITIONAL SCHOOL VOCABULARY

> For concepts of thought, see Section 22

answer	responder (v)	rehs-pohn-'dehr
• answer	respuesta	reha-'pwehs-tah
• brief	breve (adj)	'breh-beh
• long	largo (adj)	'lahr-goh
• short	corto (adj)	'kohr-toh
• right	correcto (adj)	koh-'rrehk-toh
• wrong	incorrecto (adj)	een-koh-'rrehk-toh
apply for	solicitar (v)	soh-lee-see-'tahr
assignments, homework	tarea	tah-'reh-ah

attend school	asistir (v) a la escuela	ah-sees-'teer ah lah ehs-'kweh-lah
be absent	estar* ausente	ehs-'tahr ow-'sehn-teh
be present	estar* presente	ehs-'tahr preh-'sehn-teh
be promoted	pasar de año	pah-'sahr deh ah-'nyoh
class (*students*)	clase (f)	'klah-seh
• class	clase (f)	'klah-seh
• have a class	tener* una clase	teh-'nehr 'oo-nah 'klah-seh
• skip class	dejar (v) de ir a clase	deh-'hahr deh eer ah 'klah-seh
• There's no class today.	No hay clase hoy.	noh 'ah·ee 'klah-seh oy
composition	composición (f)	kohm-poh-see-see-'ohn
copy	copia	'koh-pee·ah
• good copy	buena copia	'bweh-nah 'koh-pee·ah
• rough draft	borrador (m)	boh-rrah-'dohr
course	curso	'koor-soh
• take a course	tomar (v) un curso	toh-'mahr oon 'koor-soh
degree (*university*)	título	'tee-too-loh
• get a degree	recibir (v) un título	reh-see-'beer oon 'tee-too-loh
dictation	dictado	deek-'tah-doh
diploma	diploma (m)	dee-'ploh-mah
• get a diploma	obtener* un diploma	ohb-teh-'nehr oon dee-'ploh-mah
draw	dibujar (v)	dee-boo-'hahr
• drawing	dibujo	dee-'boo-hoh
education	educación (f)	eh-doo-kah-see-'ohn
• get an education	recibir (v) una educación	reh-see-'beer 'oo-nah eh-doo-kah-see-'ohn
error	error (m)	eh-'rrohr
essay	ensayo	ehn-'sah-yoh
exam	examen (m)	ehks-'ah-mehn
• entrance exam	examen de ingreso	ehks-'ah-mehn deh een-'greh-soh
• oral exam	examen oral	ehk-'sah-mehn oh-'rahl
• pass	salir* bien	sah-'leer bee-'ehn
• fail	salir* mal	sah-'leer mahl
• take exams	tomar (v) exámenes	toh-'mahr ehks-'ah-meh-nehs
• written exam	examen escrito	ehks-'ah-mehn ehs-'kree-toh
exercise	ejercicio	eh-hehr-'see-see·oh
explanation	explicación (f)	ehks-plee-kah-see-'ohn
• explain	explicar (v)	ehks-plee-'kahr
field (of study)	campo (de estudio)	'kahm-poh (deh ehs-'too-dee·oh)

give back	devolver*	deh-bohl-'behr
grade	nota	'noh-tah
grammar	gramática	grah-'mah-tee-kah
learn	aprender (v)	ah-prehn-'dehr
• learn by heart	aprender (v) de memoria	ah-'prehn-dehr deh meh-'moh-ree·ah
lecture	conferencia	kohn-feh-'rehn-see·ah
• lecture	dar* una conferencia	dahr 'oo-nah kohn-feh-'rehn-see·ah
listen to	escuchar (v)	ehs-koo-'chahr
mistake	error (m)	eh-'rrohr
• make a mistake	equivocarse	eh-kee-boh-'kahr-seh
notes	apuntes (m)	ah-'poon-tehs
• take notes	tomar (v) apuntes	toh-'mahr ah-'poon-tehs
problem	problema (m)	proh-'bleh-mah
• solve a problem	resolver* un problema	reh-sohl-'behr 'oon proh-'bleh-mah
quarter	trimestre (m)	tree-'mehs-treh
question	pregunta	preh-'goon-tah
• ask a question	hacer* una pregunta	'ah-sehr 'oo-nah preh-'goon-tah
read	leer (v)	leh-'ehr
• reading passage	lectura	lehk-'too-rah
registration	matrícula	mah-'tree-koo-lah
• registration fees	derechos de matrícula	deh-'reh-chohs deh mah-'tree-koo-lah
repeat	repetir*	reh-peh-'teer
review	repasar (v)	reh-pah-'sahr
• review	repaso	reh-'pah-soh
school	escuela	ehs-'kweh-lah
semester	semestre (m)	seh-'mehs-treh
study	estudiar (v)	ehs-too-dee·'ahr
take attendance	pasar (v) lista	pah-'sahr 'lees-tah
teach	enseñar	ehn-seh-'nyahr
test	examen	ehks-'ah-mehn
thesis	tesis (f)	'teh-sees
type	escribir a máquina	ehs-kree-'beer ah 'mah-kee-nah
understand	comprender (v)	kohm-prehn-'dehr
	entender*	ehn-tehn-'dehr
write	escribir	ehs-kree-'beer

38. WORK

a. JOBS AND PROFESSIONS

| accountant | contador | kohn-tah-'dohr |
| actor | actor (m) | ahk-'tohr |

actress	actriz (f)	ahk-'trees
architect	arquitecto	ahr-kee-'tehk-toh
baker	panadero	pah-nah-'deh-roh
banker	banquero	bahn-'keh-roh
barber	barbero	bahr-'beh-roh
bricklayer	albañil (m/f)	ahl-bah-'nyeel
bus driver	conductor	kohn-dook-'tohr
businessman	comerciante (m/f)	koh-mehr-see-'ahn-teh
butcher	carnicero	kahr-nee-'seh-roh
carpenter	carpintero	kahr-peen-'teh-roh
cook	cocinero	koh-see-'neh-roh
dentist	dentista (m/f)	dehn-'tees-tah
doctor	doctor	doh-'tohr
	médico	'meh-dee-koh
editor	director	dee-rehk-'tohr
	redactor	rreh-dahk-'tohr
electrician	electricista (m/f)	eh-'lehk-tree-'sees-tah
engineer	ingeniero	een-heh-nee-'eh-roh
eye doctor	médico oculista	'meh-dee-koh oh-koo-'lees-tah
factory worker	obrero	oh-'breh-roh
farmer	campesino	kahm-peh-'see-noh
fireman	bombero	bohm-'beh-roh
hairdresser	peluquero	peh-loo-'keh-roh
job	trabajo	trah-'bah-hoh
	puesto	'pwehs-toh
journalist	periodista (m/f)	preh-ree-oh-'dees-tah
lawyer	abogado	ah-boh-'gah-doh
mechanic	mecánico	meh-'kah-nee-koh
movie director	director cinematográfico	dee-rehk-'tohr see-neh-mah-toh-'grah-fee-koh
musician	músico	'moo-see-koh
notary public	notario público	noh-'tah-ree-oh 'poo-blee-koh
nurse	enfermero	ehn-fehr-'meh-roh
occupation	profesión (f)	proh-feh-see-'ohn
painter	pintor	peen-'tohr
pharmacist	farmacéutico	fahr-mah-'seh-oo-tee-koh
pilot	piloto (m/f)	pee-'loh-toh
plumber	plomero	ploh-'meh-roh
policeman	policía (m/f)	poh-lee-'see-ah
profession	profesión (f)	proh-feh-see-'ohn
professor	profesor	proh-feh-'sohr
psychiatrist	psiquiatra (m/f)	see-kee-'ah-trah
psychologist	psicólogo	see-'koh-loh-goh
scientist	científico	see-ehn-'tee-fee-koh
seamstress	costurera (f)	kohs-too-'reh-rah

secretary	secretario	*seh-kreh-'tah-ree·oh*
surgeon	cirujano	*see-roo-'hah-noh*
tailor	sastre (*m/f*)	*'sahs-treh*
teacher	maestro	*mah-'ehs-troh*
typist	mecanógrafo	*meh-kah-'noh-grah-foh*
writer	escritor	*ehs-kree-'tohr*

b. INTERVIEWING FOR A JOB

> See also Section 11—Basic Personal Information.

name	nombre (*m*)	*'nohm-breh*
• first name	nombre (de pila)	*'nohm-breh deh 'pee-lah*
• signature	firma	*'feer-mah*
address	dirección (*f*)	*dee-rehk-see·'ohn*
• street	calle (*f*)	*'kah-yeh*
• number	número	*'noo-meh-roh*
• city	ciudad (*f*)	*see·oo-'dahd*
• postal code	código postal	*'koh-dee-goh poh-'stahl*
date of birth	fecha de nacimiento	*'feh-chah deh nah-see-mee·'ehn-toh*
place of birth	lugar (*m*) de nacimiento	*loo-'gahr deh nah-see-mee·'ehn-toh*
age	edad (*f*)	*eh-'dahd*
sex	sexo	*'seh-ksoh*
• male	hombre	*'ohm-breh*
• female	mujer	*moo-'hehr*
marital status	estado civil	*ehs-'tah-doh see-'beel*
• married	casado(a)	*kah-'sah-doh (-dah)*
• single	soltero(a)	*sohl-'teh-roh (-rah)*
• be divorced	estar* divorciado(a)	*dee-bohr-see·'ahdo (-see·'adah)*
• be widowed	ser* viudo(a)	*bee·'oo-doh (-dah)*
nationality	nacionalidad (*f*)	*nah-see·oh-nah-lee-'dahd*

> See also Section 30—Nationalities and Languages.

education	enseñanza	*ehn-seh-'nyahn-sah*
elementary school	escuela primaria	*ehs-'kweh-lah pree-'mah-ree·ah*

junior high school	instituto de bachillerato elemental	*eens-tee-'too-toh deh bah-chee-yeh-'rah-toh eh-leh-mehn-'tahl*
secondary school	escuela secundaria, colegio	*ehs-'kweh-lah seh-koon-'dah-ree·ah, koh-'leh-hee·oh*
university	universidad (*f*)	*oo-nee-behr-see-'dahd*
profession	profesión (*f*)	*proh-feh-see-'ohn*
resumé	curriculum vitae (*m*)	*koo-'rree-koo-loom 'bee-teh*
application	solicitud (*f*)	*soh-lee-see-'tood*

c. THE OFFICE

See also Sections 20 and 25.

adhesive tape	cinta adhesiva	*'seen-tah ahd-eh-'see-bah*
appointment book	agenda (*f*) de entrevistas	*ah-'hehn-dah deh ehn-treh-'bees-tahs*
briefcase	maletín (*m*)	*mah-leh-'teen*
	portafolio	*pohr-tah-'foh-lee·oh*
calendar	calendario	*kah-lehn-'dah-ree·oh*
chair	silla	*'see-yah*
computer	computadora	*kohm-poo-tah-'doh-rah*
	ordenador (*m*)	*ohr-deh-nah-'dohr*
desk	escritorio	*ehs-kree-'toh-ree·oh*
file	archivo	*ahr-'chee-boh*
• **file card**	ficha	*'fee-chah*
• **file folder**	carpeta	*kahr-'peh-tah*
• **filing cabinet**	archivo	*ahr-'chee-boh*
	fichero	*fee-'cheh-roh*
intercom	interfono	*een-tehr-'foh-noh*
	intercomunicador (*m*)	*een-tehr-koh-moo-nee-kah-'dohr*
pen (*ballpoint*)	bolígrafo	*boh-'lee-grah-foh*
pencil	lápiz (*m*)	*'lah-pees*
photocopier	fotocopiadora	*foh-toh-koh-pee·ah-'doh-rah*
ruler	regla	*'reh-glah*
scissors	tijeras	*tee-'heh-rahs*
staple	grapa	*'grah-pah*
stapler	engrapador (*m*)	*ehn-grah-pah-'dohr*

tack	tachuela	*tah-'chweh-lah*
telephone	teléfono	*teh-'leh-foh-noh*
typewriter	máquina de escribir	*'mah-kee-nah deh ehs-kree-'beer*
wastebasket	papelero	*pah-peh-'leh-roh*
word processor	procesador de texto (*m*)	*proh-seh-sah-'dohr deh 'tehks-toh*

d. ADDITIONAL WORK VOCABULARY

advertising	publicidad (*f*)	*poo-blee-see-'dahd*
boss (*in an office*)	jefe(a)	*'heh-feh (-fah)*
branch (*company*)	sucursal (*m*)	*soo-koor-'sahl*
career	carrera	*kah-'rreh-rah*
Christmas bonus	aguinaldo	*ah-gee-'nahl-doh*
classified ad	anuncios clasificados	*ah-'noon-see·ohs kla-see-fee-'kah-dohs*
commerce	comercio	*koh-'mehr-see·oh*
company	compañía	*kom-pan-'nyee-ah*
contract	contratar (*v*)	*kohn-trah-'tahr*
• contract	contrato	*kohn-'trah-toh*
earn	ganar (*v*)	*gah-'nahr*
employee	empleado(a)	*ehm-pleh-'ah-doh (-dah)*
employer	empresario(a)	*ehm-preh-'sah-ree·oh (-ree·ah)*
	empleador (*m*)	*ehm-pleh-ah-'dohr*
employment agency	agencia de colocaciones	*ah-'hehn-see·ah de koh-loh-kah-see-'oh-nehs*
factory	fábrica	*'fah-bree-kah*
fire	echar (*v*)	*eh-'chahr*
hire	contratar (*v*)	*kohn-trah-'tahr*
manager	gerente (*m/f*)	*heh-'rehn-teh*
market	mercado	*mehr-'kah-doh*
office	oficina	*oh-fee-'see-nah*
plant	fábrica	*'fah-bree-kah*
	planta	*'plahn-tah*
retirement, pension	jubilación (*f*)	*hoo-bee-lah-see-'ohn*
• retire	jubilarse (*v*)	*hoo-bee-'lahr-seh*
severance pay	indemnización por despido	*een-dehm-nee-sah-see·'ohn pohr dehs-'pee-doh*
unemployment	desempleo	*dehs-ehm-'pleh-oh*
wage, salary	sueldo	*soo-'ehl-doh*
work	trabajo	*trah-'bah-hoh*
• work	trabajar (*v*)	*trah-bah-'hahr*
• work associate	colega (*m/f*)	*koh-'leh-gah*

EMERGENCIES

39. REPORTING AN EMERGENCY

a. FIRE

alarm	alarma (f)	ah-'lahr-mah
ambulance	ambulancia	ahm-boo-'lahn-see·ah
building	edificio	eh-dee-'fee-see·oh
burn	quemar (v)	keh-'mahr
	arder (v)	ahr-'dehr
• burn	quemadura	keh-mah-'doo-rah
call the fire department	llamar a los bomberos	yah-'mahr ah lohs bohm-'beh-rohs
catch fire	encenderse*	ehn-sehn-'dehr-seh
	incendiarse (v)	een-sehn-dee-'ahr-seh
danger	peligro	peh-'lee-groh
destroy	destruir*	dehs-troo-'eer
emergency exit	salida de emergencia	sah-'lee-dah deh eh-mehr-'gehn-see·ah
escape, get out	escaparse (v)	ehs-kah-'pahr-seh
extinguish, put out	extinguir (v)	eks-teen-'geer
fire	fuego	'fweh-goh
• be on fire	estar* ardiendo	ehs-'tahr ahr-dee-'ehn-doh
• Fire!	¡Fuego!	'fweh-goh
• fire alarm	alarma (f) de incendios	ah-'lahr-mah deh een-'sehn-dee·ohs
• fire escape	escalera de incendios	ehs-kah-'leh-rah deh een-'sehn-dee·ohs
• fire extinguisher	extinguidor (m) de incendios	eks-teen-gee-'dohr deh een-'sehn-dee·ohs
• firefighter	bombero	bohm-'beh-roh
• fire hydrant	boca de incendio	'boh-kah deh een-'sehn-dee·oh
• fireproof	incombustible (adj)	een-kohm-boos-'tee-bleh
first aid	primeros auxilios	pree-'meh-rohs ow-'ksee-lee-ohs
flame	llama	'yah-mah
help	ayudar (v)	ah-yoh-'dahr
• Help!	¡Socorro!	soh-'koh-rroh
ladder	escalera	ehs-kah-'leh-rah
out	afuera (adv)	ah-'fweh-rah
• Everybody out!	¡Todos afuera!	'toh-dohs ah-'fweh-rah
paramedics	asistentes médicos	ah-sees-'tehn-tehs 'meh-dee-kohs

protect	proteger*	*proh-teh-'hehr*
rescue	rescatar (v)	*rehs-kah-'tahr*
shout	gritar (v)	*gree-'tahr*
• shout	grito	*'gree-toh*
siren	sirena	*see-'reh-nah*
smoke	humo	*'oo-moh*
victim	víctima (m/f)	*'beek-tee-mah*

b. ROBBERY AND ASSAULT

argue	reñir*	*reh-'nyeer*
arrest	detener*	*deh-teh-'nehr*
	arrestar (v)	*ah-rrehs-'tahr*
assault	asalto	*ah-'sahl-toh*
Come quickly!	¡Venga inmediatamente!	*'behn-gah een-meh-dee·ah-tah-'mehn-teh*
crime	crimen (m)	*'kree-mehn*
	delito	*deh-'lee-toh*
• crime wave	ola de crímenes	*'oh-lah deh 'kree-meh-nehs*
• criminal	criminal (m/f)	*kree-mee-'nahl*
description	descripción	*dehs-kreep-see-'ohn*
fight	luchar (v)	*loo-'chahr*
	pelear (v)	*peh-leh-'ahr*
fingerprints	huellas digitales	*'weh-yahs dee-hee-'tah-lehs*
firearm	arma (f) de fuego	*'ahr-mah deh 'fweh-goh*
gun	pistola	*pees-'toh-lah*
handcuffs	esposas	*ehs-'poh-sahs*
hurry	darse* prisa	*'dahr-seh 'pree-sah*
injure, wound	herir*	*eh-'reer*
• injury, wound	herida	*eh-'ree-dah*
kill	matar (v)	*mah-'tahr*
• killer	asesino(a)	*ah-seh-'see-noh (-nah)*
knife	cuchillo	*koo-'chee-yoh*
• switchblade	navaja de muelle	*nah-'bah-hah deh 'mweh-yeh*
murder	asesinato	*ah-seh-see-'nah-toh*
	homicidio	*oh-mee-'see-dee·oh*
pickpocket	ratero(a)	*rah-teh-roh (-rah)*
	carterista (m/f)	*kahr-teh-'rees-tah*
police	policía (f)	*poh-lee-'see-ah*
• call the police	llamar (v) a la policía	*yah-'mahr ah lah poh-lee-'see-ah*
• policeman	policía (m)	*poh-lee-'see-ah*
• policewoman	policía (f)	*poh-lee-'see-ah*

rape	violar (v)	bee-oh-'lahr
• rape	violación (f)	bee-oh-lah-see·'ohn
rifle	rifle (m)	'ree-fleh
rob	robar (v)	roh-'bahr
• robber, thief	ladrón(a)	lah-'drohn ('droh-nah)
• armed robbery	robo a mano armada	'roh-boh ah 'mah-noh ahr-'mah-dah
• robbery	robo	'roh-boh
• Stop thief!	¡Ladrón!	lah-'drohn
steal	robar (v)	roh-'bahr
victim	víctima (m/f)	'beek-tee-mah
violence	violencia	bee·oh-'lehn-see·ah
weapon	arma	'ahr-mah
• shoot	disparar (v)	dees-pah-'rahr

Hurry!	¡Dese prisa!
Someone assaulted me!	¡Alguien me asalto!
Someone stole . . .	Alquien robó . . .

c. TRAFFIC ACCIDENTS

accident	accidente (m)	ahk-see-'dehn-teh
• serious accident	accidente serio	ahk-see-'dehn-teh 'seh-ree·oh
• traffic accident	accidente de circulación	ahk-see-'dehn-teh deh seer-koo-lah-see·'ohn
ambulance	ambulancia	ahm-boo-'lahn-see·ah
• call an ambulance	llamar una ambulancia	yah-'mahr 'oo-nah ahm-boo-'lahn-see·ah
be run over	ser* atropellado(a)	sehr ah-troh-peh-'yah-doh (-dah)
bite	mordedura	mohr-deh-'doo-rah
bleed	sangrar (v)	sahn-'grahr
• blood	sangre (f)	'sahn-greh
broken bone	hueso fracturado	'weh-soh frahk-too-'rah-doh
bump into	tropezar* con	troh-peh-'sahr kohn
collide, smash into	chocar (v) con	choh-'kahr kohn
• collision	choque (m)	'choh-keh
crash	choque (m)	'choh-keh
• crash into	chocar (v) con	choh-'kahr kohn

doctor	médico(a)	'meh-dee-koh (-ah)
• get a doctor	llamar a un médico	yah-'mahr ah oon 'meh-dee-koh
first aid	primeros auxilios	pree-'meh-rohs ow-'ksee-lee·ohs
• antiseptic	antiséptico	ahn-tee-'sehp-tee-koh
• bandage	venda	'behn-dah
• gauze	gasa	'gah-sah
• iodine	yodo	'yoh-doh
• scissors	tijeras	tee-'heh-rahs
• splint	tablilla	tah-'blee-yah
fracture	fractura	frahk-'too-rah
Help!	¡Socorro!	soh-'koh-rroh
hospital	hospital (m)	ohs-pee-'tahl
• emergency room	sala de emergencia	'sah-lah deh eh-mehr-'gehn-see·ah
intensive care	cuidado intensivo	kwee-'dah-doh een-tehn-'see-boh
police	policía (f)	poh-lee-'see-ah
• call the police	llamar (v) a la policía	yah-'mahr ah lah poh-lee-'see-ah
shock	choque (m)	'choh-keh
sprain	la torcedura	lah tohr-seh-'doo-rah
stretcher	camilla	kah-'mee-yah
wound, injury	herida	eh-'ree-dah

40. MEDICAL CARE

> See also Section 12—The Body.

a. THE DOCTOR

acne	acné (f)	ahk-'neh
AIDS	el SIDA	ehl 'see-dah
allergy	alergia	ah-'lehr-gee·ah
antibiotic	antibiótico	ahn-tee-bee·'oh-tee-koh
appendicitis	apendicitis (f)	ah'pehn-dee-'see-tees
• appendix	apéndice (m)	ah-'pehn-dee-seh
appointment	cita	'see-tah
artery	arteria	ahr-'teh-ree·ah
arthritis	artritis (f)	ahr-'tree-tees
aspirin	aspirina	ahs-pee-'ree-nah

asthma	asma	'ahs-mah
backache	dolor de espalda	doh-'lohr deh ehs-'pahl-dah
• have a backache	tener* un dolor de espalda	teh-'nehr oon doh-'lohr deh ehs-'pahl-dah
bandage	venda	'behn-dah
• bandage	vendar (v)	behn-'dahr
blood	sangre (f)	'sahn-greh
• blood pressure	presión arterial	preh-see-'ohn ahr-teh-ree-'ahl
• blood test	análisis (m) de sangre	ah-'nah-lee-sees deh 'sahn-greh
bone	hueso	'weh-soh
brain	cerebro	seh-'reh-broh
breathe	respirar (v)	rehs-pee-'rahr
bronchitis	bronquitis (f)	brohn-'kee-tees
bruise	contusión (f)	kohn-too-see-'ohn
bunion	juanete (m)	hwah-'neh-teh
burn	quemadura	keh-mah-'doo-rah
chills	escalofríos (m)	ehs-kah-loh-'free-ohs
choke	atragantarse (v)	ah-trah-gahn-'tahr-seh
cold	resfriado	rehs-free-'ah-doh
constipation	estreñimiento	ehs-treh-nyee-mee-'ehn-toh
• be constipated	estar* estreñido	ehs-'tahr ehs-treh-'nyee-doh
contraceptives	contraceptivos	kohn-trah-sehp-'tee-bohs
convalescence	convalecencia	kohn-bah-leh-'sehn-see-ah
• convalesce	convalecer*	kohn-bah-leh-'sehr
cough	toser (v)	toh-'sehr
• cough	tos (f)	tohs
• cough drops	pastillas para la tos	pahs-'tee-yahs 'pah-rah lah tohs
• cough syrup	jarabe para la tos	hah-'rah-beh 'pah-rah lah tohs
cramps	calambres (m)	kah-'lahm-brehs
crutches	muletas (f)	moo-'leh-tahs
cure	cura	'koo-rah
• cure, heal	curar (v)	koo-'rahr
	sanar (v)	sah-'nahr
cut	cortadura	kohr-tah-'doo-rah
• heal	cicatrizar (v)	see-kah-tree-'sahr
cyst	quiste (m)	'kees-teh
dandruff	caspa	'kahs-pah
diagnose	diagnosticar (v)	dee-ahg-nohs-tee-'kahr
diarrhea	diarrea	dee-ah-'rreh-ah

diet	régimen (*m*)	*'reh-hee-mehn*
	dieta (*f*)	*dee·'eh-tah*
• be on a diet	estar a dieta	*ehs-'tahr ah dee·'eh-tah*
digest	digerir*	*dee-heh-'reer*
digestive system	aparato digestivo	*ah-pah-'rah-toh dee-hehs-'tee-boh*
• anus	ano	*'ah-noh*
• defecate	defecar (*v*)	*deh-feh-'kahr*
• esophagus	esófago	*eh-'soh-fah-goh*
• rectum	recto	*'rehk-toh*
• stomach	estómago	*ehs-'toh-mah-goh*
• have a stomach ache	tener* un dolor de estómago	*teh-'nehr oon doh-'lohr deh ehs-'toh-mah-goh*
doctor	médico(a)	*'meh-dee-koh (-kah)*
doctor's instruments	instrumentos del médico	*eens-troo-'mehn-tohs dehl 'meh-dee-koh*
• stethoscope	estetoscopio	*ehs-teh-toh-'skoh-pee·oh*
• syringe	jeringa	*heh-'reen-gah*
• thermometer	termómetro	*tehr-'moh-meh-troh*
eardrops	gotas para los oídos	*'goh tahs 'pah-rah lohs oh·'ee-dohs*
electrocardiograph	electrocardiógrafo	*eh-lehk-troh-kahr-dee·'oh-grah-foh*
examination	examen físico	*eh-'ksah-mehn 'fee-see-koh*
• examine	examinar (*v*)	*ehks-ah-mee-'nahr*
eye doctor	oculista (*m/f*)	*oh-koo-'lees-tah*
• contact lenses	lentes (*m*) de contacto	*'lehn-tehs deh kohn-'tahk-toh*
• eyeglasses	antejos (*m*)	*ahn-teh-'oh-hohs*
	gafas	*'gah-fahs*
• farsighted	hipermétrope (*adj*)	*ee-pehr-'meh-troh-peh*
• nearsighted	miope (*adj*)	*mee·'oh-peh*
	corto de vista	*'kohr-toh deh 'bees-tah*
• sight	vista	*'bees-tah*
• eye drops	gotas para los ojos	*'goh-tahs 'pah-rah lohs 'oh-hohs*
feel	sentirse*	*sehn-'teer-seh*
• feel badly	sentirse* mal	*sehn-'teer-seh mahl*
• feel well	sentirse* bien	*sehn-'teer-seh bee·'ehn*
• strong	fuerte (*adj*)	*'fwehr-teh*
• weak	débil (*adj*)	*'deh-beel*
• How do you feel?	¿Cómo se siente Ud.?	*'koh-moh seh see·'ehn-teh oos-'tehd*
fever	fiebre (*f*)	*fee·'eh-breh*
flu	gripe (*f*)	*'gree-peh*
headache	dolor (*m*) de cabeza	*doh-'lohr deh kah-'beh-sah*

• **have a headache**	tener* un dolor de cabeza	*teh-'nehr oon doh-'lohr deh kah-'beh-sah*
• **migraine headache**	migraña	*mee-'grah-nyah*
health	salud (*f*)	*sah-'lood*
• **healthy**	sano (*adj*)	*'sah-noh*
heart	corazón (*m*)	*koh-rah-'sohn*
• **heart attack**	ataque (*m*) cardíaco	*ah-'tah-keh kahr-'dee-ah-koh*
hurt	doler*	*doh-'lehr*
ilnesses	enfermedades (*f*)	*ehn-fehr-meh-'dah-dehs*
• **blood clot**	coágulo de sangre	*koh-'ah-goo-loh deh 'sahn-greh*
• **cancer**	cáncer (*m*)	*'kahn-sehr*
• **chicken pox**	varicela	*bah-ree-'seh-lah*
• **depression**	depresión (*f*)	*deh-preh-see-'ohn*
• **diabetes**	diabetes (*f*)	*dee·ah-'beh-tehs*
• **laryngitis**	laringitis (*f*)	*lah-reen-'hee-tees*
• **leukemia**	leucemia	*leh-oo-'seh-mee·ah*
• **measles**	sarampión (*m*)	*sah-rahm-pee-'ohn*
• **mumps**	paperas	*pah-'peh-rahs*
• **muscular dystrophy**	distrofia muscular	*dees-'troh-fee·ah moos-koo-'lahr*
• **schizophrenia**	esquizofrenia	*ehs-kee-soh-'freh-nee·ah*
• **stroke**	derrame cerebral (*m*)	*deh-'rrah-meh seh-reh-'brahl*
• **ulcer**	úlcera	*'ool-seh-rah*
• **venereal disease**	enfermedad venérea	*ehn-fehr-meh-'dahd beh-'neh-reh·ah*
indigestion	indigestión (*f*)	*een-dee-hehs-tee-'ohn*
infection	infección (*f*)	*een-fehk-see-'ohn*
injection	inyección (*f*)	*een-yehk-see-'ohn*
itch	comezón (*f*)	*koh-meh-'sohn*
lose consciousness	perder* el conocimiento	*pehr-'dehr ehl koh-noh-see-mee-'ehn-toh*
lump	bulto	*'bool-toh*
lymphatic system	sistema linfático	*sees-'teh-mah leen-'fah-tee-koh*
medical records	antecedentes (*m*) médicos	*ahn-teh-seh-'dehn-tehs 'meh-dee-kohs*
medicine	medicina	*meh-dee-'see-nah*
muscle	músculo	*'moos-koo-loh*
nerves	nervios	*'nehr-bee·ohs*
• **nervous system**	sistema nervioso (*m*)	*sees-'teh-mah nehr-bee-'oh-soh*
nurse	enfermero(a)	*ehn-fehr-'meh-roh (-rah)*
operate	operar (*v*)	*oh-peh-'rahr*

operation	operación (*f*)	*oh-peh-rah-see·'ohn*
• **operating room**	sala de operaciones	*'sah-lah deh oh-peh-rah-see·'oh-nehs*
pain	dolor (*m*)	*doh-'lohr*
• **painful**	doloroso (*adj*)	*doh-loh-'roh-soh*
patient	paciente (*adj*)	*pah-see·'ehn-teh*
pill	píldora	*'peel-doh-rah*
pimple	grano	*'grah-noh*
pneumonia	pulmonía	*pool-moh-'nee·ah*
	neumonía	*neh·oo-moh-'nee·ah*
poisoning	envenenamiento	*ehn-beh-neh-nah-mee·'ehn-toh*
• **poison**	veneno (*n*)	*beh-'neh-noh*
	envenenar (*v*)	*ehn-beh-neh-'nahr*
pregnant	embarazada (*adj*)	*ehm-bah-rah-'sah-dah*
prescription	receta	*reh-'seh-tah*
pulse	pulso	*'pool-soh*
• **take someone's pulse**	tomar el pulso	*toh-'mahr ehl 'pool-soh*
rash	sarpullido	*sahr-poo-'yee·doh*
recover	recobrarse (*v*)	*reh-koh-'brahr-seh*
respiratory system	sistema respiratorio	*sees-'teh-mah rehs-pee-rah-'toh-ree·oh*
• **breathe**	respirar (*v*)	*rehs-pee-'rahr*
• **breathing**	respiración (*f*)	*rehs-pee-rah-see·'ohn*
• **bad breath**	mal aliento	*mahl ah-lee·'ehn-toh*
• **be out of breath**	estar* sin aliento	*ehs-'tahr seen ah-lee·'ehn-toh*
• **lung**	pulmón (*m*)	*pool-'mohn*
• **nostril**	ventana de la náriz	*behn-'tah-nah deh lah nah-'rees*
rheumatism	reumatismo	*reh·oo-mah-'tees-moh*
	reuma	*reh·'oo-mah*
secretary	secretario(a)	*seh-kreh-'tah-ree·oh (·ah)*
sedative	sedante (*m*)	*seh-'dahn-teh*
	calmante (*m*)	*kahl-'mahn-teh*
sick	enfermo(a)	*ehn-'fehr-moh (-ah)*
• **get sick**	enfermarse (*v*)	*ehn-fehr-'mahr-seh*
• **sickness, disease**	enfermedad (*f*)	*ehn-fehr-meh-'dahd*
sneeze	estornudar (*v*)	*ehs-tohr-noo-'dahr*
• **sneeze**	estornudo	*ehs-tohr-'noo-doh*
specialist	especialista (*m/f*)	*ehs-peh-see·ah-'lees-tah*
• **anesthetist**	anestesista	*ah-nehs-teh-'sees-tah*
• **cardiologist**	cardiólogo	*kahr-dee·'oh-loh-goh*
• **dermatologist**	dermatólogo	*dehr-mah-'toh-loh-goh*
• **gynecologist**	ginecólogo	*hee-neh-'koh-loh-goh*
• **internist**	internista	*een-tehr-'nees-tah*

• neurologist	neurólogo	*neh-oo-'roh-loh-goh*
• ophthalmologist	oftalmólogo	*ohf-tahl-'moh-loh-goh*
• pediatrician	pediatra	*peh-dee-'ah-trah*
• podiatrist	pedicuro	*peh-dee-'koo-roh*
• psychiatrist	psiquiatra	*see-kee-'ah-trah*
• urologist	urólogo	*oo-'roh-loh-goh*
suffer	sufrir (v)	*soo-'freer*
suffer from	padecer* de	*pah-deh-'sehr deh*
sunburn	quemadura del sol	*keh-mah-'doo-rah dehl sohl*
suppository	supositorio	*soo-poh-see-'toh-ree·oh*
surgeon	cirujano	*see-roo-'hah-noh*
• surgery	cirugía	*see-roo-'hee·ah*
swallow	tragar (v)	*trah-'gahr*
swell	hinchar (v)	*een-'chahr*
swollen	hinchado (adj)	*een-'chah-doh*
tablet	pastilla	*pahs-'tee-yah*
temperature	fiebre (f)	*fee-'eh-breh*
• take one's temperature	tomar la temperatura	*toh-'mahr lah tehm-peh-rah-'too-rah*
throat	garganta	*gahr-'gahn-tah*
• have a sore throat	tener un dolor de garganta	*teh-'nehr oon doh-'lohr deh gahr-'gahn-tah*
throw up	devolver* (v)	*deh-bohl-'behr*
tonsils	amígdalas	*ah-'meeg-dah-lahs*
urinary system	sistema urinario	*sees-'teh-mah oo-ree-'nah-ree·oh*
• bladder	vejiga	*beh-'hee-gah*
• kidney	riñón (m)	*ree-'nyohn*
• urinate	orinar (v)	*oh-ree-'nahr*
vaccinate	vacunar (v)	*bah-koo-'nahr*
vein	vena	*'beh-nah*
vitamin	vitamina	*bee-tah-'mee-nah*
vomit	vomitar (v)	*boh-mee-'tahr*
wheelchair	silla de ruedas	*'see-yah deh roo-'eh-dahs*

b. THE DENTIST

anesthetic	anestético	*ah-nehs-'teh-tee-koh*
appointment	cita	*'see-tah*
bridge	puente (m)	*poo-'ehn-teh*
cavity, tooth decay	caries (f)	*'kah-ree·ehs*
clean, brush	cepillarse (v)	*seh-pee-'yahr-seh*
crown	corona	*koh-'roh-nah*
dental floss	hilo dental	*'ee-loh dehn-'tahl*

dentist	dentista	*dehn-'tees-tah*
• dentist's office	oficina del dentista	*oh-fee-'see-nah dehl dehn-'tees-tah*
• go to the dentist	ir* al dentista	*eer ahl dehn-'tees-tah*
dentures	dientes postizos	*dee·'ehn-tehs poh-'stee-sohs*
drill	taladro	*tah-'lah-droh*
examine	examinar (v)	*ehk-sah-mee-'nahr*
filling	empaste (m)	*ehm-'pah-steh*
mouth	boca	*'boh-kah*
• gums	encías	*ehn-'see-ahs*
• jaw	mandíbula	*mahn-'dee-boo-lah*
• lip	labio	*'lah-bee·oh*
• Open your mouth.	Abra Ud. la boca.	*'ah-brah oos-'tehd lah 'boh-kah*
• palate	paladar (m)	*pah-lah-'dahr*
• tongue	lengua	*'lehn-gwah*
needle	aguja	*ah-'goo-hah*
Novocaine	Novocaína	*noh-boh-cah-'ee-nah*
office hours	horas de consulta	*'oh-rahs deh kohn-'sool-tah*
rinse	enjuagar(se) (v)	*ehn-hoo·ah-'gahr (-seh)*
spit	escupir (v)	*ehs-koo-'peer*
tooth	diente (m)	*dee-'ehn-teh*
• canine tooth	canino (m)	*kah-'nee-noh*
• incisor	diente incisivo	*dee-'ehn-teh een-see-'see-boh*
• molar	muela	*'mweh-lah*
• root	raíz (f)	*rah-'ees*
• wisdom tooth	muela del juicio	*'mweh-lah dehl hoo-'ee-see·oh*
toothache	dolor de muelas	*doh-'lohr deh 'mweh-lahs*
• have a toothache	tener* un dolor de muelas	*teh-'nehr oon doh-'lohr deh 'mweh-lahs*
• My tooth hurts.	Me duele el diente.	*meh 'dweh-leh ehl dee-'ehn-teh*
toothbrush	cepillo de dientes	*seh-'pee-yoh deh dee-'ehn-tehs*
toothpaste	pasta dentífrica	*'pahs-tah dehn-'tee-free-kah*
x-rays	rayos X	*'rah-yohs 'eh-kees*

41. LEGAL MATTERS

accusation	acusación (f)	ah-koo-sah-see·'ohn
• accuse	acusar (v)	ah-koo-'sahr
• accused person	acusado (adj)	ah-koo-'sah-doh
• bring an accusation against	formular (v) una acusación contra	fohr-moo-'lahr 'oo-nah ah-koo-sah-see·'ohn 'kohn-trah
address oneself to	hablar (v) a	ah-'blahr ah
admit	admitir (v)	ahd-mee-'teer
agree	consentir*	kohn-sehn-'teer
	estar* de acuerdo	ehs-'tahr deh ah-'kwehr-doh
bail	fianza	fee·'ahn-sah
controversy	controversia	kohn-troh-'behr-see·ah
convince	convencer*	kohn-behn-'sehr
coroner	médico forense	'meh-dee-koh foh-'rehn-seh
court	tribunal (m)	tree-boo-'nahl
• court of appeals	tribunal (m) de apelación	tree-boo-'nahl deh ah-peh-lah-see·'ohn
courtroom	sala de un tribunal	'sah-lah deh oon tree-boo-'nahl
debate	debatir (v)	deh-bah-'teer
• debate	debate (m)	deh-'bah-teh
defend oneself	defenderse*	deh-fehn-'dehr-seh
defense attorney	abogado(a) defensor(a)	ah-boh-'gah-doh (ah) deh-fehn-'sohr (rah)
disagree	no estar* de acuerdo	noh ehs-'tahr deh ah-'kwehr-doh
discuss	discutir (v)	dees-koo-'teer
district attorney	fiscal (m/f)	fees-'kahl
fine	multar (v)	mool-'tahr
guilt	culpa	'kool-pah
• guilty	culpable (adj)	kool-'pah-bleh
innocence	inocencia	ee-noh-'sehn-see·ah
• innocent	inocente (adj)	ee-noh-'sehn-teh
jail, prison	cárcel (f)	'kahr-sehl
• jail	encarcelar (v)	ehn-kahr-seh-'lahr
• imprison	aprisionar (v)	ah-pree-see·oh-'nahr
	encerrar*	ehn-seh-'rrahr
judge	juez (m)	hoo-'ehs
• judge	juzgar (v)	hoos-'gahr
• judgment	juicio	hoo·'ee-see·oh
	sentencia	sehn-'tehn-see·ah
jury	jurado	hoo-'rah-doh
• sit on a jury	ser miembro del jurado	sehr mee·'ehm-broh dehl hoo-'rah-doh

justice	justicia	*hoo-'stee-see·ah*
kidnap	secuestrar (*v*)	*seh-kwehs-'trahr*
law	ley (*f*)	*'leh·ee*
• **civil law**	derecho civil	*deh-'reh-choh see-'beel*
• **criminal law**	derecho penal	*deh-'reh-choh peh-'nahl*
• **illegal**	ilegal (*adj*)	*ee-leh-'gahl*
• **lawful, legal**	legal (*adj*)	*leh-'gahl*
lawsuit	pleito	*pleh·'ee-toh*
	demanda	*deh-'mahn-dah*
lawyer	abogado	*ah-boh-'gah-doh*
	jurista (*m/f*)	*hoo-'rees-tah*
litigation	litigio	*lee-'tee-hee·oh*
	pleito	*pleh·'ee-toh*
• **litigate**	litigar (*v*) sobre	*lee-tee-'gahr 'soh-breh*
magistrate	magistrado	*mah-hees-'trah-doh*
notarize	legalizar (*v*)	*leh-gah-lee-'sahr*
	certificar (*v*)	*sehr-tee-fee-'kahr*
persuade	persuadir (*v*)	*pehr-swah-'deer*
plea	alegato	*ah-leh-'gah-toh*
plead guilty	declararse (*v*) culpable	*deh-klah-'rahr-seh kool-'pah-bleh*
plead not guilty	declararse (*v*) inocente	*deh-klah-'rahr-seh ee-noh-'sehn-teh*
police station	comisaría de policía	*koh-meee-sah-'ree·ah deh poh-lee-'see·ah*
public prosecutor	acusador público	*ah-koo-sah-'dohr 'poo-blee-koh*
punish	castigar (*v*)	*kahs-tee-'gahr*
right	derecho	*deh-'reh-choh*
sentence	sentencia	*sehn-'tehn-see·ah*
• **death sentence**	pena de muerte	*'peh-nah deh 'mwehr-teh*
• **life sentence**	condena perpetua	*kohn-'deh-nah pehr-'peh-twah*
• **pass sentence**	sentenciar (*v*)	*sehn-tehn-see·'ahr*
• **prison sentence**	sentencia	*sehn-'tehn-see·ah*
sue	demandar (*v*)	*deh-mahn-'dahr*
	poner* pleito a	*poh'nehr 'pleh·ee-toh ah*
summons	citación (*f*) judicial	*see-tah-see-'ohn hoo-dee-see·'ahl*
testify	atestiguar (*v*)	*ah-tehs-tee-'gwahr*
trial	proceso	*proh-'seh-soh*
verdict	veredicto	*beh-reh-'deek-toh*
	juicio	*'hwee-see·oh*
will	testamento	*tehs-tah-'mehn-toh*
witness	testigo (*m*)	*tehs-'tee-goh*

THE CONTEMPORARY WORLD

42. SCIENCE AND TECHNOLOGY

a. THE CHANGING WORLD

For more vocabulary on basic matter, see Section 13.

---

antenna	antena (f)	ahn-'teh-nah
astronaut	astronauta (m/f)	ahs-troh-'now-tah
atom	átomo	'ah-toh-moh
• electron	electrón (m)	eh-lehk-'trohn
• molecule	molécula	moh-'leh-koo-lah
• neutron	neutrón (m)	neh-oo-'trohn
• proton	protón (m)	proh-'tohn
compact disc	disco compacto	'dees-koh kohm-'pahk-toh
fax machine	fax (m)	fahks
laser	láser (m)	'lah-sehr
• laser beam	rayo láser	'rah-yoh 'lah-sehr
microwave	microonda	mee-kroh-'ohn-dah
missile	proyectil (m)	proh-yehk-'teel
• launch	lanzar (v)	lahn-'sahr
• launch pad	plataforma de lanzamiento	plah-tah-'fohr-mah deh lahn-sah-mee-'ehn-toh
monorail	monocarril (m)	moh-noh-kah-'rreel
nuclear industry	industria nuclear	een-'doos-tree-ah noo-kleh-'ahr
• fusion reactor	reactor (m) de fusión	reh-ahk-'tohr deh foo-see-'ohn
• nuclear energy	energía nuclear	eh-nehr-'hee-ah noo-kleh-'ahr
• nuclear fuel	combustible (m) nuclear	kohm-boos-'tee-bleh noo-kleh-'ahr
• nuclear reactor	reactor (m) nuclear	reh-ahk-'tohr noo-kleh-'ahr
robot	robot (m)	roh-'boht
satellite	satélite (m)	sah-'teh-lee-teh
• artificial satellite	satélite (m) artificial	sah-'teh-lee-teh ahr-tee-fee-see-'ahl
scientific research	investigación (f) científica	een-behs-tee-gah-see-'ohn see-ehn-'tee-fee-kah

spacecraft	nave (f) espacial	*'nah-beh ehs-pah-see-'ahl*
• **lunar module**	módulo lunar	*'moh-doo-loh loo-'nahr*
• **space shuttle**	transbordador (m) espacial	*trahns-bohr-dah-'dohr ehs-pah-see-'ahl*
technology	tecnología	*tehk-noh-loh-'hee-ah*
telecommunications	telecomunicaciones (f)	*teh-leh-koh-moo-nee-kah-see-'oh-nehs*
• **teleconference**	teleconferencia	*teh-leh-kohn-feh-'rehn-see·ah*
• **telex machine**	télex (m)	*'teh-lehks*
theory of relativity	teoría de relatividad	*teh-oh-'ree·ah deh reh-lah-tee-bee-'dahd*
• **quantum theory**	teoría cuántica	*teh-oh-'ree·ah 'kwahn-tee-kah*

b. COMPUTERS

byte	byte (m)	*'bee-teh*
	octeto	*ohk-'teh-toh*
compatible	compatible (adj)	*kohm-pah-'tee-bleh*
computer	computadora	*kohm-poo-tah-'doh-rah*
	ordenador (m)	*ohr-deh-nah-'dohr*
computer language	lenguaje (m) de máquina	*lehn-'gwah-heh deh 'mah-kee-nah*
data	datos	*'dah-tohs*
data base	base de texto (f)	*'bah-seh deh 'tehks-toh*
data processing	informática	*een-fohr-'mah-tee-kah*
disk	disco	*'dees-koh*
• **floppy disk**	disco flexible	*'dees-koh fleh-'ksee-bleh*
• **hard disk**	disco duro	*'dees-koh 'doo-roh*
file, menu	archivo	*ahr-'chee-boh*
flow chart	organigrama (m)	*ohr-gah-nee-'grah-mah*
function	función (f)	*foon-see-'ohn*
hardware	hardware (m)	*hahrd-'wehr*
	elemento físico	*eh-leh-'mehn-toh 'fee-see-koh*
interface	conector (m) entre unidades	*koh-nehk-'tohr 'ehn-treh oo-nee-'dah-dehs*
keyboard	teclado	*teh-'klah-doh*
memory	memoria	*meh-'moh-ree·ah*
microcomputer	microcomputadora	*mee-kroh-kohm-poo-tah-'doh-rah*
modem	módem (m)	*'moh-dehm*
monitor	monitor (m)	*moh-nee-'tohr*
office automation	automatización (f) de oficina	*ow-toh-mah-tee-sah-see-'ohn deh oh-fee-'see-nah*

peripherals	equipo periférico	*eh-'kee-poh peh-ree-'feh-ree-koh*
personal computer	computadora personal	*kohm-poo-tah-'doh-rah pehr-soh-nahl*
print	imprimir (*v*)	*eem-pree-'meer*
printer	impresora	*eem-preh-'soh-rah*
• **laser printer**	impresora láser	*eem-preh-'soh-rah 'lah-sehr*
program	programa (*m*)	*proh-'grah-mah*
• **programmer**	programador(a)	*proh-grah-mah-'dohr (-rah)*
• **programming**	programación (*f*)	*proh-grah-mah-see-'ohn*
random access memory (RAM)	memoria (RAM)	*meh-'moh-ree·ah (rahm)*
screen	pantalla	*pahn-'tah-yah*
software	software (*m*)	*sohft-'wehr*
	logicial (*m*)	*loh-hee-see-'ahl*
spreadsheet	hojas de cálculo	*'oh-hahs deh 'kahl-koo-loh*
terminal	terminal (*m*)	*tehr-mee-'nahl*
user-friendly	fácil de manejar	*'fah-seel deh mah-neh-'hahr*
word processing	procesamiento de texto	*proh-seh-sah-mee-'ehn-toh deh 'tehks-toh*
• **word processor**	procesador de texto	*proh-seh-sah-'dohr deh 'tehks-toh*

43. POLITICS

> For vocabulary related to expressing yourself, see Sections 16, 17, 21, and 22.

arms reduction	disminución (*f*) de las armas	*dees-mee-noo-see-'ohn deh lahs 'ahr-mahs*
• **demonstration** (*public*)	manifestación (*f*) (pública)	*mah-nee-fehs-tah-see-'ohn ('poo-blee-kah)*
• **unilateral**	unilateral (*adj*)	*oo-nee-lah-teh-'rahl*
assembly	asamblea	*ah-sahm-'bleh-ah*
association	asociación (*f*)	*ah-soh-see-ah-see-'ohn*
communism	comunismo	*koh-moo-'nees-moh*
• **communist**	comunista (*m/f*)	*koh-moo-'nees-tah*
conservative	conservador(a)	*kohn-sehr-bah-'dohr (ah)*

council	consejo	*kohn-'seh-hoh*
coup d'etat	golpe (*m*) de estado	*'gohl-peh deh ehs-'tah-doh*
democracy	democracia	*deh-moh-'krah-see·ah*
• democrat	demócrata (*m/f*)	*deh-'moh-krah-tah*
• democratic	democrático (*adj*)	*deh-moh-'krah-tee-koh*
dictator	dictador	*deek-tah-'dohr*
dictatorship	dictadura	*deek-tah-'doo-rah*
economy	economía	*eh-koh-noh-'mee·ah*
elect	elegir*	*eh-leh-'heer*
• elections	elecciones (*f*)	*eh-lehk-'see·oh-nehs*
elected political representative	representante elegido	*reh-pre-sehn-'tahn-teh eh-leh-'hee-doh*
govern	gobernar*	*goh-behr-'nahr*
• government	gobierno	*goh-bee·'ehr-noh*
house of representatives	cámara de representantes	*'kah-mah-rah deh reh-preh sehn-'tahn-tehs*
ideology	ideología	*ee-deh-oh-loh-'hee·ah*
inflation	inflación (*f*)	*een-flah-see·'ohn*
labor/trade union	sindicato	*seen-dee-'kah-toh*
legislation	legislación (*f*)	*leh-hee-slah-see·'ohn*
liberal	liberal (*adj*)	*lee-beh-'rahl*
minister	ministro	*mee-'nees-troh*
monarchy	monarquía	*moh-nahr-'kee·ah*
• king	rey (*m*)	*'reh·ee*
• queen	reina	*'reh·ee-nah*
• prince	príncipe	*'preen-see-peh*
• princess	princesa	*preen-'seh-sah*
nuclear disarmament	desarme (*m*) nuclear	*dehs-'ahr-meh noo-kleh-'ahr*
parliament	parlamento	*pahr-lah-'mehn-toh*
peace	paz (*f*)	*pahs*
policy	política	*poh-'lee-tee-kah*
political	político (*adj*)	*poh-'lee-tee-koh*
politician	político(a)	*poh-'lee-tee-koh (-ah)*
politics	política	*poh-'lee-tee-kah*
• political party	partido político	*pahr-'tee-doh poh-'lee-tee-koh*
• political power	poder político	*poh-'dehr poh-'lee-tee-koh*
president	presidente(a)	*preh-see-'dehn-teh (-tah)*
protest	protestar (*v*)	*proh-tehs-'tahr*
• protest	protesta	*proh-'tehs-tah*
reform	reformar (*v*)	*reh-fohr-'mahr*
• reform	reforma	*reh-'fohr-mah*
republic	república	*reh-'poo-blee-kah*
revolt, riot	motín (*m*)	*moh-'teen*
revolution	revolución (*f*)	*reh-boh-loo-see·'ohn*

senate	senado	*seh-'nah-doh*
socialism	socialismo	*soh-see·ah-'lees-moh*
• socialist	socialista (*m/f*)	*soh-see·ah-'lees-tah*
state	estado	*ehs-'tah-doh*
• head of state	jefe de estado	*'heh-feh deh ehs-'tah-doh*
strike	declararse en huelga	*deh-klah-rahr-seh ehn 'wehl-gah*
• strike	huelga	*'wehl-gah*
third world	Tercer Mundo	*tehr-'sehr 'moon-doh*
underdeveloped countries	países subdesarrollados	*pah·'ee-sehs soob-dehs-ah-rroh-'yah-dohs*
vote	votar (*v*)	*boh-'tahr*
• vote	voto (*m*)	*'boh-toh*
war	guerra	*'geh-rrah*
welfare	asistencia pública	*ah-sees-'tehn-see·ah 'poo-blee-kah*

44. CONTROVERSIAL ISSUES

a. THE ENVIRONMENT

> See also Sections 13 and 42.

acid rain	lluvia ácida	*'yoo-bee·ah 'ah-see-dah*
air pollution	contaminación (*f*) del aire	*kohn-tah-mee-nah-see·'ohn dehl 'ah-ee-reh*
conservation	preservación (*f*)	*preh-sehr-bah-see·'ohn*
consumption	consumo	*kohn-'soo-moh*
ecosystem	ecosistema (*m*)	*eh-koh-sees-'teh-mah*
energy	energía	*eh-nehr-'hee·ah*
• energy crisis	crisis (*f*) energética	*'kree-sees eh-nehr-'heh-tee-kah*
• energy needs	necesidades de energía	*neh-seh-see-'dah-dehs deh eh-nehr-'hee·ah*
• energy source	fuente (*f*) de energía	*'fwehn-teh deh eh-nehr-'hee·ah*
• energy waste	malgasto de energía	*mahl-'gahs-toh deh eh-nehr-'hee·ah*
environment	medio ambiente (*m*)	*'meh-dee·oh ahm-bee·'ehn-teh*
food chain	cadena alimenticia	*kah-'deh-nah ah-lee-mehn-'tee-see·ah*

fossil fuel	combustible (*m*) fósil	*kohm-boos-'tee-bleh 'foh-seel*
geothermal energy	energía geotérmica	*eh-nehr-'hee-ah heh-oh-'tehr-mee-kah*
incinerator	incinerador (*m*)	*een-see-neh-rah-'dohr*
landfill	terraplén (*m*) de desperdicios	*teh-rrah-'plehn deh dehs-pehr-'dee-see-ohs*
natural resources	recursos naturales	*reh-'koor-sohs nah-too-'rah-lehs*
petroleum	petróleo	*peh-'troh-leh-oh*
pollution	contaminación (*f*)	*kohn-tah-mee-nah-see-'ohn*
radiation	radiación (*f*)	*rah-dee-ah-see-'ohn*
• **radioactive waste**	desechos radioactivos	*deh-'seh-chohs rah-dee-oh-ahk-'tee-bohs*
solar cell	célula solar	*'seh-loo-lah soh-'lahr*
solar energy	energía solar	*eh-nehr-'hee-ah soh-'lahr*
thermal energy	energía térmica	*eh-nehr-'hee-ah 'tehr-mee-kah*
toxic waste	desechos tóxicos de fabricación	*dehs-'eh-chohs 'tohk-see-kohs deh fah-bree-kah-see-'ohn*
water pollution	contaminación (*f*) del agua	*kohn-tah-mee-nah-see-'ohn dehl 'ah-gwah*
wind energy	energía del viento	*eh-nehr-'hee-ah dehl bee-'ehn-toh*

b. SOCIETY

abortion	aborto	*ah-'bohr-toh*
• **fetus**	feto	*'feh-toh*
AIDS	el SIDA	*ehl 'see-dah*
censorship	censura	*sehn-'soo-rah*
drugs	drogas	*'droh-gahs*
• **drug addict**	drogadicto(a)	*drohg-ah-'deek-toh (-tah)*
• **drug addiction**	toxicomanía	*toh-ksee-koh-mah-'nee-ah*
• **drug pusher**	vendedor(a) traficante de drogas	*behn-deh-'dohr (-rah) trah-fee-'kahn-teh deh 'droh-gahs*
• **take drugs**	tomar (*v*) drogas	*toh-'mahr 'droh-gahs*
feminism	feminismo	*feh-mee-'nees-moh*
• **feminist**	feminista (*m/f*)	*feh-mee-'nees-tah*

homosexuality	homosexualidad (f)	oh-moh-seh-ksoo·ah-lee-'dahd
• homosexual	homosexual (m)	oh-moh-seh-ksoo·'ahl
• lesbian	lesbiana	lehs-bee·'ah-nah
• lesbianism	lesbianismo	lehs-bee·ah·'nees-moh
morality	moralidad (f)	moh-rah-lee-'dahd
nuclear weapon	arma nuclear	'ahr-mah noo-kleh-'ahr
• antinuclear protest	manifestación (f) antinuclear	mah-nee-fehs-tah-see·'ohn ahn-tee-noo-kleh-'ahr
• atomic bomb	bomba atómica	'bohm-bah ah-'toh-mee-kah
• chemical weapon	arma química	'ahr-mah 'kee-mee-kah
pornography	pornografía	pohr-noh-grah-'fee-ah
prostitution	prostitución (f)	prohs-tee-too-see·'ohn
racism	racismo	rah-'sees-moh

c. EXPRESSING YOUR OPINION

according to . . .	según . . .	seh-'goon
as a matter of fact	en realidad	ehn reh-ah-lee-'dahd
by the way	a propósito	ah proh-'poh-see-toh
for example	por ejemplo	pohr eh-'hehm-ploh
from my point of view	desde mi punto de vista	'dehs-deh mee 'poon-toh deh 'bees-tah
I believe that . . .	Creo que . . .	'kreh-oh keh
I don't know if . . .	No sé si . . .	noh seh see
I doubt that . . .	Dudo que . . .	'doo-doh keh
I think that . . .	Pienso que . . .	pee·'ehn-soh keh
I would like to say that . . .	Me gustaría decir que . . .	meh goos-tah-'ree-ah deh-'seer keh
I'm not sure that . . .	No estoy seguro(a) de que . . .	noh ehs-'toy seh-'goo-roh (-rah) deh keh
I'm sure that . . .	Estoy seguro(a) de que . . .	ehs-'toy seh-'goo-roh (-rah) deh keh
in conclusion	en conclusión (f)	ehn kohn-kloo-see·'ohn
in my opinion	en mi opinión (f)	ehn mee oh-pee-nee·'ohn
It seems that . . .	Parece que . . .	pah-'reh-seh keh
It's clear that . . .	Es claro que . . .	ehs 'klah-roh keh
that is to say	es decir	ehs deh-'seer
There's no doubt that . . .	No hay duda de que . . .	noh 'ah·ee 'doo-dah deh keh
therefore	por eso	pohr 'eh-soh

APPENDIX: SPANISH VERBS

IRREGULAR VERBS

The following verbs have irregular forms in the present tense. All of them have been marked throughout the text and in the end vocabulary section with an asterisk. They are listed here only in the present tense and for your convenience are presented continuously across the page instead of in the traditional way:

me acuesto	nos acostamos
te acuestas	os acostáis
se acuesta	se acuestan

acostarse: me acuesto, te acuestas, se acuesta, nos acostamos, os acostáis, se acuestan

advertir: advierto, adviertes, advierte, advertimos, advertís, advierten

agradecer: agradezco, agradeces, agradece, agradecemos, agradecéis, agradecen

almorzar: almuerzo, almuerzas, almuerza, almorzamos, almorzáis, almuerzan

apretar: aprieto, aprietas, aprieta, apretamos, apretáis, aprietan

aprobar: apruebo, apruebas, aprueba, aprobamos, aprobáis, aprueban

aullar: aúllo, aúllas, aúlla, aullamos, aulláis, aúllan

caer: caigo, caes, cae, caemos, caéis, caen

calentarse: me caliento, te calientas, se calienta, nos calentamos, os calentáis, se calientan

coger: cojo, coges, coge, cogemos, cogéis, cogen

colgar: cuelgo, cuelgas, cuelga, colgamos, colgáis, cuelgan

comenzar: comienzo, comienzas, comienza, comenzamos, comenzáis, comienzan

concluir: concluyo, concluyes, concluye, concluimos, concluís, concluyen

conducir: conduzco, conduces, conduce, conducimos, conducís, conducen

conocer: conozco, conoces, conoce, conocemos, conocéis, conocen

consentir: consiento, consientes, consiente, consentimos, consentís, consienten

construir: construyo, construyes, construye, construimos, construís, construyen

contar: cuento, cuentas, cuenta, contamos, contáis, cuentan

continuar: continúo, continúas, continúa, continuamos, continuáis, continúan

convalecer: convalezco, convaleces, convalece, convalecemos, convalecéis, convalecen

convencer: convenzo, convences, convence, convencemos, convencéis, convencen

costar: cuesto, cuestas, cuesta, costamos, costáis, cuestan

crecer: crezco, creces, crece, crecemos, crecéis, crecen

criar: crío, crías, cría, criamos, criáis, crían

dar(se): (me) doy, (te) das, (se) da, (nos) damos, (os) dais, (se) dan

decir: digo, dices, dice, decimos, decís, dicen

defenderse: me defiendo, te defiendes, se defiende, nos defendemos, os defendéis, se defienden

demostrar: demuestro, demuestras, demuestra, demostramos, demostráis, demuestran

despertarse: me despierto, te despiertas, se despierta, nos despertamos, os despertáis, se despiertan

destruir: destruyo, destruyes, destruye, destruimos, destruís, destruyen

detener(se): *see* tener

devolver: *see* volver

digerir: digiero, digieres, digiere, digerimos, digerís, digieren

disminuir: disminuyo, disminuyes, disminuye, disminuimos, disminuís, disminuyen

divertirse: me divierto, te diviertes, se divierte, nos divertimos, os divertís, se divierten

doler: duelo, dueles, duele, dolemos, doléis, duelen

dormir: duermo, duermes, duerme, dormimos, dormís, duermen

elegir: elijo, eliges, elige, elegimos, elegís, eligen

empezar: empiezo, empiezas, empieza, empezamos, empezáis, empiezan

encender(se): (me) enciendo, (te) enciendes, (se) enciende, (nos) encendemos, (os) encendéis, (se) encienden

encerrar: encierro, encierras, encierra, encerramos, encerráis, encierran

enfriarse: me enfrío, te enfrías, se enfría, nos enfriamos, os enfriáis, se enfrían

engrandecer: engrandezco, engrandeces, engrandece, engrandecemos, engrandecéis, engrandecen

entender: entiendo, entiendes, entiende, entendemos, entendéis, entienden

entristecerse: me entristezco, te entristeces, se entristece, nos entristecemos, os entristecéis, se entristecen

envejecerse: me envejezco, te envejeces, se envejece, nos envejecemos, os envejecéis, se envejecen

esquiar: esquío, esquías, esquía, esquiamos, esquiáis, esquían

estar: estoy, estás, está, estamos, estáis, están

extinguir: extingo, extingues, extingue, extinguimos, extinguís, extinguen

extraer: extraigo, extraes, extrae, extraemos, extraéis, extraen

fluir: fluyo, fluyes, fluye, fluimos, fluís, fluyen

gobernar: gobierno, gobiernas, gobierna, gobernamos, gobernáis, gobiernan

hacer (se): (me) hago, (te) haces, (se) hace, (nos) hacemos, (os) hacéis, (se) hacen

helar: hielo, hielas, hiela, helamos, heláis, hielan

herir: hiero, hieres, hiere, herimos, herís, hieren

invertir: invierto, inviertes, invierte, invertimos, invertís, invierten

ir: voy, vas, va, vamos, vais, van

irse: me voy, te vas, se va, nos vamos, os vais, se van

jugar: juego, juegas, juega, jugamos, jugáis, juegan

llover: llueve *(invariable)*

maldecir: *see decir*

maullar: maúllo, maúlles, maúlle, maullamos, maulláis, maúllan

medir: mido, mides, mide, medimos, medís, miden

mentir: miento, mientes, miente, mentimos, mentís, mienten

merendar: meriendo, meriendas, merienda, merendamos, merendáis, meriendan

morir: muero, mueres, muere, morimos, morís, mueren

mover: muevo, mueves, mueve, movemos, movéis, mueven

nacer: nazco, naces, nace, nacemos, nacéis, nacen

negar: niego, niegas, niega, negamos negáis, niegan

nevar: nieva *(invariable)*

obtener: *see tener*

oir: oigo, oyes, oye, oímos, oís, oyen

oler: huelo, hueles, huele, olemos, oléis, huelen

padecer: padezco, padeces, padece, padecemos, padecéis, padecen

parecerse: me parezco, te pareces, se parece, nos parecemos, os parecéis, se parecen

pedir: pido, pides, pide, pedimos, pedís, piden

pensar: pienso, piensas, piensa, pensamos, pensáis, piensan

perder: pierdo, pierdes, pierde, perdemos, perdéis, pierden

poder: puedo, puedes, puede, podemos, podéis, pueden

poner(se): (me) pongo, (te) pones, (se) pone, (nos) ponemos, (os) ponéis, (se) ponen

predecir: *see decir*

preferir: prefiero, prefieres, prefiere, preferimos, preferís, prefieren

probar: pruebo, pruebas, prueba, probamos, probáis, prueban

proponer: *see poner*

proteger: protejo, proteges, protege, protegemos, protegéis, protegen

querer: quiero, quieres, quiere, queremos, queréis, quieren

recoger: recojo, recoges, recoge, recogemos, recogéis, recogen

recomendar: recomiendo, recomiendas, recomienda, recomendamos, recomendáis, recomiendan

recordar: recuerdo, recuerdas, recuerda, recordamos, recordáis, recuerdan

regar: riego, riegas, riega, regamos, regáis, riegan

reír(se): (me) río, (te) ríes, (se) ríe, (nos) reímos, (os) reís, (se) ríen

remendar: remiendo, remiendas, remienda, remendamos, remendáis, remiendan

reñir: riño, riñes, riñe, reñimos, reñís, riñen

repetir: repito, repites, repite, repetimos, repetís, repiten

reproducir: reproduzco, reproduces, reproduce, reproducimos, reproducís, reproducen

resolver: resuelvo, resuelves, resuelve, resolvemos, resolvéis, resuelven

rogar: ruego, ruegas, ruega, rogamos, rogáis, ruegan

rugir: rujo, ruges, ruge, rugimos, rugís, rugen

saber: sé, sabes, sabe, sabemos, sabéis, saben

salir: salgo, sales, sale, salimos, salís, salen

satisfacer: satisfago, satisfaces, satisface, satisfacemos, satisfacéis, satisfacen

seguir: sigo, sigues, sigue, seguimos, seguís, siguen

sembrar: siembro, siembras, siembra, sembramos, sembráis, siembran

sentarse: me siento, te sientas, se sienta, nos sentamos, os sentáis, se sientan

sentirse: me siento, te sientes, se siente, nos sentimos, os sentís, se sienten

ser: soy, eres, es somos, sois, son

servir: sirvo, sirves, sirve, servimos, servís, sirven

sonar: sueno, suenas, suena, sonamos, sonáis, suenan

sonreír: *see reír*

sugerir: sugiero, sugieres, sugiere, sugerimos, sugerís, sugieren

tender(se): (me) tiendo, (te) tiendes, (se) tiende, (nos) tendemos, (os) tendéis, (se) tienden

tener: tengo, tienes, tiene, tenemos, tenéis, tienen

teñir: tiño, tiñes, tiñe, teñimos, teñís, tiñen

tostar: tuesto, tuestas, tuesta, tostamos, tostáis, tuestan

traducir: traduzco, traduces, traduce, traducimos, traducís, traducen

traer: traigo, traes, trae, traemos, traéis, traen

tronar: trueno, truenas, truena, tronamos, tronáis, truenan

tropezar: tropiezo, tropiezas, tropieza, tropezamos, tropezáis, tropiezan

vaciar: vacío, vacías, vacía, vaciamos, vaciáis, vacían

venir: vengo, vienes, viene, venimos, venís, vienen

ver: veo, ves, ve, vemos, véis, ven

verter: vierto, viertes, vierte, vertimos, vertís, vierten

vestirse: me visto, te vistes, se viste, nos vestimos, os vestís, se visten

volar: vuelo, vuelas, vuela, volamos, voláis, vuelan

volver: vuelvo, vuelves, vuelve, volvemos, volvéis, vuelven

ENGLISH-SPANISH WORDFINDER

This alphabetical listing of all of the English words in *Spanish Vocabulary* will enable you to find the information you need quickly and efficiently. If all you want is the Spanish equivalent of an entry word, you will find it here. If you also want pronunciation and usage aids, or closely associated words and phrases, use the reference number(s) and letter(s) to locate the section(s) in which the entry appears. This is especially important for words that have multiple meanings.

A

a, an un, uno, una, unos, unas 8c

abbreviation la abreviatura 19c

able to poder 21a

abortion el aborto 44b

above arriba, sobre 3d

abroad al extranjero 19e, 30a

absent ausente 37f

accent el acento 8a, 19c

accept aceptar 21b

acceptable aceptable 21b

accident el accidente 33c, 39c

according to según 44c

accordion el acordeón 28c

account la cuenta 26

accountant el (la) contador (ra) 38a

accounting la contabilidad 37e

accusation la acusación 41

accuse acusar 41

accused el (la) acusado (a) 41

acid el ácido 13c

acid rain la lluvia ácida 44a

acne la acné 40a

acquaintance el (la) conocido (a) 10b

across a través de 3d, 36c

act actuar 28e

active activo 8a, 11e

activity la actividad 11e

actor el actor 28a, 38a

actress la actriz 28a, 38a

actually en realidad 17b

acute agudo 2b

adapt adaptar 11e

adaptable adaptable 11e

add sumar 1e

addict el (la) adicto (a) 11e

addition la suma 1e

address la dirección, las señas 11f, 19e, 38b

adhesive tape la cinta adhesiva 19d, 25c, 38c

adjacent adyacente 2b

adjective adjetivo 8a

admit admitir 41

adolescence la juventud 11b

adolescent el (la) joven 11b

adult el (la) adulto(a) 11b

adventure la aventura 20a

adverb el adverbio 8a

advertising la publicidad, la propaganda 20a, 38d

advice el consejo 17a

advise aconsejar 17a

affection el afecto, el cariño 11e, 21a

affectionate afectuoso, cariñoso 11e

Africa Africa 30b

after después (de) 4e, 8o

afternoon la tarde 4a

again otra vez 4e

age la edad 11b, 38b

aggressive agresivo 11e

agnostic el (la) agnóstico (a) 11d

ago hace 4e

agree estar* de acuerdo 21a, 22b, 41

agriculture la agricultura 14a

ahead delante, adelante 3d, 36c

Spanish nouns are denoted with the definite article **el, la, los,** or **las.** To avoid dissonance, some Spanish feminine nouns that begin with a stressed *a* take the masculine definite article **el;** these are identified by *(f).*

AIDS el SIDA 40a, 44b
air el aire 6a, 13c
air conditioning el aire acondicionado 23e, 33e
air pollution la contaminación del aire 44a
airline la línea aérea 32a
airmail por avión 19e
airplane el avión 32c
airport el aeropuerto 32a
aisle el pasillo 28a, 32c
alarm el alarma 39a
alarm clock el despertador 4d, 25i
albatross el albatros 15b
alcoholic drink la bebida alcohólica 24k
algebra el álgebra (f) 1f
algebraic algebraico 1f
all todo 3c
All aboard! ¡Todos a bordo! 34
all day toda el día 4a
allegory la alegoría 17a
allergy la alergia 40a
allude aludir 17a
almost casi 3c
almost never casi nunca 4e
alphabet el alfabeto 8a
already ya 4e
also también 44c
although aunque 8o
altitude la altitud 32c
altruism el altruismo 11e
altruist el (la) altruista 11e
altruistic altruista 11e
always siempre 4e
amateur aficionado 27b
ambition la ambición 11e
ambitious ambicioso 11e
ambulance la ambulancia 33a, 39a, 39c
America América 30b
American americano(a) (adj, n) 30d
amethyst la amatista 25i
ammonia el amoniaco 13c
among entre 3d, 8g
amphitheater el anfiteatro 36a
analogy la analogía 17a, 28d
anatomy la anatomía 37e
anchovy la anchoa 24d
and y 8o

anesthetic el anestético 40b
anesthetist el (la) anestesista 40a
anger el enojo 11e, 21a
angle el ángulo 2b
angry enojado 11e
animal el animal 15a
ankle el tobillo 12a
anniversary el aniversario 11c, 29a
announce anunciar 17a
announcement el anuncio 17a
annually anualmente 4c
answer la respuesta (n); responder (v) 9, 17a, 18b, 37f
answering machine el contestador automático 18a
ant la hormiga 15d
Antarctic Antártico 13b
Antarctic Circle el Círculo Antártico 13e
antenna la antena 20b, 42a
anthropology la antropología 37e
antibiotic el antibiótico 25h, 40a
antinuclear protest la manifestación antinuclear 44b
antique la antigüedad 25a
antiseptic el antiséptico 39c
antithesis la antítesis 28d
anus el ano 40a
anxiety el ansia (f) 21a
anxious inquieto 11e, 21a
anxiousness la inquietud 11e, 21a
apartment el apartamento, el piso 23g
apartment building la casa de pisos 23g
aperitif el aperitivo 24g
apostrophe el apóstrofo 19c
appendicitis la apendicitis 40a
appendix el apéndice 20a, 28d, 40a
appetizer la tapa, el bocadillo 24g
appetizing apetitoso 24p
applaud aplaudir 28e
applause el aplauso 28e
apple la manzana 14d, 24f

apple tree   el manzano   14c
application   la solicitud   38b
apply for   solicitar   37f
appointment   la cita   40a, 40b
appointment book   la agenda de entrevistas   38c
approval   la aprobación   21b
approve   aprobar*   21b
approximately   aproximadamente   3c
apricot   el albaricoque   14d, 24f
April   abril   5b
Aquarius   Acuario   5d
Arabic   árabe   *(adj, n)*   30d
Arabic numerals   la numeración arábica   1d
archaeology   la arqueología   37e
archipelago   el archipiélago   13b
architect   el (la) arquitecto (a)   38a
architecture   la arquitectura   28b, 37e
Arctic   Ártico   13b
Arctic Circle   el Círculo Ártico   13e
area   el área   *(f)*   3a, 13d
area code   la zona telefónica   18b
Argentinian   argentino(a)   *(adj, n)*   30d
argue   reñir*   17a, 39b
argument   la disputa   17a
Aries   Aries   5d
arithmetic   la aritmética   1f
arithmetical   arimético   1e
arm   el brazo   12a
armchair   el sillón   23c, 35c
armed robbery   robo a mano armada   39b
arms reduction   la disminución de las armas   43
arrest   detener*, arrestar   39b
arrival   la llegada   32a
arrive   llegar   3e
arrogant   arrogante   11e
art   el (la) arte   28b, 37e
art museum   el museo de arte   36a
artery   la arteria   40a
arthritis   la artritis   40a

artichoke   la alcachofa   14e, 24e
article   el artículo   8a, 20a
articulate   articular   17a
artificial   artificial   13d, 25i
artificial satellite   el satélite artificial   42a
artist   el (la) artista   28b
artistic   artístico   11e
as   como   8o
as a matter of fact   en realidad   17b, 44c
as if   como si   8o
ashtray   el cenicero   23c
Asia   Asia   30b
ask   preguntar   9, 17a
ask a question   hacer* una pregunta   9
asparagus   el espárrago   14e, 24e
aspirin   la aspirina   25h, 40a
assault   el asalto   39b
assembly   la asamblea   43
assignments   la tarea   37f
assistant   el (la) ayudante   37d
association   la asociación   43
assure   asegurar   21a
asterisk   el asterisco   19c
asthma   el asma   *(f)*   40a
astronaut   el (la) astronauta   42a
astronomy   la astronomía   13a, 37e
astute   astuto   11e
astuteness   la astucia   11e
at   en   8g
at home   en casa   23f
at midnight   a la medianoche   4a
at night   de noche   4a
at noon   al mediodía   4a
at the end of   al final de   36c
at the top   en lo alto de   36c
At what time?   ¿A qué hora?   4b
atheism   el ateísmo   11d
atheist   el (la) ateísta   11d
athlete   el (la) atleta   27b
Atlantic   el Atlántico   13b
atlas   el atlas   20a, 37b
atmosphere   la atmósfera   6a, 13b

atmospheric atmosférico 13b

atmospheric conditions las condiciones atmosféricas 6a

atom el átomo 13c, 42a

atomic bomb la bomba atómica 44b

attend asistir 37f

attic el ático 23a

attitude la actitud 21a

attractive atractivo 11a, 11e

audience el público 28e

audio equipment el equipo auditivo 20b

August agosto 5b

aunt la tía 10a

Australia Australia 30b

Australian australiano(a) *(adj, n)* 30d

Austria Austria 30b

authentic auténtico 13d

author el (la) autor (a) 20a

autobiography la autobiografía 28d

automobile el automóvil 33a

avarice, greed la avaricia 11e

avenue la avenida 11f, 36a

average el promedio 1f

away fuera 3d

axis el axis 2b

B

baby el (la) bebé 11b

bachelor el (la) soltero (a) 11c

backache el dolor de espalda 40a

back up retroceder 33c

bacon el tocino 24c

bad malo 11e, 24p

bad breath el mal aliento 40a

bad mood mal humor 21a

bag el saco, la bolsa 23d, 25a

baggage el equipaje 31

bagpipes la gaita 28c

bail la fianza 41

baked asado 24b, 24p

baker el panadero 38a

bakery la panadería 24n

balcony el balcón 23a, 35c

bald calvo *(adj)* 12d

ball la pelota 27b

ballad el romance 28d

ballet el ballet 28c

ballpoint pen el bolígrafo 19d, 25c, 37b

banana la banana, el plátano 14d, 24f

bandage la venda 25h, 39c, 40a vendar *(v)* 40a

bangs el flequillo 12d

bank el banco 26

bank book la libreta de depósitos 26

bank rate el tipo de descuento bancario 26

banker el banquero 38a

banknote (see *bill*)

baptism el bautismo 11d

barber el barbero 12d, 38a

barber shop la barbería 12d

bark ladrar 15a

barn el establo 15a

barometer el barómetro 6c

barometric pressure la presión barométrica 6c

baroque barroco *(n, adj)* 28d

barrel el barril 23d

bartender el cantinero 24m

baseball el béisbol 27b

basement el sótano 23a

basil la albahaca 14e, 24j

basilica la basílica 36a

basin la cuenca 13b

basket la cesta, la canasta 23d, 27b

basketball el básquetbol, el baloncesto 27b

basketball court la cancha 27b

bass drum el bombo 28c

bassoon el bajón 28c

bat el murciélago 15a

bat *(baseball)* el bate 27b

bathing suit el traje de baño 25k

bath oil el aceite de baño 25f

bathroom el cuarto de baño 23b, 35c

bathtub la bañera 23a, 35c

batter *(baseball)* el bateador

battery *(car)* la batería   25b, 33e
battery la pila   25b
bay la bahía   13b
beach la playa   13b, 36b
beak el pico   15b
beans los frijoles   14e, 24e
bear el oso   15a
beard la barba   12a
beast la bestia   15a
beautician el (la) peluquero (a)   12d
beautiful hermoso   11a, 251
because porque   8o
become hacerse*   10b, 25a
become bored aburrirse *(v)*   21a
bed la cama   23c, 35c
bedbug la chinche   15d
bedroom la alcoba, el cuarto   23b
bedside table la mesilla de noche   23c, 35c
bedspread el cubrecama   23d, 35c
bee la abeja   15d
beech tree el (la) haya *(f)*   14c
beefsteak el bistec   24c
beer la cerveza   24k
beet la remolacha   14e, 24e
before antes (de)   4e, 8o
beg rogar*   17a
begin empezar*, comenzar*   4e
behind detrás   3d, 36c
Belgian belga   30d
belief la creencia   11d
believe creer   11d, 22b
bellboy el botones   35b
bell tower el campanario   36a
below zero bajo cero   6c
belt el cinturón   25k
Berlin Berlín   30c
beside junto a   3d
besides además de   8g
best seller el éxito de librería   20a, 25o
between entre   3d, 8g
beyond más allá   3d
bible la biblia   28d
bicycle la bicicleta   33a
bicycle racing el ciclismo

big grande   3c, 11a, 251
bill la cuenta   24m, 25a, 35b
bill facturar *(v)*   25a
bill, banknote el billete   26
billiard ball la bola de billar   27a
billiard table la mesa de billar   27a
billiards el billar   27a
billionth billonésimo   1b
bingo el bingo   27a
bingo card la tarjeta de bingo   27a
biography la biografía   28d
biology la biología   37e
bird el pájaro   15b
birth el nacimiento   11c
birthday el cumpleaños   11c, 29a
bisector la bisectriz   2b
bishop *(chess)* el alfil   27a
bite la mordedura   39c
black negro   7a
blackberry la zarzamora   14d
blackbird el mirlo   15b
blackboard la pizarra   37b
blackboard eraser el borrador   37b
bladder la vejiga   40a
blade *(of knife)* la hoja   23d, 25f
blanket la manta   23d, 35c
bleat balar   15a
bleed sangrar   39c
blender la licuadora   23d
blindness la ceguera   12c
blind person el (la) ciego(a)   12c
block *(city)* la manzana, la cuadra   33c
blond(e) rubio(a)   11a
blood la sangre   12a, 39c, 40a
blood clot el coágulo de sangre   40a
blood pressure la presión arterial   40a
blood test el análisis de sangre   40a
bloom florecer   14a
blouse la blusa   25k
blue azul   7a

blueberry   el mirtilo   24f
blueprint   el cianotipo   28b
blush, rouge   el colorete   25f
board   subir a   32a
boarding   el embarque   32a
boarding house   la casa de huéspedes   35a
boarding pass   la tarjeta de embarque   32a
boat   el barco   36b
bobbypins   las horquillas   25f
body   el cuerpo   11a, 12a, 19a
body build   desarrollar la musculatura   27a
boiling point   el punto de ebullición   6c
bold   audaz   11e
Bolivian   boliviano(a)   *(adj, n)*   30d
bond   el bono   26
bone   el hueso   12a, 40a
book   el libro   20a, 25o, 37b
bookcase   el estante   23c, 37b
bookstore   la librería   25o
boot   la bota   25n
border   la frontera   13e, 31
bore   aburrir   21a
boredom   el aburrimiento   21a
boss   el (la) jefe (a)   38d
botanical   botánico   14a
botany   la botánica   14a, 37e
both   ambos   3c
bottle   la botella   23d, 24l
bottom   el fondo   3d
bouquet of flowers   el ramo de flores   14b
bow   el arco   28c
bowl   el tazón   23d, 24l
bowl   jugar* a los bolos   27a
bowling alley   la bolera   27a
bowling ball   la bola   27a
box   la caja   23d
box office   la taquilla   28a
boxing   el boxeo   27b
boxing gloves   los guantes de boxeo   27b
boxing ring   el ring   27b
boy   el chico, el muchacho   11a, 11b
boyfriend   novio, amigo   10b
bra   el sostén   25k

bracelet   la pulsera   25i
bracket   el corchete   19c
brain   el cerebro   12a, 40a
brake   el freno   33a, 33c, 33e
branch   la rama   14a
branch *(of a company)*   la sucursal   38d
brash   atrevido   11e
brass   el latón   13c
brass instruments   los cobres   28c
Brazil   el Brasil   30b
Brazilian   brasileño(a)   *(adj, n)*   30d
breakfast   el desayuno   24a, 35b
breath   el aliento   40a
breathe   respirar   12b, 40a
bricklayer   el albañil   38a
bride   la novia   11c
bridge   el puente   33c, 36a, 40b
brief   breve   4e, 37f
briefcase   la cartera, el portafolio   25c, 38c
briefly   brevemente   4e, 17b
bright   vivo   7b
brilliant   brillante   11e
bring   traer*   25a
brocade   el brocado   25l
broccoli   el brécol, el brócoli   14e, 24e
brochure   el folleto   20a, 30a
broiled   a la parrilla   24b
broken bone   el hueso fracturado   39c
broken line   la línea quebrada   2b
bronchitis   la bronquitis   40a
bronze   el bronce   13c
brooch   el broche   25i
brook   el arroyo   36b
broom   la escoba   23d
broth   el caldo   24g
brother   el hermano   10a
brother-in-law   el cuñado   10a
brown   marrón   7a
bruise   la contusión   40a
brunet(te)   moreno(a)   11a
brush   el cepillo   12d, 25f
brush *(art)*   el pincel   28b
brush   cepillarse *(v)*   12d,

40b

buckle up   abrocharse (v) 32c

bud   el brote   14a

Buddhism   el budismo   11d

Buddhist   el (la) budista (n, adj)   11d

budget   el presupuesto   26

buffalo   el búfalo   15a

bug   el insecto   15d

build   construir   23f

building   el edificio   23g, 39a

bulb   el bulbo   14a

bull   el toro   15a

bullring   la plaza de toros 36a

bumper   el parachoques   33e

bump into   tropezar* con 39c

bunion   el juanete   40a

burn   quemar   39a

burn   la quemadura   39a, 40a

bus   el autobús, el camión 33a, 34

bus driver   el conductor   34, 38a

bus station   la estación de autobuses, la camionera   34

business letter   carta comercial 19e

businessman   el comerciante 38a

businesswoman   la comerciante 38a

busy   ocupado   18b

but   pero, sino   8o

butcher   el carnicero   38a

butcher shop   la carnicería 24n

butter   la mantequilla   24h

butterfly   la mariposa   15d

buttocks   el trasero   12a

button   el botón   25g

buttonhole   el ojal   25g

buy   comprar   23f, 25a

byte   el byte, el octeto   42b

C

cabbage   la col, el repollo 14e, 24e

cabin (plane)   la cabina   32c

cable   el cable   18a, 25b

cafeteria   la cafetería   24m

cake   la torta   24g

calculate   calcular   1f

calculation   el cálculo   1f

calculus   el cálculo   37e

calendar   el calendario   5b, 38c

calf   la pantorrilla   12a

call   llamar   17a

calling card   tarjeta de visita 16b

calm   tranquilo   11e

calmness   la tranquilidad 11e

camel   el camello   15a

camera   la cámara   25d

camp   acampar   36b

campground   el acampamento 36b

campus   la ciudad universitaria, el campus   37c

can   la lata   23d

can, be able   poder*   21a

Canada   el Canadá   30b

Canadian   el (la) canadiense (n, adj)   30d

canceled   cancelado   32b

cancer   el cáncer   40a

Cancer   Cáncer   5d

canine tooth   el canino   40b

canoe   la canoa   36b

canteen   la cantimplora   36b

canvas   el lienzo   7c, 28b

cap   la gorra   36b

capacity   la capacidad   3c

cape   el cabo   13b

capital   la capital   13e

capital city   la ciudad capital 13e, 30a

capital letter   la letra mayúscula 19c

Capricorn   Capricornio   5d

car   el carro, el coche   33a

car body   la carrocería   33e

car racing   las carreras de coches   27b

car window   la ventanilla 33e

carat   el quilate   25i

carbon   el carbono   13c

carburetor   el carburador 33e

card   la tarjeta   19e

cardinal number   número

cardinal 1d
cardiologist el (la) cardiólogo(a) 40a
career la carrera 11f, 38d
carnation el clavel 14b
carpenter el carpintero 38a
carpet la alfombra 23c
carriage *(typewriter)* el carro 19d
carrot la zanahoria 14e, 24e
carry llevar 31
case el estuche 23d
cash el dinero, en efectivo 25a, 26
cash cobrar, cambiar 26
cash register la caja registradora 25a
cashier el (la) cajero (a) 25a, 26
cassette el casete 20b, 25j
cast el reparto 28e
castle el castillo 36a
cat el gato 15a
catch *(ball)* agarrar, coger* 27b
catechism el catecismo 11d
caterpillar la oruga 15d
cathedral la catedral 36a
Catholic católico(a) *(adj, n)* 11d
Catholicism el catolicismo 11d
cauliflower la coliflor 14e, 24e
caution el cuidado 33d
cave la cueva 13b
cavity la caries 40b
ceiling el techo 23a
celery el apio 14e, 24e
cell la célula 14a
cello el violoncelo 28c
Celsius Celsius 6c
censorship la censura 44b
center el centro 2a
centimeter el centímetro 3a
century el siglo 4c
chain la cadena 25i, 33a
chain guard *(bicycle)* el cárter 33a
chair la silla 23c, 38c
chalk la tiza 37b
change cambiar 4e, 25a
change gears cambiar de velocidad 33c

change the subject cambiar el tema 17a
changing room el vestuario 25k
channel el cauce 13b
channel *(TV, radio)* el canal 20b
chapter el capítulo 28d
character el carácter 11e
character *(in a book, etc.)* el personaje 28d, 28e
characteristic la característica 11e
characterize caracterizar 11e
charter flight el vuelo fletado 30a
chat charlar 17a
cheap barato 24p
check *(banking)* el cheque 25a, 26
check *(luggage)* facturar, depositar 32a
check *(restaurant)* la cuenta 24m
checkbook la libreta de cheques 26
checkerboard el tablero de damas 27a
checkers las damas 27a
checking account la cuenta corriente 26
checkmate el jaque mate 27a
cheek la mejilla 12a
cheese el queso 24h
chemical el producto químico 13c
chemical weapon el arma química *(f)* 44b
chemistry la química 13c, 37e
chemistry lab el laboratorio de química 37c
cherry la cereza 14d, 24f
cherry tree el cerezo 14c
chess el ajedrez 27a
chessboard el tablero de ajedrez 27a
chest el pecho 12a
chestnut la castaña 14d
chest of drawers la cómoda 23c, 35c
chicken el pollo 24c

child   el niño   11b
Chilean   chileno(a)   *(adj, n)*
30d
chills   los escalofríos   40a
chimney   la chimenea   23a
chin   la barbilla   12a
China   China   30b
Chinese   chino(a)   *(adj, n)*
30d
chlorine   el cloro   13c
chlorophyll   la clorofila   14a
choke   atragantarse   *(v)*   40a
Christian   cristiano(a)   *(adj, n)*
11d
Christianity   el cristianismo
11d
Christmas   la Navidad   5f,
29a
Christmas bonus   el aguinaldo
38d
Christmas Eve   la Nochebuena
5f
church   la iglesia   11d, 36a
cigar   el puro, el cigarro   25e
cigarette   el cigarrillo   25e
circle   el círculo   2a
circumference   la circunferencia
2a
citrus   la fruta agria   14d
city   la ciudad   11f, 13e,
30a, 36a, 38b
city map   el plano de la ciudad
36a
civil law   el derecho civil   41
clam   la almeja   24d
clamp   la abrazadera   25b
clarinet   el clarinete   28c
class *(of students)*   la clase
37d, 37f
classical music   la música
clásica   25j, 28c
classified ads   los anuncios
clasificados   38d
classroom   el aula   *(f)*   37c
clause   la cláusula   8a
clay   la arcilla   13c
clean   limpio   *(adj)*   11a,
clean   limpiar   23f, 25g
clean oneself   limpiarse   *(v)*
12d
clear   claro   25d
clear the table   quitar (limpiar)
la mesa   23f, 24o
clerk   el (la) dependiente

19e
clerk's window   la ventanilla
19e
climate   el clima   6a
clock   el reloj   4d
close an account   liquidar una
cuenta   26
closed   cerrado   25a
closed circuit   el circuito
cerrado   20b
closet, cupboard   el armario
23b, 35c
closing   la despedida   19c
closing time   hora de cerrar
25a
clothes   la ropa   25g
clothes basket   la cesta para la
ropa sucia   25g
clothes hanger   la percha, el
gancho   23d, 35c
clothespin   la pinza   25g
clothing store   la tienda de ropa
25k
cloud   la nube   6a, 13b
cloudy   nublado   6a
clown   (see *fool*)
clubs *(cards)*   los bastos   27a
clutch   el embrague   33e
coach *(sports)*   el (la) entrenador
(ra)   27b
coach *(train)*   el coche, el vagón
34
coach class   la segunda clase
34
coal   el carbón   13c
coal mine   la mina de carbón
13c
coal mining   la extracción del
carbón   13c
coast   la costa   13b
coat   el abrigo   25k
cockroach   la cucaracha   15d
codfish   el bacalao   15c, 24d
coed school   el colegio mixto
37a
coffee   el café   24k
coffee pot   la cafetera   23d
coffee table   la mesa de centro
23c
coin   la moneda   26, 27a
coin collecting   la numismática
27a
colander   el colador   23d
cold *(illness)*   el resfriado

40a

cold (*weather*) frío (*adj*); el frío (*n*)   6a, 24p
cold water   el agua fría   35c
collar   el cuello   25g
colleague   el (la) colega   10b
collect call   la llamada de cobro revertido   18b
collide   chocar con   39c
collision   el choque   39c
cologne   la colonia   25f
Colombian   colombiano(a) (*adj, n*)   30d
colon (*punctuation sign*)   dos puntos   19c
color   el color   7c, 25d
colored   coloreado   7c
coloring   la coloración   7c
comb   el peine   12d, 25f
comb one's hair   peinarse (*v*)   12d
come   venir*   3e
comedian, comedienne   el (la) comediante   28e
comedy   la comedia   20a, 28e
comet   el cometa   13a
comics   las tiras cómicas   20a, 25o
comma   la coma   19c
commerce   el comercio   37e, 38d
commercial   el anuncio   20b
communicate   comunicar   17a
communication   la comunicación   17a
communism   el comunismo   43
communist   el (la) comunista   43
compact car   el coche pequeño   33a
compact disc   el disco compacto   20b, 25j, 42a
company   la compañía   38d
compare   comparar   17a
comparison   la comparación   8a, 17a
compartment   el compartimiento   34
compass (*drawing instrument*)   el compás   2b, 37b
compass (*navigating instrument*)   la brújula   3d

compatible   compatible   42b
competition   la competencia   27b
complain   quejarse   21a, 35b
complaint   la queja   21a, 35b
complementary   complementario   2b
complex   complejo   1d
complex number   el número complejo   1d
complicated   complicado   22a
composer   el (la) compositor (ra)   25j, 28c
composition   la composición   28c, 37f
compound   el compuesto   13c
compound interest   el interés compuesto   26
computer   la computadora, el ordenador   19d, 38c, 42b
computer language   el lenguaje de máquina   42b
concave   cóncavo   2b
concept   el concepto   22a
concert   el concierto   28c
conclude   concluir*   17a
conclusion   la conclusión   17a
conditional   condicional   8a
condominium   el condominio   23g
conductor (*train*)   el (la) revisor(a)   34
conductor (*bus*)   el (la) conductor(a)   34
cone   el cono   2a
confirmation   la confirmación   11d
conflict   el conflicto   28d
conformist   el (la) conformista   11e
congratulate   felicitar   17a
Congratulations.   Felicitaciones.   16c, 29c
conjugation   la conjugación   8a
conjunction   la conjunción   8a
connection   la conexión, el enlace   32a, 34
conscience   la conciencia

11e, 22a

conscientious concienzudo
11e, 22a

consecutive consecutivo 2b

consent *(agree)* consentir*
41

conservation la preservación
44a

conservative conservador
11e, 43

conservatory el conservatorio
37a

consonant la consonante 8a

constipation el estreñimiento
40a

consumption el consumo
44a

contact lenses los lentes de
contacto 40a

continent el continente 13e,
30a

continental continental 6a,
13e

continually continuamente
4e

continue continuar* 4e

contraceptives los
contraceptivos 40a

contract el contrato *(n)*;
contratar *(v)* 38d

controversy la controversia
41

convalesce convalecer* 40a

convalescence la convalecencia
40a

conversation la conversación
17a

convex convexo 2b

convince convencer* 22b,
41

cook cocinar *(v)* 24o

cook el (la) cocinero (a) 38a

cool fresco 6a

coordinate la coordenada
2b

copilot el copiloto 32c

copper el cobre 13c

copy la copia 37f

corduroy la pana 25l

corkscrew el sacacorchos
23d

corn el maíz 14e, 24i

corner *(street)* la esquina
33c, 36a

coroner el médico forense
41

correspondence la
correspondencia 19e

corridor el pasillo 23a

cortisone la cortisona 25h

cosecant la cosecante 2b

cosine el coseno 2b

cosmetics store la perfumería
25f

cosmos el cosmos 13a

cost costar* 24o, 25a

cost of living el coste de vida
26

Costa Rican el (la)
costarricense *(n, adj)* 30d

cotangent la cotangente 2b

cotton el algodón 13c, 25l

cough toser *(v)*; la tos *(n)*
40a

cough drops las pastillas para
la tos 40a

cough syrup el jarabe para la
tos 40a

council el consejo 43

counter el mostrador 25a

country el país 11f, 13e,
30a

countryside el campo, la
campiña 13b, 36b

courage el valor 11e

courageous valiente 11e

courier el mensajero 19e

course *(meal)* el plato 24g

course *(school)* el curso 37f

court el tribunal 41

court of appeals el tribunal de
apelación 41

courteous cortés 11e

courtesy la cortesía 11e

courtroom la sala de un
tribunal 41

cousin el primo 10a

cover la portada 20a

cover charge el precio del
cubierto 24m

cow la vaca 15a

cramps los calambres 40a

crash el choque 39c

crash into chocar con 39c

crayon el creyón 7c

crazy loco 11e

cream la crema 24h, 25f

create crear 11e

creative creativo 11e
creativity la creatividad 11e
credit el crédito 26
credit card la tarjeta de crédito 25a, 26
crew *(plane)* la tripulación 32c
cricket el grillo 15d
crime el crimen, el delito 39b
crime wave la ola de crímenes 39b
criminal el (la) criminal 39b
criminal law el derecho penal 41
critical crítico 11e
criticism la crítica 20a, 28d
crocodile el cocodrilo 15c
cross cruzar 36c
crown la corona 40b
cruise el crucero 36b
crutches las muletas 40a
cry llorar 11e, 21a
crying el llanto 11e, 21a
Cuban cubano(a) *(adj, n)* 30d
cubed al cubo 1e
cube root la raíz cúbica 1e
cucumber el pepino 14e, 24e
cue *(billiards)* el taco 27a
cultivate cultivar 14a
cultivation el cultivo 14a
cultured culto 11e
cup la taza 23d, 24l
cure curar, sanar *(v)*; la cura *(n)* 40a
curiosity la curiosidad 11e
curler el rulo, el rizador 12d, 25f
curls los bucles 12d
curly rizado 11a
curly-haired de pelo rizado 11a
currency el dinero en circulación 26
current la corriente 35c
curtain *(theater)* el telón 28e, 35c
curtain *(window)* la cortina 23c, 35c
curve la curva 33c

cushion el cojín 23c
custodian el portero 37d
customer el (la) cliente 25a, 26
customs la aduana 31
customs officer el aduanero 31
cut cortar *(v)* 12d, 24o
cut la cortadura 40a
cutlet la chuleta 24g
cyclamen el ciclamen 14b
cylinder el cilindro 2a
cymbals los címbalos 28c
cypress tree el ciprés 14c
cyst el quiste 40a

D

dad el papá 10a
dahlia la dalia 14b
daily diario 4c
daily newspaper (el) diario *(n, adj)* 20a
dairy la lechería 24n
dairy products los productos lácteos 24h
dam el dique, la presa 13b
dance bailar *(v)*; el baile *(n)* 28c, 29b
dance music la música de baile 25j
dancer el (la) bailarín (ra) 28c
dandruff la caspa 40a
danger el peligro 33d, 39a
dangerous peligroso 33d
dangerous crossing el cruce peligroso 33d
Danish danés(-nesa) *(adj, n)* 30d
dark oscuro 6a, 7b
dark blue azul oscuro 7a
dark-haired moreno, de pelo oscuro 11a
darkroom la cámara oscura, el cuarto oscuro 25d
darts los dardos 27a
dashboard el tablero de instrumentos 33e
data los datos 42b
data base la base de texto 42b
data processing la informática 42b
date la fecha 19c

date *(fruit)*   el dátil   14d, 24f
date book   el diario   37b
daughter   la hija   10a
daughter-in-law   la nuera   10a
dawn   el amanecer   4a
day   el día   4a, 4c
day after tomorrow   pasado mañana   4a
day before yesterday   anteayer   4a
day-care center   la guardería   37a
deaf person   el (la) sordo(a)   12c
deafness   la sordera   12c
death   la muerte   11c
death sentence   la pena de muerte   41
debate   el debate *(n)*; debatir *(v)*   17a, 41
debt   la deuda   26
decade   la década   4c
decagon   el decágono   2a
December   diciembre   5b
decimal   decimal   1f
declarative   declarativo   8a
declare   declarar   17a, 31
decor   la decoración   23c
decorate   decorar   23f
decrease   disminuir* *(v)* la disminución *(n)*   3c
deer   el venado, el ciervo   15a
defecate   defecar   40a
defend oneself   defenderse*   41
defense attorney   el (la) abogado(a) defensor(a)   41
definite   definido   8a
definition   la definición   20a
degree   el grado   2b
degree   el título   37f
delicate   delicado   11e
democracy   la democracia   43
democrat   el (la) demócrata   43
democratic   democrático   43
demonstrate   demostrar*   22b
demonstration   la manifestación pública   43
Denmark   Dinamarca   30b

dense   denso   3b
density   la densidad   3b
dental floss   el hilo dental   25h, 40b
dentist   el (la) dentista   38a, 40b
dentist's office   la oficina del dentista   40b
dentures, false teeth   los dientes postizos   40b
deny   negar   17a
deodorant   el desodorante   25f
depart   salir*, partir   3e, 34
department   el departamento   25a
department store   el almacén   25a
departure   la salida   32a
deposit   el depósito *(n)*; depositar *(v)*   26
deposit slip   la hoja de depósito   26
depressed   deprimido   21a
depression   la depresión   21a, 40a
dermatologist   el dermatólogo   40a
describe   describir   17a
description   la descripción   17a, 39b
descriptive   descriptivo   8a
desert   el desierto   13b
desk *(classroom)*   el pupitre   37b
desk *(office)*   el escritorio   37b, 38c
desperate   desesperado   21a
desperation   la desesperación   21a
dessert   el postre   24g
destroy   destruir*   39a
detest   detestar, odiar   21b
detour   el desvío   33d
develop   revelar   25d
diabetes   la diabetes   40a
diagnose   diagnosticar   40a
dial   la esfera   4d, 25i
dial   marcar   18b
dial direct   marcar directo   18b
dialogue   el diálogo   28d
diameter   el diámetro   2a
diamond   el diamante   25i
diamonds *(cards)*   los diamantes

27a

diarrhea la diarrea 40a
dice los dados 27a
dictate dictar 17a
dictator el dictador 43
dictatorship la dictadura 43
dictionary el diccionario 20a, 25o, 37b
die morirse* 11c
diesel el diesel 33c
diet el régimen, la dieta; estar* a dieta 40a
difference la diferencia 1f
difficult difícil 22a
dig cavar 14a
digest digerir* 40a
digestive system el aparato digestivo 40a
digit el dígito 1d
digress divagar 17a
diligence la diligencia 11e
diligent diligente 11e
dimension la dimensión 3b
dining room el comedor 23b
dinner la cena 24a
diploma el diploma 11f, 37f
diplomatic diplomático 11e
direct directo 8a
direct dialing marcar directo 18b
direction la dirección 3d
dirty sucio 11a, 12d, 25g
disagree no estar* de acuerdo 21a, 41
disagreement el desacuerdo 21a
disappoint decepcionar 21a
disappointed decepcionado 21a
disarmament el desarme 43
discothèque la discoteca 29b
discount el descuento 25a, 26
discourse el discurso 8a
discourteous descortés 11e
discuss discutir 17a, 41
discussion la discusión 17a
disgust el disgusto 21b
disgusted disgustado 21b
dishonest deshonesto 11e
dishonesty la deshonestidad

11e
dishwasher el lavaplatos 23d
dislike tener* aversión a 21b
disorganized desorganizado 11e
dissatisfaction el descontento 21a
dissatisfied descontento *(adj)* 21a
distance la distancia 3d, 33c
district attorney el (la) fiscal 41
divide dividir 1e
division la división 1e
divorce el divorcio 11c
divorced (be) estar* divorciado(a) 11c, 38b
doctor el médico 38a, 39c, 40a
documentary el documentario 20b
documents los documentos 31
dodecahedron el dodecaedro 2a
dog el perro 15a
dollar el dólar 26
dolphin el delfín 15c
Dominican dominicano 30d
donkey el burro 15a
door la puerta 23a, 33e
doorbell el timbre 23a
doorman el portero 35b
double doble 3c
double bass el contrabajo 28c
double bed la cama matrimonial 35b, 35c
double room el cuarto doble 35b
doubt dudar *(v)* 22b
doubt la duda 22a
dove la paloma 15b
down below abajo 3d
downtown el centro 30a, 36a
draft (banking) la letra de cambio 26
drama el drama 20a, 28e
draw (lines) trazar 2b
draw (sketch) dibujar 37f

drawer   el cajón   23c
drawing   el dibujo   28b, 37f
dress   el vestido   25k
dresser   la cómoda, el tocador 23c, 35c
dried fruit   las frutas secas 14d
drill   taladrar *(v)*   25b
drill   el taladro   25b, 40b
drink   beber *(v)*   12b, 24o; tomar *(v)*   24o
drink   la bebida   24k
drive   conducir*, manejar 3e, 33c
driver   el (la) conductor(a) 33b
driver's license   la licencia para conducir   33b
drop   la gota   6a
drug addict   el (la) drogadicto(a)   44b
drug addiction   la toxicomanía 44b
drug pusher   el vendedor (traficante) de drogas   44b
drugs   las drogas   44b
drug store/pharmacy   la farmacia   25h
drums   los tambores   28c
dry   seco   6a
dry cleaner   la tintorería 25g
dryer   el secador   23d
dry oneself   secarse *(v)* 12d
duck   el pato   15b
dull   apagado   7b
during   durante   4e
Dutch   holandés   30d
duty tax   los derechos de aduana 31
dynamic   dinámico   11e

E
each   cada   3c
eagle   el águila *(f)*   15b
ear   la oreja   12a
eardrops *(medication)*   las gotas para los oídos   40a
early   temprano   4e, 32b, 34
earn   ganar   38d
earphone   el auricular   18a
earring   el arete, el pendiente 25i

Earth   la Tierra   13a
earthquake   el terremoto 13b
easel   el caballete   28b
east   el este   3d
Easter   la Pascua Florida   5f
eastern   oriental   3d
easy   fácil   22a
eat   comer   12b, 24o
eccentric   excéntrico   11e
eclipse   el eclipse   13a
economics   la economía   37e
economy   la economía   43
economy class   la clase turista 30a, 32a, 34
ecosystem   el ecosistema 44a
Ecuadorian   ecuatoriano(a) *(adj, n)*   30d
edge   el borde   3d
editor   el (la) director(a), el (la) redactor(a)   20a, 38a
editorial   el editorial   20a
education   la enseñanza   11f, 37f, 38b
eel   la anguila   15c, 24d
egg   el huevo   24h
eggplant   la berenjena   14e, 24e
egoism   el egoísmo   11e
egoist   el egoísta   11e
Egypt   Egipto   30b
elastic   elástico   13d
elbow   el codo   12a
elect   elegir*   43
elected political representative   el representante elegido   43
election   la elección   43
electric adaptor   el adaptador eléctrico   35b
electric razor   la afeitadora eléctrica   12d, 25f
electrical   eléctrico   13c, 25b
electrical system   el sistema eléctrico   33c
electrician   el (la) electricista 38a
electricity   la electricidad 13c, 23e
electrocardiograph   el electrocardiógrafo   40a
electron   el electrón   13c, 42a
elegance   la elegancia   11a

elegant elegante 11a, 251
elegantly elegantemente 11a
element el elemento 13c
elementary school la escuela primaria 37a, 38b
elementary school teacher el maestro, la maestra 37d
elephant el elefante 15a
elevator el ascensor 23g, 25a, 35b
eloquence la elocuencia 11e
eloquent elocuente 11e
emerald la esmeralda 25i
emergency la emergencia 39a
emergency exit la salida de emergencia 39a
emergency lane el carril de emergencia 33d
emergency procedures los procedimientos de emergencia 32c
emergency room la sala de emergencia 39c
emphasis el énfasis 17a
emphasize enfatizar 17a
employee el empleado 26, 38d
employer el empleador 38d
employment agency la agencia de colocaciones 38d
empty vacío 3c
encourage animar, estimular 21a
encyclopedia la enciclopedia 20a, 25o, 37b
end el fin 4e
end, finish terminar 4e
end table la mesa auxiliar 23c
ending *(verb)* la terminación 8a
endorse endosar 26
endorsement el endoso 26
enemy el enemigo 10b
energetic enérgico 11e
energy la energía 11e, 13c, 44a
energy crisis la crisis energética 44a
energy needs las necesidades de energía 44a
energy source la fuente de energía 44a
energy waste el malgasto de

energía 44a
engaged prometido, comprometido 11c
engagement el noviazgo 11c, 29a
engine el motor 33e
engineer el ingeniero 38a
engineering la ingeniería 37e
England Inglaterra 30b
English el inglés(esa) *(adj, n)* 30d
enjoyment *(fun)* la diversión 21a
enjoy oneself *(have fun)* divertirse* 21a
enlarge agrandar, ampliar 25d, 25m
enlargement la ampliación 25d
enough bastante 3c
enter entrar 3e, 36c
entire entero 3c
entrance la entrada 23a, 25a, 35b, 36c
envelope el sobre 19d, 19e, 25c
envious envidioso 11e
environment el medio ambiente 13b, 44a
envy la envidia 11e
equality la igualdad 1f
equation la ecuación 1f
equator el ecuador 13e
equilateral equilátero 2a
equinox el equinoccio 5c
eraser *(pencil)* la goma de borrar, el borrador 2b, 19d, 37b
error el error 37f
eruption la erupción 13b
escalator la escalera movediza 25a
escape escaparse *(v)* 39a
esophagus el esófago 40a
essay el ensayo 20a, 28d, 37f
euphemism el eufemismo 28d
Europe Europa 30b
even par 1d
evening la tarde 4a
evening school la escuela nocturna 37a
every cada 3c
everyone todo el mundo 3c, 8n

everything   todo   3c, 8n
everywhere   en todas partes
    36c
exam   el examen   37f
examination   el examen físico
    40a
examine   examinar   40a, 40b
exchange   cambiar, canjear *(v)*
    25a, 26
exchange   el cambio   26
exchange rate   el tipo de cambio
    26
exclamation point   el signo de
    admiración   19c
excursion   la gira   30a
excuse   la excusa   17a
excuse oneself   disculparse *(v)*
    17a
exercise   el ejercicio   37f
exhibition   la exhibición   28b
existence   la existencia   22a
exit   la salida   25a, 35b, 36c
exit   salir*   3e, 36c
expensive   caro   24p, 25a
expiration date   la fecha de
    vencimiento   26
explain   explicar   17a, 37f
explanation   la explicación
    17a, 37f
expression   la expresión   17a
express oneself   expresarse *(v)*
    17a
extension   la extensión   3b
extinguish   extinguir*   39a
extract   extraer*   1e
extraction   la extracción   1e
eye   el ojo   12a
eye doctor   el médico oculista
    38a, 40a
eyebrow   la ceja   12a
eyedrops   las gotas para los ojos
    40a
eyeglasses   las gafas, los
    anteojos   37b, 40a
eyelash   la pestaña   12a
eyelid   el párpado   12a

F
fable   la fábula   28d
fabric   la tela, el paño   251
face   la cara   12a
face powder   los polvos para la
    cara   25f
factor   el factor   1f

factory   la fábrica   38d
factory worker   el obrero
    38a
fairy tale   el cuento de hadas
    28d
faith   la fé   11d, 21a
faithful   fiel   11d, 11e
fake   falso   13d
fall   caer*   3e
fall *(season)*   el otoño   5c
fall asleep   dormirse*   12b
fall in love   enamorarse   11c
false   falso   25i
false teeth   (see *dentures*)
family   la familia   10a
fan   el ventilador   33e
fan belt   la correa de ventilador
    33e
far   lejos   3d, 36c
farm   la granja, la hacienda
    15a
farmer   el campesino, el
    labrador   15a, 38a
farmland   tierras de labrantío
    13b
farsighted   hipérmetrope *(adj)*
    40a
fascinate   fascinar   11e
fascinating   fascinante   11e
fascination   la fascinación   11e
fashion   la moda   25k
fast   rápido   3e
fasten   asegurar   32c
fat   gordo   11a
father   el padre   10a
father-in-law   el suegro   10a
faucet   el grifo   23a, 35c
fax machine   el fax   18a,
    18b, 42a
feather   la pluma   15b
February   febrero   5b
feel   sentirse*   12c (see
    sense), 21a, 40a
feel badly   sentirse* mal   12b, 40a
feel like   tener* ganas de
    21a
feel well   sentirse* bien   12b, 40a
feeling   el sentimiento   21a
felt   el fieltro   251
felt pen   el rotulador   7c, 19d
female   la hembra   11a
feminine   femenino   8a, 11a
feminism   el feminismo   44b
fence   la cerca   15a

fencing *(sport)* la esgrima
27b
fencing bout el encuentro de
esgrima   27b
fennel el hinojo   14e
fetus el feto   44b
fever la fiebre   40a
fiancé el novio   10b, 11c
fiancée la novia   10b, 11c
fiber la fibra   13c
fiction la ficción   20a, 28d
field el campo   13b, 27b
field *(of study)* el campo
(de estudio)   37f
field hockey el hockey sobre
hierba   27b
fig el higo   14d, 24f
fig tree la higuera   14c
fight luchar, pelear *(v)*; la
pelea *(n)*   39b
figure la figura   2a
figure of speech la figura
retórica   17a
file *(office)* el archivo   38c,
42b
file *(tool)* la lima   25b
file card la ficha   38c
filet el filete   24g
filing cabinet el archivo, el
fichero   38c
fill llenar   3c
filling *(dental)* el empaste
40b
film la película   25d
film projector el proyector
37f
filter el filtro   33e
fine multar, dar* una multa
41
fine, ticket la multa   33c
fine arts las bellas artes   37e
finger el dedo   12a
fingernail la uña   12a
fingerprints las huellas digitales
39b
finish, end terminar   4e
Finland Finlandia   30b
fire *(dismiss from job)* echar
38d
fire el fuego   13c, 39a
fire alarm la alarma de
incendios   39a
fire escape la escalera de
incendios   39a

fire extinguisher el extinguidor
de incendios   39a
fire hydrant la boca de
incendio   39a
firearm el arma de fuego *(f)*
39b
firefighter el bombero   39a
firefly la luciérnaga   15d
fireman el bombero   38a
fireplace la chimenea   23a
fireproof incombustible   39a
first aid los primeros auxilios
39a, 39c
first class la primera clase
30a, 32a, 34
first name nombre (de pila)
11f, 38b
fir tree el abeto   14c
fish el pescado, el pez   15c,
24d
fish pescar *(v)*   15c, 36b
fish store la pescadería   24n
fishbone la espina   15c
fisherman el pescador   15c
fishhook el anzuelo   15c
fishing la pesca   15c
fishing rod la caña de pescar
15c
fix reparar   25i, 33c
fixed price el precio fijo
24m, 25a
flame la llama   39a
flannel la franela   251
flash *(photo/camera)* el flash
25d
flashlight la linterna   25b
flatter adular *(v)*   21a
flattery la adulación   21a
flavor el sabor   12c
flea la pulga   15d
flight el vuelo   32a
flight attendant el (la)
aeromozo(a), la azafata   32c
floor el suelo   23a
floor *(level)* el piso   23a,
35b
floppy disk el disco flexible
42b
flour la harina   24i
flour sifter el cernidor de
harina   23d
flow fluir*   13b
flow chart el organigrama   42b
flower florecer *(v)*   14a

flower   la flor   14b
flowerbed   el arriate, el macizo   14b
flu   la gripe   40a
fluorescent   fluorescente   25b
flute   la flauta   25c
fly   la mosca   15d
fly   volar*   15b, 32c
focus   enfocar *(v)*   25d
fog   la neblina   6a
foggy   brumoso   6a
foliage   el follaje   14a
folklore   el folklore   28d
folk music   la música folklórica   28c
follow   seguir*   3e, 36c
food   la comida   24a
food chain   la cadena alimenticia   44a
food coloring   coloración para comida   7c
fool, clown   el (la) tonto(a), el (la) bufón(ona)   11e
foolish   tonto   11e
foot   el pie   12a
football   el fútbol americano   27f
footnote   la nota   20a
for   para, por   8g
for example   por ejemplo   44c
for sale   de venta   25c
forehead   la frente   12a
foreign currency   la moneda extranjera   31
foreign exchange   las divisas   26
foreigner   el (la) extranjero(a)   31
forest   la selva, el bosque   13b
forget   olvidar(se)   22b
fork   el tenedor   23d, 24l
form   el formulario   31
fossil   el fósil   13c
fossil fuel   el combustible de fósil   13c, 44a
fox   el zorro   15a
fraction   la fracción   1f
fracture   la fractura   39c
France   Francia   30b
free   libre   18b
freeze   helarse*, congelarse   6a

freezer   el congelador   23d
French   francés(esa)   *(adj, n)*   30d
French fries   las papas fritas   24g
frequent   frecuente   4e
frequently   con frecuencia   4e
fresco painting   el fresco   28b
Friday   el viernes   5a
fried   frito   *(adj)*   24p
friend   el (la) amigo(a)   10b
friendly   amistoso   11e
friendship   la amistad   10b
frog   la rana   15c
from   de   3d, 8g
front page   la primera plana   20a
frosted *(hair)*   escarchado   *(adj)*   12d
fruit   la fruta   14d, 24f
fruit store   la frutería   24n
fruit tree   el frutero   14c
frying pan   la sartén   23d
fuel   el combustible   13c
full   lleno   3c
fun   la alegría, la diversión   21a
function   la función   42b
funny   cómico   11e
fur coat   el abrigo de piel   25k
furniture   los muebles   23c
fuse   el fusible   25b
fusion reactor   el reactor de fusión   42b

G
galaxy   la galaxia   13a
game   el juego, el partido   27a, 27b
garage   el garaje   23a, 35b
garden   el jardín   14e, 23a
garlic   el ajo   14e, 24j
gas   el gas   13c, 23e
gas pedal   el acelerador   33e
gas station   la gasolinera   33c
gas tank   el tanque   33e
gasoline   la gasolina   13c, 33c
gate   la puerta   32a
gather   recoger*   14a
gauze   la gasa   39c

gearshift el cambio de velocidad 33e
Gemini Géminis 5d
gender el género 8a
generator el generador 33e
generosity la generosidad 11e
generous generoso 11e
genre el género 28d
gentle *(mild)* suave 11e
gentle *(tame)* manso 11e
gentleman el caballero 11a
geography la geografía 13e, 37e
geometry la geometría 2b, 37e
geothermal energy la energía geotérmica 44a
geranium el geranio 14b
German alemán(-ana) *(adj, n)* 30d
Germany Alemania 30b
gerund el gerundio 8a
get dressed vestirse* 25m
get up levantarse *(v)* 3e, 12b
gift el regalo 11c, 25a
giraffe la jirafa 15a
girl la chica, la muchacha 11a, 11b
girlfriend la novia, la amiga 10b
gladiolus el gladiolo 14b
glass *(drinking)* el vaso 23d, 241
globe el globo 13e
glossy finish el acabado brillante 25d
glove el guante 25k, 27b
glove compartment la guantera 33e
glue el pegamento 19d
go ir* 3e, 36c
go away irse *(v)* 3e
go down bajar 3e, 36c
go forward adelantarse *(v)* 33c
go out salir* 3e, 29b
go to bed acostarse* 12b
go up subir 3e, 36c
goal *(soccer)* el gol 27b
goalie *(soccer)* el (la) portero(a) 27b
goat la cabra, el cabrito 15a, 24c

God Dios 11d
gold el oro 13c, 25i
gold dorado *(adj)* 7a
golden anniversary aniversario de oro 11c
goldfish la carpa dorada 15c
golf el golf 27b
good bueno 11e, 24p
goose el ganso, el ánsar 15b
gossip chismear, el chisme 17a
govern gobernar* 43
government el gobierno 43
graceful gracioso 11e
grade *(school class)* la clase 37a
grade *(school mark)* la nota 37f
graduate graduarse 11f
grain el grano 14a, 24i
gram el gramo 3a
grammar la gramática 8a, 37f
grandchild el nieto 10a
grandfather el abuelo 10a
grandfather clock el reloj de caja 4d
grandmother la abuela 10a
grand piano el piano de cola 28c
grapefruit la toronja, el pomelo 14d, 24f
grapes las uvas 14d, 24f
grass la hierba, el césped 13b, 14e
grasshopper el saltamontes, el chapulín 15d
grater el rallador 23d
gravity la gravedad 13a
gray gris 7a
great-aunt la tía abuela 10a
great-grandchild el bisnieto 10a
great-grandfather el bisabuelo 10a
great-grandmother la bisabuela 10a
great-uncle el tío abuelo 10a
Greece Grecia 30b
greed, avarice la avaricia 11e
greedy avaro, avaricioso 11e

Greek griego(a) *(adj, n)*
30d
green verde 7a
green pepper el pimiento verde
14e
greenhouse el invernadero
14a
Greenland Groenlandia 30b
greeting el saludo 16a
grocery store la tienda de
comestibles 24n
groom el novio 11c
ground floor la planta baja
23a, 23g
grow crecer* 3c, 11b
grow up hacerse* mayor
11b
growth el crecimiento 3c
Guatemalan guatemalteco(a)
(adj, n) 30d
guide el (la) guía 36a
guidebook la guía del viajero
25o, 36a
guilt la culpa 41
guilty culpable 41
guitar la guitarra 28c
guitarist el (la) guitarrista
28c
gulf el golfo 13b
gums las encías 40b
gun la pistola 39b
gymnasium el gimnasio
27a, 37c
gynecologist el (la)
ginecólogo(a) 40a

H
habit el hábito 11e
hail el granizo 6a
hair el pelo 12a, 12b
hair dryer el secador 12d
hair spray la laca 12d, 25f
haircut el corte de pelo 12d
hairdresser el peluquero, la
peluquera 12d, 38a
hake la merluza 15c, 24d
half la mitad *(n)*; medio
(adj) 3c
hall el vestíbulo 23b
hallway el pasillo, el corredor
23a, 37c
ham el jamón 24c
hammer el martillo *(n)*;
martillar *(v)* 25b

hand la mano 12a, 25i
hand *(of watch)* la manecilla
4d, 25i
handcuffs las esposas 39b
handicapped incapacitado
11a
handkerchief el pañuelo
25k
handle *(car door)* la manija
33e
handle *(knife)* el mango
23d
handlebar el manillar 33a
handshake el apretón de manos
16a
handsome guapo 11a
hang up colgar* 18b
happen pasar, ocurrir 4e
happiness la felicidad 11e,
21a
happy alegre, contento 11e,
21a
Happy Birthday! ¡Feliz
cumpleaños! 11c, 29c
hard duro 13d
hardware *(computer)* el
elemento físico, el hardware
42b
hardware store la ferretería
25b
hard-working trabajador
11e
hare la liebre 15a
harmony la armonía 28c
harp el arpa 28c
harpsichord el clavicordio
28c
hat el sombrero 25k
hate el odio *(n)*; odiar *(v)*
11e, 21b
hateful odioso 11e
hatred el odio 21b
have to tener* que 21a
hazard flash las luces de
emergencia 33e
he él 8h
head la cabeza 12a
head of state el (la) jefe de
estado 43
headache el dolor de cabeza
40a
heading el membrete 19c
headlight el faro delantero
33e

headline el titular 20a
headphones los auriculares 20b, 32c
heal *(a cut)* cicatrizar 40a
health la salud 11a, 40a
healthy saludable, sano 11a, 40a
hear oír* 12c
hearing el oído 12c
heart el corazón 12a, 40a
heart attack el ataque cardíaco 40a
hearts *(cards)* los corazones 27a
heat el calor 13c
heater la calefacción 33e
heating la calefacción *(n)* 23e
heavy *(liquid)* espeso 3b
heavy *(weight)* pesado 3b, 11a, 13d, 31
hectare la hectárea 3a
hectogram el hectogramo 3a
hedge el seto vivo 14a
height la estatura 11a
helmet el casco 27b
help ayudar *(v)* 39a
Help! ¡Socorro! 39a, 39c
hemisphere el hemisferio 13e
hen la gallina 15b
heptagon el heptágono 2a
her su, sus 8f
herb la hierba, la yerba 24j
here aquí, acá 3d, 36c
heredity la herencia 11c
hero el héroe 28e
heroine la heroína 28e
herring el arenque 24d
herself se 8k
hesitate vacilar 17a
hesitation la vacilación 17a
hexagon el hexágono 2a
hiccup hipar *(v)* 40a
hiccup el hipo 40a
high *(temperature)* alto 6c
high school el colegio, la escuela secundaria 37d, 38b
high school teacher el profesor, la profesora 37d
highway la carretera 33c
hill la colina 13b
him lo, le 8i

himself se 8k
Hindu el (la) hindú *(adj, n)* 11d
hip la cadera 12a
hippopotamus el hipopótamo 15a
hire contratar *(v)* 38d
his su, sus 8e
history la historia 37e
hit *(ball)* pegarle a *(v)* 27b
hobby el pasatiempo 27a
hockey el hockey 27b
hole el agujero 25g
holiday *(official)* el día de fiesta 5a, 29a
Holland Holanda 30b
home base la base meta 27b
home run el jonrón 27b
homework la tarea 37f
homosexual homosexual 44b
homosexuality la homosexualidad 44b
Honduran hondureño(a) *(adj, n)* 30d
honest honesto, recto 11e
honesty la honradez 11e
honey la miel 24j
honeymoon la luna de miel 11c
hood el capó 33e
hope la esperanza *(n)*; esperar *(v)* 21a
horizontal horizontal 3d
horn la corneta 28c
horn *(car)* la bocina 33e
horoscope el horóscopo 5d
horse el caballo 15a
horse racing las carreras de caballo 27b
horsepower el caballo de fuerza 33e
horseradish el rábano picante 24j
horticulture la horticultura 14a
hospital el hospital 39c
hot caliente 24p
hot water el agua caliente 35c
hotel el hotel 35a
hour la hora 4c
hourly por hora, cada hora 4c

house   la casa   23a
house of representatives   la cámara de representantes   43
How?   ¿Cómo?   9
How much?   ¿Cuánto?   3c, 9
howl   aullar*   15a
hug   el abrazo   19b
human   humano   11d, 15a
human being   el ser humano   11d
humanitarian   humanitario   11e
humanity   la humanidad   11d
humble   humilde   11e
humid   húmedo   6a
humidity   la humedad   6a
humility   la humildad   11e
humor   el humor   11e
hunger   el hambre   *(f)*   12b
hunt   cazar   15a
hunter   el cazador   15a
hunting   la caza   *(n)*   15a
hurricane   el huracán   6a, 13b
hurry   darse* prisa   39b
hurt   doler*   40a, 40b
husband   el marido   10a, 11c
hydrogen   el hidrógeno   13c
hyena   la hiena   15a
hygiene   la higiene   12d
hygienic   higiénico   12d
hyperbole   la hipérbole   28d
hyphen   el guión   19c
hypothesis   la hipótesis   22a

I
I   yo   8h
ice   el hielo   6a, 13b
ice cream   el helado   24h
ice cream parlor   la heladería   24n
ice cubes   los cubitos de hielo   35b
ice hockey   el hockey sobre hielo   27b
icosahedron   el icosaedro   2a
idea   la idea   22a
idealism   el idealismo   11e
idealist   el (la) idealista   11e
identification   la identificación   11f
identification card   la tarjeta de identificación   31, 35b
identify   identificar   17a

ideology   la ideología   43
idiom   el modismo   28d
if   si   8o
ignition   el encendido   33e
ignorance   la ignorancia   11e
ignorant   ignorante   11e, 22a
illegal   ilegal   41
illustration   la ilustración   20a
imaginary   imaginario   1d
imagination   la imaginación   11e, 22a
imaginative   imaginativo   11e
imagine   imaginar   22b
impatient   impaciente   11e
imperative   imperativo   8a
imperfect   imperfecto   8a
import   importar   31
impossible   imposible   21c
imprison   aprisionar, encerrar*   41
imprudent   imprudente   11e
impudence   la insolencia   11e
impudent   insolente   11e
impulse   el impulso   11e
impulsive   impulsivo   11e
in   en   3d, 8g
in front of   delante de, en frente de   3d, 36c
incinerator   el incinerador   44a
incisor   el diente incisivo   40b
income   los ingresos   26
increase   aumentar   3c
indecision   la indecisión   11e
indecisive   indecisivo   11e
indefinite   indefinido   8a
independent   independiente   11e
index   el índice   20a
index finger   el dedo índice   12a
Indian   indio(a)   *(adj, n)*   13b
indicate   señalar   17a
indication   la indicación   17a
indicative   indicativo   8a
indifference   la indiferencia   11e, 21a
indifferent   indiferente   11e, 21a

indigestion la indigestión 40a
indirect indirecto 8a
industrial industrial 13c
industry la industria 13c
inexpensive barato 25a
infection la infección 40a
infinitive el infinitivo 8a
inflation la inflación 43
inform avisar 17a
information la información 18b
infrared light la luz infrarroja 13c
ingenious ingenioso 11e
inherit heredar 11c
injection la inyección 25h, 40a
injure herir* 39b
injury la herida 39b
ink la tinta 19d, 37b
innocence la inocencia 11e, 41
innocent inocente 11e, 41
insect el insecto 15d
inside (of) dentro (de) 3d, 36c
instant instante (adj, n) 4c
instrument el instrumento 27a, 28c
insulation wire el alambre aislante 25b
insulin la insulina 25h
insurance el seguro 26, 30a
insurance card la tarjeta de seguro 33b
insurance policy la póliza de seguros 26
insurance premium la prima de seguros 26
integer entero 1d
intelligence la inteligencia 11e
intelligent inteligente 11e
intensive care el cuidado intensivo 39c
intercom el interfono, el intercomunicador 18a, 38c
interest el interés 26
interest rate la tasa de interés 26
interesting interesante 22a
interface el conector entre unidades 42b

intermission el entreacto 28e
internist el internista 40a
interrogative interrogativo 8a
interrupt interrumpir 17a
interruption la interrupción 17a
intersection la bocacalle, el cruce 33c, 33d, 36a
interview la entrevista 20a, 20b, 21o
intransitive intransitivo 8a
introduce (someone) presentar 16b
invertebrate invertebrado (adj, n) 15a
invest invertir* 26
investment la inversión 26
invite invitar 17a
invitation la invitación 17a, 29b
iodine el yodo 13c, 39c
irascible colérico 11e
Ireland Irlanda 30b
Irish irlandés(-desa) (adj, n) 30d
iron (metal) el hierro 13c
iron (appliance) planchar (v); la plancha (n) 23d, 25g
ironic irónico 11e
ironing board la tabla de planchar 25g
irony la ironía 11e, 28d
irrational number el número irracional 1d
irregular irregular 8a
irritable irritable 11e
Islamic islámico 11d
island la isla 13b
isosceles isósceles 2a
Israel el Israel 30b
it lo, la 8i
Italian italiano(a) (adj, n) 30d
italics la bastardilla 19c
Italy Italia 30b
itch la comezón 40a
its su, sus 8e

J
jack (car) el gato 33e
jacket la chaqueta 25k
jail la cárcel 41

jail encarcelar 41
jam la mermelada 24j
January enero 5b
Japan el Japón 30b
Japanese japonés *(adj, n)* 30d
jaw la mandíbula 12a, 40b
jazz el jazz 25j, 28c
jealous celoso 11e
jealousy los celos 11e
jest bromear 17a
jewel la joya 25i
jewelry store la joyería 25i
Jewish judío(a) *(adj, n)* 11d
job el trabajo, el puesto 11f, 38a
jog correr a trote corto 27a
joke el chiste 17a
journalist el (la) periodista 20a, 38a
journey el viaje 30a
joy la alegría 21a
Judaism el judaísmo 11d
judge el juez *(n)*; juzgar *(v)* 41
judgment el juicio 22a, 41
juice el jugo, el zumo 24k
July julio 5b
June junio 5b
junior high school el instituto de bachillerato elemental 37a, 38b
Jupiter Júpiter 13a
jury el jurado 41
just justo 4e
justice la justicia 22a, 41

K

keep quiet callarse *(v)* 17a
Keep to the right. Conserve su derecha. 33d
ketchup la salsa de tomate 24j
kettle el hervidor, la cafetera 23d
key la llave 23d, 35b
keyboard el teclado 19d, 42b
keyboard instruments los instrumentos de teclado 28c
kick *(ball)* patear 27b
kidnap secuestrar 41
kidney el riñón 40a

kill matar 39b
killer el asesino 39b
kilogram el kilogramo 3a
kilometer el kilómetro 3a
kindergarten la escuela de párvulos 37a
king el rey 27a, 43
kiss besar 11c, 21b
kiss el beso 11c
kitchen la cocina 23b
knapsack la mochila 27a, 31
knee la rodilla 12a
knife el cuchillo 23d, 241, 39b
knight *(chess)* el caballo 27a
know saber*, conocer* 16b, 22b
knowledge el conocimiento 22a
knowledgeable informado 22a
knuckle el nudillo 12a

L

lab technician el (la) ayudante de laboratorio 37d
label la etiqueta 25a
laboratory el laboratorio 13c, 37c
labor union el sindicato 43
lace el encaje 251
lack faltar 25a
ladder la escalera 39a
ladle el cucharón 23d
lady la señora 11a
laity el laicado 11d
lake el lago 13b, 36b
lamb el cordero 15a, 24c
lamp la lámpara 23c, 35c
land la tierra, el terreno 13b
land aterrizar *(v)* 32c
landfill el terraplén de desperdicios 44a
landing el aterrizaje 32c
landing gear el tren de aterrizaje 32c
landlord el propietario, el patrón 23g
landscape el paisaje 13b
lane *(traffic)* el carril 33c
language lab el laboratorio de lenguas 37c

languages (foreign) las lenguas
(extranjeras) 37e
large grande 3c, 11a
laryngitis la laringitis 40a
laser el láser 42a
laser beam el rayo láser
42a
last durar 4e
late tarde 4e, 32b, 34
Latin America Latinoamérica
30b
latitude la latitud 13e
laugh reírse* 11e, 21a
laughter la risa 11e, 21a
launch lanzar 42a
launch pad la plataforma de
lanzamiento 42a
laundry la lavandería 25g
lava la lava 13b
law el derecho, las leyes
37e, 41
lawful legal 41
lawsuit el pleito, la demanda
41
lawyer el abogado 38a, 41
laxative el laxante 25h
lay person el laico 11d
layer el estrato 13b
laziness la pereza 11e
lazy perezoso 11e
lead el plomo 13c
leaded gas la gasolina con
plomo 33c
leaf la hoja 14a
leaf through *(pages)* hojear
20a
leap year el año bisiesto 5b
learn aprender 22b, 37f
leather de cuero, de piel *(adj)*
13c
leather el cuero 25l
leave salir*, partir 3e, 34
lecture la conferencia *(n)*;
dar* *(v)* una conferencia
17a, 37f
left izquierdo 3d
leg la pierna 12a
legal legal 41
legend la leyenda 28d
legislation la legislación 43
lemon el limón 14d, 24f
lemon tree el limonero 14c
length la longitud 3a
lengthen alargar 25m

lentil la lenteja 14e
Leo Leo 5d
leopard el leopardo 15a
lesbian la lesbiana 44b
lesbianism el lesbianismo
44b
less menos 3c
letter *(of the alphabet)* la letra
8a, 19c
letter la carta 19d
letter carrier el cartero 19e
letterhead el papel con
membrete 19d
lettuce la lechuga 14e, 24e
leukemia la leucemia 40a
level llano 3d
liberal liberal 11e, 43
Libra Libra 5d
librarian el (la) bibliotecario(a)
37d
library la biblioteca 37c
license plate la placa 33e
lid la tapa 23d
lie mentir* *(v)*; la mentira
(n) 17a
lie down acostarse*, tumbarse
3e
life la vida 11c
life jacket el chaleco salvavidas
32c
life sentence la condena
perpetua 41
lift levantar 3e
liftoff el despegue 32c
light la luz 6a, 13a
light *(color)* claro *(adj)* 7b
light *(weight)* ligero *(adj)*
3b, 13d
light blue azul claro 7a
light bulb la bombilla 25b
lighter el mechero, el
encendedor 25e
lightning relampaguear *(v)*
6a, 6b
lightning el relámpago 6a
lights las luces 35c
like gustarle a uno *(v)* 21b
lily la azucena 14b
lima bean el frijol de media
luna 14e
line la línea 2b
line *(queue)* la cola 26
line up hacer* cola 26
lining el forro 25g

lion   el león   15a
lip   el labio   12a, 40b
lipstick   el lápiz de labios   25f
liqueur   el licor   24k
liquid   el líquido   13c
Lisbon   Lisboa   30c
listen to   escuchar   12c, 17a, 37f
liter   el litro   3a
literal   literal   17a
literature   la literatura   28d, 37e
litigate   litigar sobre   41
litigation   el litigio, el pleito   41
little   pequeño   3c, 11a
little finger   el dedo meñique   12a
live   vivir   11c, 23f
lively   vivo   7b, 11e
liver   el hígado   24c
living room   la sala   23b
loan   el préstamo   26
lobby   el vestíbulo   28a, 35b
lobster   la langosta   24d
locate   localizar   13e
location   la localización   13e
logarithm   logaritmo   1f
London   Londres   30c
long   largo   3b, 37f
long-distance call   la llamada de larga distancia   18b
longitude   la longitud   13e
look after   cuidar   14a, 40a
look at   mirar   12c, 20b
look for   buscar   25a
look forward to   esperar con placer anticipado   4e
loose   suelto   25l
lose   perder*   27b
lose consciousness   perder* el conocimiento   40a
loss   la pérdida   26, 27b
lost and found   la oficina de objetos perdidos   32a
lotion   la loción   25f
loudspeaker   el altavoz   20b
louse   el piojo   15d
lovable   amable   11e
love   querer*, amar   (v); el amor   (n)   11c, 11e, 21b
love affair   el amorío   10b
lover   el (la) amante   10b
loving   cariñoso   11e

low   bajo   6c
luggage   el equipaje   31, 35b
luggage rack   el portaequipajes   35b
lump   el bulto   40a
lunar   lunar   13a
lunar eclipse   el eclipse lunar   13a
lunar module   el módulo lunar   42a
lunch   el almuerzo   24a
lung   el pulmón   12a, 40a
Lutheran   luterano(a)   (adj, n)   11d
Luxembourg   Luxemburgo   30b
luxury hotel   el hotel de primera categoría   35a
lymphatic system   el sistema linfático   40a

M

mad   enojado, enfadado   11e
madness   la locura   11e
magazine   la revista   20a, 25o, 37b
magistrate   el magistrado   41
maid   la criada   35b
mail   el correo   19e
mail delivery   la distribución de correo   19e
mailbox   el buzón   19e, 23a
mailman   el cartero   19e
main   principal   8a
main character   el (la) protagonista   28d
main office   la oficina central   37c
make a call   hacer* una llamada   18b
make a mistake   equivocarse   (v)   37f
make a stop   hacer* una escala   32c
make the bed   hacer* la cama   23f
makeup   el maquillaje   12d, 25f
male   el macho   11a, 38b
malicious   malévolo   11e
malign   hablar mal de   (v)   17a
malleable   maleable   13d
mammal   el mamífero   15a

man el hombre 11a
manager el (la) gerente 26, 35b, 38d
mandolin la mandolina 28c
manicure la manicura 12d
many muchos 8n
map el mapa 13e, 37b
maple tree el arce 14c
March marzo 5b
margarine la margarina 24h
margin el márgen 19c, 19d
marker el marcador 19d, 25c
market el mercado 24n, 38d
marital status el estado civil 11c, 38b
marriage el matrimonio 11c
marriage ceremony la boda 11c
marry *(someone)* casar 11c
Mars Marte 13a
mascara el rimel 12d, 25f
masculine masculino 8a, 11a
masking tape la cinta adhesiva 25b
mass la masa 3b
Mass la misa 11d
massage el masaje 12d
masterpiece la obra maestra 28b
matches las (los) cerillas(-os), los fósforos 25e
mathematics las matemáticas 37e
matrimony el matrimonio 11c
matte finish el acabado mate 25d
matter la materia 13c
matter importar 21a
maximum máximo 3b, 6c, 31
May el mayo 5b
mayonnaise la mayonesa 24j
me me 8i, 8j
meadow el prado 13b
meal la comida 24a
mean querer* decir, significar *(v)* 17a
meaning el significado 17a
meanness la maldad 11e
measles el sarampión 40a
measure medir* 3b

measuring cups juego de tazas de medir 23d
measuring spoons juego de cucharitas de medir 23d
measuring tape cinta métrica 3b
meat la carne 24c
mechanic el mecánico 33c, 38a
mechanical mecánico 25b, 33c
medical records los antecedentes médicos 40a
medicine la medicina 25h, 37e, 40a
mediocre mediocre 21b
Mediterranean Mediterráneo 6a
medium mediano 11a
meet conocer* 16b
melon el melón 14d
melting point punto de fusión 6c
membrane la membrana 14a
memory la memoria 22a, 42b
mend remendar* 25g
mention mencionar 17a
menu el menú, la lista de platos 24g
meow maullar* 15a
mercury mercurio 6c, 13c
Mercury Mercurio 13a
merge el empalme 33d
meridian meridiano 13e
Merry Christmas. Feliz Navidad. 16c, 29c
message el mensaje 18b, 35b
metal el metal 13c
metamorphosis la metamorfosis 15d
metaphor la metáfora 17a, 28d
meteor el meteoro 13a
meter el metro 3a
methane el metano 13c
Methodist el (la) metodista *(adj, n)* 11d
Mexico México 30b
Mexico City la Ciudad de México 30c
microcomputer la microcomputadora 42b

microphone   el micrófono   20b

microscope   el microscopio   13c

microwave   la microonda   42a

microwave oven   el horno de microondas   23d

middle finger   el dedo medio   12a

midnight   la medianoche   4a

mild *(weather)*   templado   6a, 6b

mild *(flavor)*   suave   24p

mileage   el kilometraje   33e

milk   la leche   24h

millimeter   el milímetro   3a

millionth   millonésimo   1b

mind   la mente   22a

mineral   el mineral   13c

mineral water   el agua mineral *(f)*   24k

minimum   mínimo   3b, 6c

minister   el ministro   11d, 43

mint   la menta   14e, 24j

minus   menos   1e, 6c

minute   el minuto   4c

mirror   el espejo   23c, 35c

mischievous   travieso   11e

miss *(the train)*   perder*   34

Miss   Señorita (Srta.)   11f, 16b

missile   el proyectil   42a

mistake   el error   37f

mixer   la batidora   23d

model   el modelo   13c

modem   el módem   42b

molar   la muela   40b

mole   el topo   15a

molecular   molecular   13c

molecule   la molécula   13c, 42a

mom   la mamá   10a

moment   el momento   4c

monarchy   la monarquía   43

Monday   el lunes   5a

money   el dinero   26

money order   el giro postal   19e, 26

monitor   el monitor   42b

monk   el monje   11d

monkey   el mono   15a

monologue   monólogo   28d

monorail   el monocarril   42a

month   el mes   4c

monthly   mensualmente   4c, 5b

monument   el monumento   36a

mood *(grammar)*   el modo   8a

mood   el humor   11e, 21a

moon   la luna   5c, 6a, 13a

moonbeam   el rayo de luna   13a

morality   la moralidad   44b

more   más   3c

morning   la mañana   4a

mortgage   la hipoteca   26

mosque   la mezquita   11d

mosquito   el mosquito   15d

moth   la polilla   15d

mother   la madre   10a

mother-in-law   la suegra   10a

motion   la moción   3e

motor   el motor   33e

motorcycle   la motocicleta   33a

mountain   la montaña   13b

mountain climbing   el alpinismo   27a, 36b

mountainous   montañoso   13b

mountain range   la cordillera   13b

mouse   el ratón   15a

mouth   la boca   12a, 40b

move   mover*   3e

move *(residence)*   mudarse *(v)*   23f

movement   el movimiento   3e

movie   la película   28a

movie camera   la cámara cinematográfica   25d

movie director   el director cinematográfico   38a

movie star   la estrella de cine   28a

Mr.   Señor (Sr.)   11f, 16b

Mrs.   Señora (Sra.)   11f, 16b

much   mucho   3c

muffler   el mofle   33e

mugginess   el bochorno   6a

muggy   bochornoso   6a, 6b

mule   el mulo   15a

multiple   múltiple   1f

multiplication   la multiplicación   1e

multiplication table la tabla de multiplicación 1e
multiply multiplicar 1e
mumble mascullar 17a
mumps las paperas 40a
murder el asesinato, el homicidio 39b
murmur murmurar 17a
muscle el músculo 12a, 40a
muscular dystrophy la distrofia muscular 40a
museum el museo 36a
mushroom la seta, el hongo 14e, 24e
music la música 25j, 28c, 37e
musician el (la) músico(a) 28c, 38a
mussels los mejillones 24d
mustache el bigote 12a
mustard la mostaza 24j
mute person el (la) mudo(a) 12c
my mi, mis 8e
myself me 8k
mystery el misterio 20a, 25o
myth el mito 11d, 28d
mythology la mitología 28d

N
nag regañar 17a
nail el clavo (n); clavar (v) 25b
nail polish esmalte para las uñas 12d, 25f
name el nombre 11f, 38b
napkin la servilleta 23d, 24l
narrow estrecho 3b
nation la nación 13e, 30a
national nacional 13e
nationality la nacionalidad 11f, 38b
natural natural 1d, 13b
natural gas el gas natural 13c
natural resources los recursos naturales 13c, 44a
nature la naturaleza 13b
navigable navegable 13b
navy blue azul marino 7a
near cerca 3d, 36c
nearsighted miope (adj)

neat limpio 11e
neck el cuello 12a
necklace el collar 25i
need necesitar (v); la necesidad (n) 21a
needle la aguja 40b
negative negativo 1d
neigh rebuznar 15a
neon light el alumbrado de neón 25b
nephew el sobrino 10a
Neptune Neptuno 13a
nerves los nervios 40a
nervous system el sistema nervioso 40a
net la red 27c
network la cadena 20b
neurologist el neurólogo 40a
neutron el neutrón 13c, 42a
never nunca 4e
New York Nueva York 30c
news report las noticias 20a
newscast el noticiario 20b
newspaper el periódico 20a, 25o
newsstand el kiosko 34
next to al lado de 3d
Nicaraguan el (la) nicaragüense (n, adj) 30d
nice simpático 11e
niece la sobrina 10a
night la noche 4a
nightingale el ruiseñor 15b
no no 16c
no one nadie 3c, 8n
no smoking no fumar 32a, 34
no smoking section la sección de no fumar 32a, 34
noise el ruido 12c
noisy ruidoso 12c
nonconformist el (la) disidente 11e
non-fiction la literatura no novelesca 20a
noodles los fideos 24i
noon el mediodía 4a
north el norte 3d
North America Norteamérica 30b
North Pole el Polo Norte 13e

Norway   Noruega   30b
Norwegian   noruego(a) *(adj, n)*   30d
nose   la nariz   12a
nostril   la ventana de la nariz   12a, 40a
notarize   legalizar, certificar   41
notary public   el notario público   41
note   la nota   19e, 20a, 28c
note pad   el bloc de papel   25c
notebook   el cuaderno   37b
notes   los apuntes   37f
nothing   nada   3c
noun   el sustantivo   8a
novel *(literature)*   la novela   20a, 25o, 28d
November   noviembre   5b
Novocain   la novocaína   40b
now   ahora   4e, 17b
nowadays   hoy día   4e
nowhere   en ninguna parte   3d
nuclear   nuclear   42a
nuclear disarmament   el desarme nuclear   42a
nuclear energy   la energía nuclear   13c, 42a
nuclear industry   la industria nuclear   42a
nuclear reactor   el reactor nuclear   42a
nuclear weapon   el arma nuclear *(f)*   44b
nucleus   el núcleo   13c, 14a
number   el número   1d, 8a, 38b
numeral   el número   1d
numerical   numérico   1d
nun   la monja   11d
nurse   el (la) enfermero(a)   38a, 40a
nursery school   la escuela de párvulos   37a
nut   la tuerca   25b
nylon   el nailon, el nilón   251

O

oak tree   el roble   14c
oat   la avena   24i
obesity   la obesidad   11a

obituaries   la necrología   20a
obituary   el obituario   20a
object   el objeto   8a
oboe   el oboe   28c
obstinate   obstinado   11e
obtuse   obtuso   2b
occasionally   de vez en cuando   4e
occupation   la profesión   38d
occur   occurrir, suceder   4e
ocean   océano   13b
octagon   el octógono   2a
octahedron   el octaedro   2a
October   octubre   5b
octopus   el pulpo   15c
odd   impar *(adj, n)*   1d
of   de   8g
offend   ofender   17a
office   la oficina   38d
office automation   la automatización de oficina   42b
office hours   las horas de consulta   40b
often   con frecuencia   4e
oil   el aceite   13c, 24j, 33e
ointment   el ungüento   25h
old   viejo   11b
old age   la vejez   11c
older *(in age)*   mayor   11b
olive   la aceituna   14d, 24e
olive tree   el olivo   14c
omelette   la tortilla   24h
on   encima de   3d, 8g
on time   a tiempo   32b, 34
once   una vez   4e
one way *(road sign)*   la dirección única   33d
onion   la cebolla   14e, 24e
only   solo, único *(adj)*   4e
only   sólo, solamente *(adv)*   4e
onomatopoeia   la onomatopeya   28d
opal   el ópalo   25i
opaque   opaco   7b, 13d
open   abierto *(pp)*, abrir *(v)*   25a
open *(a play)*   estrenar   28e
open an account   abrir una cuenta   26
opening hour   hora de abrir   25a
opening night   el estreno   28e

opera la ópera 28c
operate operar 40a
operating room la sala de operaciones 40a
operation la operación 40a
operator el operador 18b
ophthalmologist el oftalmólogo 40a
opinion la opinión 22a
opposite opuesto 2b
optimism el optimismo 11e
optimist el (la) optimista 11e
optimistic optimista 11e
oral oral 17a
orally oralmente 17a
orange (color) anaranjado 7a
orange (fruit) la naranja 14d, 24f
orange tree el naranjo 14c
orbit estar* en órbita, órbita 13a
orchestra la orquesta 28c
orchestra conductor el director de orquesta 28c
orchid la orquídea 14b
order mandar (v); el mandato (n) 17a, 24o
order pedir* 24o
ordinal ordinal 1d
organ el órgano 28c
organic orgánico 13c
organism el organismo 14a
oriental oriental 11d
original original 11e
ostrich el avestruz 15b
others otros 8n
our nuestro, nuestra, nuestros, nuestras 8e
ourselves nos 8k
out afuera (adv) 39a
outlet (electrical, telephone) la toma 18a, 25b
outside fuera 3d, 36c
outskirts las afueras 30a
outspoken franco 17a
owl el búho 15b
ox el buey 15a
oxygen el oxígeno 13c, 32c
oyster la ostra 24d

P
Pacific el Pacífico 13b

package el paquete 19e, 25a
pad el bloc 19d
pagan pagano (adj, n) 11d
page la página 19d, 20a
pail el cubo 23d
pain el dolor 40a
painful doloroso 40a
paint la pintura 7c, 23f, 28b
paintbrush la brocha 25b
painter el pintor, la pintora 7c, 28b
painting la pintura, el cuadro 23c, 28b
pair el par 3c, 25n
pajamas las pijamas 25k
palate el paladar 40b
palette la paleta 28b
palm tree la palma 14c
pamphlet el folleto 20a
pan la cacerola 23d
Panamanian panameño(a) (adj, n) 30d
panties las bragas 25k
pantry la despensa 23a
pants los pantalones 25k
paper el papel 19d, 25c, 37b
paper clip el sujetapapeles 19d
paperback book el libro en rústica 25o
parable la parábola 28d
paradox la paradoja 28d
paragraph el párrafo 19c
Paraguayan paraguayo(a) (adj, n) 30d
parakeet el perico 15b
parallel paralelo 2b
parallelogram paralelogramo 2a
paramedics los asistentes médicos 39a
parents los padres 10a
Paris París 30c
park aparcar, estacionar (v) 33c
park el parque 36a
parkbench el banco 36a
parking el estacionamiento 33c
parking meter el parquímetro 36a

parliament   el parlamento
43
parrot   el loro   15b
parsley   el perejil   14e, 24j
part   la parte   3c
participle   el participio   8a
particle   la partícula   13c
party   la fiesta   29b
party *(political)*   el partido
43
pass   pasar, adelantar *(v)*
33c
pass *(ball)*   pasar *(v)*   27b
pass *(football)*   el pase   27b
pass by   pasar   3e
passenger   el pasajero   32c,
33b
passive   pasivo   8a
passport   el pasaporte   31,
35b
past   pasado   4e, 8a
pastel *(art)*   el pastel   28b
pastry   el pastel   24i
pastry shop   la pastelería
24n
patience   la paciencia   11e,
21a
patient   paciente   11e, 40a
paw   la pata   15a
pawn *(chess)*   el peón   27a
pay   pagar   25a, 26, 35b
pay telephone   el teléfono
público   18a
payment   el pago   26
pea   el guisante   14e, 24e
peace   la paz   43
peach   el melocotón, el durazno
14d, 24f
peach tree   el melocotonero, el
duraznero   14c
peak   el pico   13b
peanut   el cacahuete   24f
pear   la pera   14d
pear tree   el peral   14c
pearl   la perla   25i
pedal   el pedal   33a
pedestrian   el peatón   33b
pedestrian crossing   el paso de
peatones   33c, 33d, 36a
pediatrician   el pediatra   40a
peel   pelar *(v)*   24o
pelican   el pelícano   15b
pen   la pluma   2b, 7c, 19d,
25c, 37b, 38c

pen name   el seudónimo
28d
penalty *(soccer)*   el tiro penal
27b
pencil   el lápiz   2b, 19d,
37b, 38c
pencil sharpener   el sacapuntas
25c
penicillin   la penicilina   25h
peninsula   la península   13b
pension   la jubilación   38d
pentagon   el pentágono   2a
people   la gente   11d
pepper   la pimienta   24j
perceive   percibir   12c
percent   el porcentaje   1f
perception   la percepción
12c
percussion instruments   los
instrumentos de percusión   28c
perfect   perfecto   8a
perfection   la perfección   11e
perfectionist   el (la)
perfeccionista   11e
perform   representar   28e
performance   la representación
28e
perfume   el perfume   12d,
25f
period *(punctuation sign)*   el
punto   19c
peripherals   el equipo periférico
42b
permanent press   inarrugable
(adj)   25l
permanent wave   el permanente
12d
person   la persona   8a, 11d
personal   personal   8a
personal computer   la
computadora personal   42b
personality   la personalidad
11e
personification   la
personificación   28d
personify   personificar   28d
perspire   sudar   6b
persuade   persuadir   22b, 41
Peruvian   peruano(a)   *(adj, n)*
30d
pessimism   el pesimismo
11e
pessimist   el (la) pesimista
11e

pessimistic pesimista 11e
pet el animal doméstico 15a
petal el pétalo 14b
petroleum el petróleo 13c, 44a
petunia la petunia 14b
pharmacist el (la) farmacéutico(a) 25h, 38a
philosophy la filosofía 37e
phone llamar por teléfono 18b
phonetics la fonética 8a
photocopier la fotocopiadora 38c
photo(graph) la foto(grafía) 20a, 25d
photosynthesis la fotosíntesis 14a
phrase la frase 19c
physical físico 13c
physics la física 13c, 37e
pianist el (la) pianista 28c
piano el piano 28c
pick la piqueta 25b
pickpocket el ratero, el carterista 39b
picky difícil 11e
pie el pastel 24g
piece el pedazo 3c
piece of furniture el mueble 23c
pig el cerdo 15a
pigeon el pichón 15b
pill la píldora 25h, 40a
pillow la almohada 23d, 35c
pilot el (la) piloto 32c, 38a
pimple el grano 40a
pincers las tenazas 25b
pineapple la piña 14d, 24f
pine tree el pino 14c
pink rosado 7a
pipe (*smoking*) la pipa 25e
Pisces Piscis 5d
place el lugar 3d, 19c, 38b
plagiarism el plagio 28d
plain el llano 13b
plane figures las figuras planas 2a
planet el planeta 13a
plant la planta 14a
plant (*factory*) la fábrica 38d
plastic el plástico 13c
plate el plato 23d, 241

platform la plataforma 34
platinum el platino 13c
play (*a record*) tocar 20a, 28c
play (*a sport*) jugar* 27a
play (*sports*) la jugada (*n*) 27b
play (*theater*) el drama (*n*) 20a
player (*music*) el (la) músico (a) 28c
player (*sports*) el jugador, la jugadora 27b
playing cards las cartas, los naipes 27a
playoffs el partido de desempate 27b
playwright el dramaturgo 28e
plea el alegato 41
plead guilty declararse culpable 41
plead not guilty declararse inocente 41
pleasant agradable 11e, 21b
please (*courtesy*) por favor 16c
pliers los alicates 25b
plot la trama, el argumento 20a, 28d, 28e
plug (*telephone*) la clavija 18a
plug (*electric*) el enchufe 25b
plum la ciruela 14d, 24f
plumage el plumaje 15b
plumber el plomero 38a
plumbing la fontanería 25b
plural plural 8a
plus más 1e, 6b
Pluto Plutón 13a
pneumonia la pulmonía, la neumonía 40a
pocket el bolsillo 25g, 27a
podiatrist el pedicuro 40a
poem el poema 20a
poet el (la) poeta(tisa) 28d
poetry la poesía 20a, 25o
point el punto 2b
point (*score*) el punto, el tanto 27b
point of view el punto de vista 28d
poison el veneno (*n*); envenenar (*v*) 40a

poisoning el envenenamiento
40a
Poland Polonia 30b
pole el polo 13e
police la policía 33b, 39b,
39c 42b
police station la comisaría
41
policeman el policía 33b,
39b, 42b
policewoman la policía 33b
policy la política 43
policy (insurance) la póliza
26
Polish polaco(a) *(adj, n)* 30d
political político 43
political party el partido
político 43
political science la ciencia
política 37e
politician el político 43
politics la política 43
pollen el polen 14a
pollution la contaminación
13c, 44a
polyester el poliester 25l
polyhedron el poliedro 2a
pond el estanque 13b, 37b
pool la alberca, la piscina 35b
poor pobre 11e
poplar tree el álamo 14c
poppy la amapola 14a
porch el portal, la terraza
cubierta 23a
pork el cerdo 24c
pork chop la chuleta de cerdo
24c
pornography la pornografía
44b
portable phone el teléfono
remoto 18a
porter el maletero 32a, 34,
35b
portion la porción 3c
portrait el retrato 28b
Portugal Portugal 30b
Portuguese portugués (esa)
(adj, n) 30d
position la posición 3d
positive positivo 1d
possessive posesivo 8e, 8f,
11e
postal code el código postal
19e, 38b

postal rate la tarifa postal
19e
postcard la tarjeta postal
19e
postdate posfechar *(v)*; la
posfecha *(n)* 26
pot la olla 23d
potato la papa, la patata
14e, 24e
pour echar, verter* 24o
powder el polvo 25h
power la potencia 1e, 43
practice practicar 27b
praise alabar 17a
pray orar, rezar 11d, 17a
prayer la oración 11d, 17a
precious precioso 25i
predicate el predicado 8a
preface el prefacio 28d
prefer preferir* 21b
pregnancy el embarazo 11c
pregnant embarazada 11c,
40a
prelude el preludio 28c
preposition la preposición
8g
Presbyterian el présbiteriano
(n, adj) 11d
prescription la receta 25h,
40a
present el presente 4e, 8a
present presente *(adj)* 4e
president el presidente 43
president (of a university) el
rector 37d
presumptuous presuntuoso
11e
pretentious pretencioso 11e
preterite el pretérito 8a
previous anterior 4e
price el precio 24m, 25a,
35b
price tag la etiqueta 25a
priest el cura, el sacerdote
11d
primate el primate 15a
prime (number) primo 1d
prince el príncipe 43
princess la princesa 43
principal (school) el director, la
directora 37d
print la impresión, imprimir *(v)*
20a
print escribir con letras de

molde *(v)* 11f
printed matter los impresos 19e
printer la impresora 42b
printing la imprenta 20a, 42b
prison la cárcel 41
private school la escuela privada 39a
problem el problema 1f, 22a, 37f
product el producto 1f
profession la profesión 11f, 38a, 38b
professional profesional 11f, 27b
professor el (la) profesor(a) 37d, 38a
profit la ganancia 26
program el programa 20b, 28e, 42b
programmer el programador 42b
programming la programación 42b
projector el proyector 20b
prologue el prólogo 28d
promise prometer *(v)*; la promesa *(n)* 17a
pronoun el pronombre 8a
pronounce pronunciar 17a
pronunciation la pronunciación 8a, 17a
propose proponer* 17a
prostitution la prostitución 44b
protect proteger* 39a
protest la protesta *(n)*; protestar *(v)* 43
Protestant el (la) protestante *(n, adj)* 11d
Protestantism el protestantismo 11d
proton el protón 13c, 42a
protractor *(drawing instrument)* el transportador 2b
proud orgulloso 11e
proverb el proverbio 28d
provided that con tal que 8o
province la provincia 13e
prudent prudente 11e
prune la ciruela pasa 14d, 24f
P.S. PD 19c

psychiatrist el (la) psiquiatra 38a, 40a
psychologist el (la) psicólogo(a) 38a
psychology la psicología 37e
public garden el jardín público 36a
public notices los avisos públicos 36a
public parking el estacionamiento público 33c
public prosecutor el acusador público 41
public washroom el servicio público 36a
publish publicar 20a
publisher el (la) editor(a) 20a
puck el disco 27b
pudding el budín 24g
Puerto Rican puertorriqueño(a) *(adj, n)* 30d
pull tirar 3e
pulse el pulso 40a
pumpkin la calabaza 14e
pun el retruécano 28d
punch el punzón 25b
punctuation la puntuación 19c
punish castigar 41
purchase la compra *(n)*; comprar *(v)* 25a
pure puro 7b, 13d
purple morado 7a
purse la bolsa 25n
push empujar 3e
put poner* 3e
put on ponerse* 25m
pyramid la pirámide 2a

Q

quadratic equation la ecuación de segundo grado 1f
quantity la cantidad 3c
quantum theory la teoría cuántica 42a
quart el cuarto 3a
quarter, trimester el trimestre 37f
queen la reina 27a, 43
question la pregunta 37f
question mark el signo de interrogación 19c
quickly rápidamente 3e

quotation mark las comillas 19c

quotient el cociente 1f

R

rabbi el rabino, el rabí 11d

rabbit el conejo 15a

race *(sports)* la carrera 27b

race la raza 11d

racetrack el hipódromo 27b

racism el racismo 44b

radiation la radiación 44a

radio el radio 20b, 23d, 35c

radioactive radioactivo 44a

radioactive waste los desechos radioactivos 44a

radish el rábano 14e

radius el radio 2a

railroad el ferrocarril 34

railroad station la estación del ferrocarril 34

railway crossing el cruce de vías 36a

rain llover* 6a

rain la lluvia 6a

rainbow el arco iris 6a

raincoat el impermeable 25k

rainy lluvioso 6a

raise someone criar 11c

ramp la rampa 33c

random access memory la memoria RAM 42b

rape violar *(v)*; la violación *(n)* 39b

rare raro 4e, 24b

rarely raramente, raras veces 4e

rash el sarpullido 40a

raspberry la frambuesa 14d, 24f

rat la rata 15a

ratio la proporción 1e

rational racional 1d

razor la afeitadora 12d, 25f

read leer 20a, 37f

reader el (la) lector(a) 20a

reading lamp la lámpara para leer 35c

reading passage la lectura 37f

real real 1d

real estate los bienes raíces 26

reason la razón 22a

reason razonar *(v)* 22b

rebellious rebelde 11e

receipt el recibo 26, 35b

receive recibir 19e

receiver el receptor 18a, 20b

recent reciente 4e

recently recientemente 4e

reception la recepción 11c

reception desk la recepción 35b

reciprocal recíproco 1d

recommend recomendar* 17a

record *(audio)* el disco 20a, 25i

record *(audio)* grabar 20b

record player el tocadiscos 20b, 37b

recover recobrarse *(v)* 40a

rectangle el rectángulo 2a

rectum el recto 40a

red rojo 7a

red-haired pelirrojo 11a

red snapper el huachinango 15c

referee el árbitro 27b

reference book el libro de consulta 20a, 25o

refined refinado 11e

reflect reflexionar, meditar 22b

reflexive reflexivo 8a, 8k

reform la reforma *(n)*; reformar *(v)* 43

refrigerator la nevera, el frigorífico 23d

refund reembolsar *(v)* 25a

refund el reembolso 25a

region la región 13e

registered letter la carta certificada 19e

registration la matrícula 37f

registration fees los derechos de matrícula 37f

regular regular 4e, 8a

rehearsal el ensayo 28e

rehearse ensayar 28e

relate relatar 17a

relative relativo 8a, 8m

relatives los parientes 10a

relax relajarse *(v)* 12b

relief el alivio 21a

relieve aliviar 21a

religion la religión 11d

religious religioso 11d
remain quedarse *(v)* 29b
remember recordar* 22b
remote control el control remoto 20b
rent alquilar *(v)*; el alquiler *(n)* 23g
rented car el coche alquilado 33a
repeat repetir* 17a, 37f
repetition la repetición 17a
reply responder, contestar 19e
reporter el reportero 20a
representative el(la) representante 43
reproach reprochar 17a
reproduce reproducir* 14a
reproduction la reproducción 14a
reptile el reptil 15c
republic la república 43
request pedir* *(v)*; la petición *(n)* 17a
rescue rescatar, el rescate 39a
reservation la reservación, la reserva 24m, 32a, 35b
reserved reservado 11e, 24m
residence la residencia 11f
resistant resistente 13d
respiratory system el sistema respiratorio 40a
rest descansar 12b
restaurant el restaurante 24m
restore restaurar 23f
résumé el curriculum vitae 38d
retail la venta al por menor 26
retire jubilarse *(v)* 38d
retirement la jubilación 38d
return volver*, regresar 3e
return *(an object)* devolver* 3e, 25a
return address la dirección del remitente 19e
return ticket el boleto de regreso 30a
review repasar *(v)*; el repaso *(n)* 37f
review *(book)* la reseña 20a

revolt el motín 43
revolution la revolución 43
rhetoric la retórica 17a, 28d
rhetorical retórico 17a
rheumatism el reumatismo, la reuma 40a
rhinoceros el rinoceronte 15a
rhombus el rombo 2a
rhubarb el ruibarbo 14e
rhyme la rima 28d
rhythm el ritmo 28c
ribbon *(typewriter)* la cinta de máquina de escribir 19d
rice el arroz 24i
rich rico 11e
rifle el rifle 39b
right correcto *(adj)* 37f
right recto *(adj)* 2b
right el derecho *(n)* 3d, 41
ring sonar *(v)* 18b
ring el anillo, la sortija 25i
ring finger el dedo anular 12a
rinse enjuagar(se) *(v)* 40b
rinse el enjuague 12d, 40b
riot el motín 43
ripe maduro 14a
rite el rito 11d
river el río 13b, 36b
road el camino 33c
road map el mapa de carreteras 33b
roar rugir* 15a
rob robar 39b
robber el ladrón 39b
robbery el robo 39b
robot el robot 42a
robust robusto 13d
rock la roca, la peña 13b
rock music la música rock 25j, 28c
role el papel 28e
rollerskating el patinaje sobre ruedas 27a
Roman numeral el número romano 1d
romantic romántico 11e
Rome Roma 30c
roof el tejado 23a
rook *(chess)* la torre 27a
room el cuarto, la habitación 23b, 35b

rooster el gallo 15b
root la raíz 1e, 14a, 40b
rope la cuerda 27a, 36b
rose la rosa 14b
rosemary el romero 14e, 24j
rough áspero 11e, 13d
rough draft el borrador 37f
round-trip ticket el boleto de ida y vuelta 30a
row la fila 28a
ruby el rubí 25i
rude mal educado 11e
rug la alfombra 23c
ruler la regla 2b, 19d, 37b, 38c
rumor el rumor 17a
run correr 3e, 12b, 27b
run over atropellar 39c
runway la pista 32c
rush hour la hora de punta 33c
Russia Rusia 30b
Russian ruso *(a)* *(adj, n)* 30d

S
sad triste 11e, 21a
sadness la tristeza 11e, 21a
safe la caja fuerte 26
safe deposit box la caja de seguridad 26
Sagittarius Sagitario 5d
salad la ensalada 24g
salamander la salamandra 15c
salary el salario, el sueldo 26, 38d
sale la venta 25a
salmon el salmón 15c, 24d
salt la sal 13c, 24j
salty salado 24p
salutation la salutación, el saludo 19c
Salvadoran salvadoreño *(a)* *(adj, n)* 30d
sand la arena 13b
sandwich la torta, el bocadillo 24g
sanitary napkins las servilletas higiénicas 25h
sapphire el zafiro 25i
sarcasm el sarcasmo 11e
sarcastic sarcástico 11e

sardine la sardina 15c, 24d
satellite el satélite 13a, 42a
satire la sátira 28d
satisfaction la satisfacción 21a
satisfied satisfecho 21a
satisfy satisfacer* 21a
Saturday el sábado 5a
Saturn Saturno 13a
saucer el platillo 23d, 24l
sausage la salchicha 24c
save ahorrar 26
savings los ahorros 26
savings account la cuenta de ahorros 26
savings bank la caja de ahorros 26
saw la sierra 25b
saxophone el saxofón 28c
say decir* 17a
scalene escaleno 2a
scarf la bufanda 25k
scene la escena 28e, 38c
scenery el decorado 28e
schedule el horario 4e, 34
schizophrenia la esquizofrenia 40a
school la escuela 37f
school bag la mochila 37b
schoolmate el (la) compañero(a) de clase 37d
school yard el patio 37c
school year el año escolar 5b, 37a
science la ciencia 37e
science fiction la ciencia ficción 20a, 25o
scientific research la investigación científica 42a
scientist el científico 38a
scissors las tijeras 12d, 19d, 38c, 39c
scorch chamuscar 25g
score marcar 27b
Scorpio Escorpión 5d
scorpion el alacrán 15d
Scotland Escocia 30b
screen la pantalla 25d, 28a, 42b
screw el tornillo *(n)*; atornillar *(v)* 25b
screwdriver el destornillador 25b
sculpt esculpir 28b

sculptor el escultor 28b
sculptress la escultora 28b
sculpture la escultura 28b
sea el mar 6a, 13b, 36b
seafood el pescado, el marisco 24d
seagull la gaviota 15b
seamstress la costurera 38a
search registrar 41
season la estación 5c
seat el asiento 28a, 32c, 34
seat (bicycle) el sillín 33a
seat belt el cinturón de seguridad 32c
secant la secante 2b
second el segundo 4c, 8a
secretary el (la) secretario(a) 37d, 38a, 40a
securities (stocks and bonds) los valores 26
sedative el sedante, el calmante 40a
seduction la seducción 11e
seductive seductivo 11e
see ver* 12c, 30a
seed la semilla (n); sembrar* (v) 14a
segment el segmento 2b
selfish egoísta 11e
self-service el autoservicio 33c
self-sufficient independiente 11e
sell vender 23f, 25a
semester el semestre 37f
semicolon el punto y coma 19c
senate el senado 43
send mandar 3e, 19e
sender el remitente 19e
sense, feel sentirse* 12c
sense el sentido 12c
sensitive sensible 11e
sentence (grammar) la frase, la oración 8a, 19c
sentence la sentencia 41
sentimental sentimental 11e
separate separado 11c
separation (marital) la separación matrimonial 11c
September septiembre 5b
series la serie 20b
serious serio 11e
serve servir* 24o

services los servicios 24m, 35b
set (hair) el peinado 12d
set el conjunto 1f
set the table poner* la mesa 23f, 24o
several varios 3c
severance pay la indemnización por despido 38d
sew coser 25g
sewing machine la máquina de coser 23d
sex el sexo 11a, 38b
sexy atractivo 11a
shade, shadow la sombra 6a
shame la vergüenza 21a
shampoo el champú 12d, 25f, 35c
share (see stock)
shark el tiburón 15c
shave afeitarse (v) 12d
she ella 8h
sheep el carnero, la oveja 15a
sheet (bed) la sábana 23d, 35c
sheet (of paper) la hoja 25c
shelf el estante 23a
shirt la camisa 25k
shock el choque 39c
shoe el zapato 25n
shoe store la zapatería 25n
shoelaces los cordones 25n
shoot disparar 39b
shop la tienda (n); ir* de compras (v) 25a
short (length) corto 3b, 12d
short (stature) bajo 11a
short story el cuento 20a, 28d
shorten acortar 25m
shorts (underwear) los calzoncillos 25k
shorts los pantalones cortos 25k
shoulder el hombro 12a
shout gritar (v); el grito (n) 17a, 39a
shovel la pala 25b
show la función 20b, 28c
shower la ducha 23a, 35c
shrewd sagaz, listo 11e
shrimp la (las) gamba(s), el (los) camarón(-rones) 24d

shuffle cards   barajar   27a
shut up   callarse   17a
shy   tímido   11e
sick   enfermo   11a, 40a
sickness   la enfermedad   11a, 40a
side   el lado   2b
sidewalk   la acera   36a
sight   la vista   12c, 40a
sign   firmar   11f, 19c, 26
signal   la señal   33c
signature   la firma   11f, 19c, 26, 38b
silence   el silencio   17a
silent   silencioso   17a
silk   la seda   13c, 25l
sill   (see *window ledge*)
silver   la plata   13c, 25i
silver   plateado *(adj)*   7a
silver anniversary   el aniversario de plata   11c
simile   el símil   28d
simple   sencillo   11e, 22a
simultaneous   simultáneo   4e
since   desde   4e, 8n
sincere   sincero   11e
sincerity   la sinceridad   11e
sine *(mathematics)*   el seno   2b
sing   cantar   28c
singer   el (la) cantante   25j, 28c
single   el (la) soltero(a)   38b
single bed   la cama sencilla   35b
single room   el cuarto sencillo   35b
singular   singular   8a
sink   el lavabo   23a, 35c
siren   la sirena   39a
sister   la hermana   10a
sister-in-law   la cuñada   10a
sit down   sentarse*   3e, 32c
size   tamaño   3b
size *(of clothes)*   la talla   25k
size *(of shoe)*   el número   25n
skate   patinar   27a
skating   el patinaje   27a
ski   esquiar*   27b
ski   el esquí   27b
ski resort   el lugar para esquiar   36b
skillet   la sartén   23d

skin   la piel   12a
skirt   la falda   25k
sky   el cielo   6a, 13b
sleep   dormir*   12b
sleeping bag   el saco de dormir   36b
sleeve   la manga   25g
slice   rebanar, tajar   24o
slide *(photo)*   la diapositiva   25d
slide projector   el proyector de diapositivas   20b, 37b
sliding door   la puerta corrediza   35c
slim   delgado   11a
slip   la combinación   25k
slipper   la zapatilla   25n
slippery   resbaladizo   33d
sloppy   desorganizado   11e
slot *(for tokens)*   la ranura   18a
slow   lento   3e, 4e
slow down   ir *(v)* más despacio   33c
slowly   despacio, lentamente   3e, 4e
small   pequeño   3c, 11a, 25l
small letter *(lowercase)*   la minúscula   19c
smart   listo, inteligente   11e
smell   oler*   12c
smell *(sense of)*   el olfato   12c
smile   sonreír* *(v)*; la sonrisa *(n)*   11e, 21a
smoke   el humo   13c, 39a
smoking section   la sección de fumar   32a, 34
smooth   liso   13d
snack   comer(se) *(v)* un bocadillo   24a
snack   el bocadillo   24a
snake   la serpiente   15c
sneeze   estornudar *(v)*; el estornudo *(n)*   40a
snobbish   presuntuoso   11e
snow   nevar* *(v)*; la nieve *(n)*   6a, 6b
soap   el jabón   12d, 25f
soap bar   la pastilla de jabón   35c
soap opera   la telenovela   20b
soap powder   el jabón en polvo   25g

soccer   el fútbol   27b
soccer ball   el balón de fútbol
27b
soccer player   el (la) futbolista
27b
socialism   el socialismo   43
socialist   el (la) socialista   43
sociology   la sociología   37e
sock   el calcetín   25n
sodium   el sodio   13c
sodium bicarbonate   el
bicarbonato de sodio   25h
sofa   el sofá   23c
soft   blando   13d
soft drink   el refresco   24k
software   el software, el logicial
42b
solar   solar   13a
solar cell   la célula solar
44a
solar eclipse   el eclipse solar
13a
solar energy   la energía solar
44a
solar system   el sistema solar
13a
sole fish   el lenguado   15c,
24d
solid   sólido   2a
soliloquy   el soliloquio   28d
solstice   el solsticio   5c
soluble   soluble   13d
solution   la solución   1f
solve   resolver*   1f, 37f
some   algunos   3c, 8n
someone   alguien   8n
something   algo   8n
somewhere   en alguna parte
3d
son   el hijo   10a
song   la canción   25j, 28c
son-in-law   el yerno   10a
sonnet   el soneto   28d
sorrow   el dolor, la pena
21a
soul   el alma   (f)   11d
sound   el sonido   12c
soundtrack   la banda sonora
28a
soup   la sopa   24g
sour   agrio   24p
south   el sur   3d
South America   Sudamérica
30b

South Pole   el Polo Sur   13e
souvenir   el recuerdo   25a
space   el espacio   2b, 13a
space bar (typewriter)   el
espaciador   19d
space shuttle   el transbordador
espacial   42a
spacecraft   la nave espacial
42a
spades (cards)   las espadas, los
picos   27a
Spain   España   30b
Spanish   español(a)   (adj, n)
30d
spark plug   la bujía   33e
sparrow   el gorrión   15b
spatula   la espátula   23d
speak   hablar   17a
speaker   el altavoz   20b
special delivery   el correo
urgente   19e
specialist   el (la) especialista
40a
species   la especie   14a
speech   el discurso   17a
speed   la velocidad   3a, 33c
speed limit   el límite de
velocidad   33d
speed up   acelerar   33c
spelling   la ortografía   19c
spend   gastar   25a
spend (time)   pasar   4e
sphere   la esfera   2a
spice   la especia   24j
spicy   picante   24p
spider   la araña   15d
spinach   la espinaca   14e,
24e
spirit   el espíritu   11d
spiritual   espiritual   11d
spit   escupir   40b
splint   la tablilla   39c
spoke   el radio   33a
spoon   la cuchara   23d, 24l
sporadic   esporádico   4e
sport   el deporte   27b
sports car   el coche deportivo
33a
sports event   el encuentro
deportivo   27b
sports fan   el aficionado
deportivo   27b
spot, stain   la mancha   25g
sprain   la torcedura   39c

spreadsheet las hojas de cálculo
42b
spring la primavera   5c
spring *(of watch)* el muelle
25i
square el cuadro   2a
square la plaza   11f, 36a
square centimeter el centímetro
cuadrado   3a
square kilometer el kilómetro
cuadrado   3a
square meter el metro cuadrado
3a
square millimeter el milímetro
cuadrado   3a
squared al cuadrado   1e
squid el (los) calamar(es)
24d
stable estable   13d
stadium el estadio   27b
stage el escenario   28e
stain (see *spot*)
stainless steel el acero
inoxidable   13c
stairs la escalera   23a, 35b
stamp el timbre, la estampilla,
el sello   19e, 27a
stamp collecting la filatelia
27a
staple la grapa   19d, 25c,
38c
stapler el grapador   19d,
25c, 38c
star la estrella   6a, 13a
starch el almidón   25g
starched almidonado   25g
start *(the car)* arrancar   33c
starter *(car)* el arranque
33e
state el estado   11f, 13e, 43
state declarar *(v)*   17a
statement la declaración
17a
station la estación   20b
stationery store la papelería
25c
statistics la estadística   1f,
37e
stay quedarse *(v)*   29b
steal robar   39b
steel el acero   13c
steering wheel el volante
33e
stem el tallo   14a

stepbrother el hermanastro
10a
stepdaughter la hijastra   10a
stepfather el padrastro   10a
stepmother la madrastra
10a
stepsister la hermanastra
10a
stepson el hijastro   10a
stereo (phonic) el equipo
estreofónico   20b
stethoscope el estetoscopio
40a
still todavía, aún   4e
stinginess la mezquindad
11e
stingy tacaño, mezquino
11e
stitch coser   25g
stock market la bolsa de
valores   26
stock, share la acción   26
Stockholm Estocolmo   30c
stockings las medias   25n
stomach el estómago   12a,
40a
stone la piedra   13b
Stop *(sign)* Alto   33d
stop parar, detener*   3e
stop *(e.g., bus)* la parada
34
store la tienda   25a
store clerk el (la) dependiente,
(also) la dependienta   25a
storm la tormenta, la tempestad
6a
story el cuento   17a
stove la estufa   23d
straight plano   2b
straight ahead derecho   36c
strait el estrecho   13b
strawberry la fresa   14d,
24f
street la calle   11e, 36a, 38b
streetcar el tranvía   33a
strength la fuerza   11a
stretcher la camilla   39c
strike la huelga   43
strike declararse *(v)* en huelga
43
string el cordel   19d, 25c
string bean la judía verde
14e, 24e
string instruments los

instrumentos de cuerda 28c

striped rayado 25l
stroke el derrame cerebral 40a
strong fuerte 11a, 11e, 13d, 40a
structure la estructura 13c
stubborn terco 11e
student el (la) estudiante 37d
study estudiar 22b, 37f
stupid estúpido 11e
style el estilo 28d
subject *(school)* la asignatura 37e
subject *(grammar)* el sujeto 8a
subjunctive subjuntivo 8a
subordinate subordinado 8a
substance la substancia 13c
subtract restar 1e
subtraction la resta 1e
suburbs las afueras 30a
subway el metro, el subterráneo 34
subway station la estación del metro 34
sue demandar, poner* pleito a 41
suede la gamuza 25l
suffer sufrir 40a
suffer from padecer de 40a
suffice bastar 3c
sufficient suficiente 3c
sugar el azúcar 24j
suggest sugerir* 17a
suit el traje 25k
suitcase la maleta 31
sulphur el azufre 13c
summarize resumir 17a
summary el resumen 17a
summer el verano 5c
summons la citación judicial 41
sum up sumar 1f
sun el sol 5c, 6a, 13a
Sunday el domingo 5a
sunlight la luz del sol 13a
sunrise la salida del sol 4a
sunset la puesta del sol 4a
supermarket el supermercado 24n
superstitious supersticioso 11e

supplementary suplementario 2b
suppository el supositorio 25h, 40a
surgeon el cirujano 38a, 40a
surgery la cirugía 40a
surname el apellido 11f, 38b
surprise la sorpresa *(n)*; sorprender *(v)* 21a
swallow tragar 15b, 40a
swan el cisne 15b
swear *(in court)* jurar 41
swear *(profanity)* maldecir* 17a
sweater el suéter 25k
sweatshirt la sudadera 25k
Sweden Suecia 30b
Swedish sueco(a) *(adj, n)* 30d
sweet dulce 11e, 24p
swell hinchar 40a
swim nadar 27b
swimming la natación 27b
Swiss suizo(a) *(adj, n)* 30d
switch el interruptor 23a, 35c
switchblade la navaja de muelle 39b
Switzerland Suiza 30b
swollen hinchado 40a
swordfish el pez espada 15c
symbol el símbolo 1f, 17a, 28d
sympathetic compasivo 21a
sympathy *(over a death)* la condolencia, el pésame 21a
symphony la sinfonía 28c
synagogue la sinagoga 11d
synthesizer el sintetizador 28c
synthetic sintético 13d
syringe la jeringa 40a
syrup el jarabe 25h

T
tab el tabulador 19d
table la mesa 23c, 24l, 35c
tablecloth el mantel 23d, 24l
tablet *(medicine)* la pastilla 25h, 40a
tack la tachuela 37b, 38c

tag   la etiqueta   25a
tail   la cola   15a
tailor   el sastre   25k, 38a
take *(the train, etc)*   tomar
  34
take attendance   pasar lista
  37f
take off   quitarse *(v)*   25m
take off *(plane)*   despegar
  32c
take-off   el despegue   32c
talcum powder   el talco   25f
tall   alto   3b, 11a
tampons   los tapones   25h
tangent   la tangente   2a, 2b
tangerine   la mandarina
  14d, 24f
tape   la cinta   25j
tape recorder   la grabadora
  20b, 37b
tapestry   la tapicería   28b
tariff   la tarifa   31
taste   probar*   12c
tasty   sabroso   24p
Taurus   Tauro   5d
tax   el impuesto   26
tax exemption   la exención del
  impuesto   26
taxi   el taxi   33a
taxi driver   el (la) taxista
  33a
tea   el té   25k
teach   enseñar   37f
teacher   el (la) profesor(a)
  37d, 38a
team   el equipo   27b
teapot   la tetera   23d
teaspoon   la cucharita   23d,
  24l
teaspoonful   la cucharadita
  23d
technical school   el instituto
  laboral   37a
technology   la tecnología
  42a
teenager   el (la) joven   11b
telecommunication   la
  telecomunicación   18a, 42a
teleconference   la
  teleconferencia   42a
telephone   el teléfono   18a,
  23e, 37c, 38c
telephone book   la guía de
  teléfonos   18a

telephone booth   la cabina
  telefónica   18a
telephone line   línea telefónica
  18b
telephone number   el número
  de teléfono   11f, 18b, 38b
television   la televisión   20b
television set   el televisor
  20b, 23d, 24d, 35c
telex machine   el télex   18a,
  42a
tell   decir*   17a
temperature   la temperatura
  6c, 40a
temple   el templo   11d, 36a
temporary   temporáneo   4e
tenant   el arrendatario   23g
tennis   el tenis   27b
tennis racket   la raqueta   27b
tense   el tiempo   8a
tent   la tienda   36b
terminal *(computer)*   el terminal
  42b
terminal *(e.g., airline)*   la
  terminal   32a
termite   el comején   15d
terrace   la terraza   23a
terrible   terrible   6b, 11e
territory   el territorio   13e
test   el examen, la prueba   37f
testify   atestiguar   41
tetrahedron   el tetraedro   2a
text   el texto   19c, 20a
textbook   el libro de texto
  25o, 37b
textile   el textil, el tejido   13c
thank   agradecer*   17a, 21a
thankful   agredecido   21a
thankfulness   el agradecimiento
  21a
that   ese, esa, eso   8d
that   que   8m
the   el, la, los, las   8b
theater   el teatro   25o, 28e
their   su, sus   8e
them   los, las, les   8i, 8j
theme   el tema   28d
themselves   se   8k
then   entonces   4e
theory of relativity   la teoría de
  relatividad   42b
there   allí, allá   3d, 36c
therefore   por eso   44c
thermal energy   la energía

térmica   44a
thermometer   el termómetro
  6c, 25h, 40a
thermostat   el termostato
  6c, 35c
these   estos, estas *(adj)*   8d
thesis   la tesis   37f
they   ellos, ellas   8h
thick   espeso   3b
thief   el ladrón   39b
thigh   el muslo   12a
thin   delgado   3b, 11a
think   pensar*   22b
third world   el Tercer Mundo
  43
thirst   la sed   12b
this   este, esta *(adj)*; esto
  (pron)   8d
thorn   la espina   14b
those   esos, esas, aquellos,
  aquellas *(adj)*   8d
thought   el pensamiento   22a
thousandth   milésimo   1b
threat   la amenaza   17a
threaten   amenazar   17a
throat   la garganta   12a, 40a
through   a través de   3d,
  36c
throw (ball)   lanzar   27b
throw up (vomit)   devolver*
  40a
thumb   el pulgar   12a
thunder   el trueno *(n)*; tronar*
  (v)   6a, 6b
Thursday   el jueves   5a
tick   la garrapata   15d
ticket   el boleto, el billete
  27b, 30a, 32a, 34
ticket agent   el vendedor de
  boletos   32a, 34
ticket counter   la taquilla, la
  boletería   34
tide   la marea   13b
tie (clothing)   la corbata   25k
tie (the score)   el empate *(n)*;
  empatar *(v)*   27b
tiger   el tigre   15a
tight   ceñido   25l
tighten   apretar*   25m
time   el tiempo   4a
timpani   los timbales   28c
tin   el estaño   13c
tint   el tinte *(n)*; teñir* *(v)*
  7c

tip   la propina   24m
tire   la llanta   33a, 33e
tissue (paper handkerchief)   el
  pañuelo de papel   25h
title   el título   11f, 16b, 20a
title of ownership   el título
  33b
to   a   3d, 8g
to her   le   8j
to him   le   8j
to me   me   8j
to them   les   8j
to us   nos   8j
to you   te, le, os, les   8j
toad   el sapo   15c
toast (in drinking)   brindar *(v)*;
  el brindis *(n)*   17a
toast   tostar*   24o
toaster   el tostador   23d
tobacco   el tabaco   25e
tobacco shop   la tabaquería
  25e
today   hoy   4a
toe   el dedo del pie   12a
toilet   el inodoro, el retrete, el
  excusado   23a, 32c, 35c
toilet paper   el papel higiénico
  35c
token   la ficha   18a
Tokyo   Tokio   30c
tolerance   la tolerancia   21a
tolerate   tolerar   21a
toll   el peaje   33c, 33d
toll booth   la barrera de peaje
  33c
tomato   el tomate   14e, 24e
tomorrow   mañana   4a
tongue   la lengua   12a, 40a
tonight   esta noche   4a
tonsils   las amígdalas   40a
too much   demasiado   3c
tools   las herramientas   25b,
  33c
tooth   el diente   12a, 40b
toothache   el dolor de muelas
  40b
toothbrush   el cepillo de dientes
  12d, 25h, 40b
toothpaste   la pasta dentífrica
  12d, 25h, 40b
toothpick   el palillo   23d, 24l
top   la cumbre   3d
topaz   el topacio   25i
tornado   el tornado   6a

touch   tocar   12c
touch *(sense of)*   el sentido del tacto   12c
touch up   el retoque   12d
tour   la gira   30a
tour guide   el (la) guía de turismo   30a
touring bus   el autobús de turismo   30a
tourist   el (la) turista   30a
tow truck   la grúa de remolque   33a
toward   hacia   3d, 36c
towel   la toalla   12d, 35c
tower   la torre   36a
town   el pueblo   11f
track *(sports)*   la pista   27b
track *(train)*   la vía   34
track and field   el atletismo en pista   27b
traditional   tradicional   11e
traffic   el tráfico, la circulación   33c, 39c
traffic accident   el accidente de circulación   39c
traffic light   el semáforo   33c, 36a
traffic policeman   el guardia   33b
traffic policewoman   la guardia   33b
tragedy   la tragedia   20a, 28e
trailer   el remolque   33a
train   el tren   34
train station   la estación de trenes   34
transformer   el transformador   25b
transitive   transitivo   8a
translate   traducir*   17a
translation   la traducción   17a
transmission   la transmisión   20b, 33e
transparent   transparente   7b, 13c, 13d
transplant   trasplantar, el trasplante   14a
trapezoid   el trapecio   2a
travel   viajar   30a
travel agency   el (la) agente de viajes   30a
traveler's check   el cheque de viajero   26, 35b

tray   la bandeja   23d, 24l, 32c
tree   el árbol   14c
trial   el proceso   41
triangle   el triángulo   2a
trigonometry   la trigonometría   2b
trim   recortar   12d
trimester   (see quarter)
trip   el viaje   30a, 36b
triple   triple   3c
trombone   el trombón   28c
tropic   el trópico   13e
Tropic of Cancer   el trópico de Cáncer   13e
Tropic of Capricorn   el trópico de Capricornio   13e
tropical   tropical   6a, 13e
troublemaker   el perturbador   11e
trout   la trucha   15c, 24d
truck   el camión   33a
truck driver   el camionero   33a
true   verdadero   25i
trumpet   la trompeta   28c
trunk *(tree)*   el tronco   14a
trunk *(car)*   el baúl, la valija   33e
trust   la confianza *(n)*; tener* *(v)* confianza   21a
try on   probar*   25m
T-shirt   la camiseta   25k
tuba   la tuba   28c
Tuesday   el martes   5a
tulip   el tulipán   14b
tuna   el atún   15c, 24d
tuner *(audio)*   el receptor   20a
tunnel   el túnel   33c
turbulence   la turbulencia   32c
turkey   el pavo   15b, 24c
turn   volver*, girar   3e
turn   dar* la vuelta   33c, 36c
turn *(pages)*   hojear   20a
turnip   el nabo   14e
turn off   apagar   20b, 35c
turn on   poner*   20b, 35c
turn signal   el indicador de dirección   33e
turtle   la tortuga   15c
twin   el (la) gemelo(a)   10a
type   escribir a máquina   37f

typewriter la máquina de escribir 19d, 38c

typist el (la) mecanógrafo(a) 38a

typography la tipografía 20a

U

ugly feo 11a, 25l

ugliness la fealdad 11a

ulcer la úlcera 40a

ultraviolet light la luz ultravioleta 13a

unbuckle desabrocharse 32c

uncle el tío 10a

under debajo (de) 3d

underdeveloped countries los países subdesarrollados 43

underlining el subrayado *(n)* 19c

underpass el paso subterráneo 33d

understand comprender, entender* 22b, 37f

underwear la ropa interior 25k

undress desnudarse *(v)* 25m

unemployment el desempleo 38d, 43

United States los Estados Unidos 30b

universe el universo 13a

university la universidad 37a, 38b

unleaded gas la gasolina sin plomo 33c

unless a menos que 8o

unmarried soltero 11c

unpleasant desagradable 21b

unscrew destornillar 25b

until hasta 4e

up arriba 3d

Uranus Urano 13a

urinary system el sistema urinario 40a

urinate orinar 12b, 40a

urologist el urólogo 40a

Uruguayan uruguayo(a) *(adj, n)* 30d

us nos 8i, 8j

user friendly fácil de manejar 42b

usher el acomodador 28e

usually normalmente 4e

utensils los utensilios 23d

utter pronunciar 17a

V

vacation las vacaciones 29a, 36b

vaccinate vacunar 40a

vacuum cleaner la aspiradora 23d

vain vanidoso 11e

valley el valle 13b

van el furgón 33a

vapor el vapor 13c

variable variable 1f, 26

vase el florero 23d

VCR la videocasetera 20b

veal la ternera 24c

vector el vector 2b

vegetable la legumbre, el vegetal 14e, 24e

vegetation la vegetación 13b

vehicle el vehículo 33a

vein la vena 40a

velvet el terciopelo 25l

venereal disease la enfermedad venérea 40a

venetian blinds las persianas 23c

Venezuelan venezolano(a) *(adj, n)* 30d

Venus Venus 13a

verb el verbo 8a

verdict el veredicto, el juicio 41

versatile versátil 11e

verse el verso 28d

vertebrate vertebrado 15a

vertex el vértice 2b

vertical vertical 3d

vibrant vibrante 7b

victim el (la) víctima 39a, 39b

video game el juego eléctronico 20b

videocamera la cámara de vídeo 25d

videocassette el videocasete 20b

videotape la cinta (magnética) de video 20b

view la vista 35b

vinegar   el vinagre   24j
viola   la viola   28c
violence   la violencia   39b
violet   violeta   14b
violin   el violín   28c
violinist   el (la) violinista   28c
Virgo   Virgo   5d
virile   viril   11a
visa   el visado, la visa   31
visit   visitar   29b
vitamin   la vitamina   25h, 40a
vocabulary   el vocabulario   17a
vocational school   la escuela vocacional   37a
volcano   el volcán   13b
volleyball   el volibol   27b
volume   el volumen   3a
vomit   vomitar   40a
vote   el voto *(n)*; votar *(v)*   43
vowel   la vocal   8a
vulture   el buitre   15b

W

wage   el sueldo   38d
waist   la cintura   12a
wait for   esperar   4e, 19e, 34
waiter   el camarero, el mesero   24m
waitress   la camarera   24m
waiting room   la sala de espera   32a
wake up   despertarse*   12b
wake-up call   despertar(se)* con una llamada   35b
walk   andar, caminar   3e, 12b
walk   la caminata   3e
walkie-talkie   el radioteléfono portátil   20b
wall *(exterior)*   el muro   23a
wall *(inside)*   la pared   23a
wallpaper   el empapelado   23c
walnut   la nuez   14d
walnut tree   el nogal   14c
want to   querer*   21a
war   la guerra   43
warm up   calentarse*   6b
warn   advertir*   17a
warning   el aviso, la advertencia   17a

wash   lavar *(v)*   23f, 25g
wash oneself   lavarse *(v)*   12d
washable   lavable   25g
washing machine   la lavadora   23d
washroom *(public)*   los servicios   23b, 36a
wasp   la avispa   15d
wastebasket   el papelero   38c
watch   el reloj   4d, 25i
watchband   la correa de reloj   4d
water   el agua   13c, 14a, 23e, 25k
water fountain   la fuente   36a
water pollution   la contaminación del agua   44a
watercolor   la acuarela   28b
watermelon   la sandía   14d, 24f
wave   la ola   13b, 39b
we   nosotros   8h
weak   débil   11a, 11e, 13d, 40a
weakness   la debilidad   11a
weapon   el arma *(f)*   39b
wear   llevar   25g, 25m
weather   el tiempo   6a
weather forecast   el pronóstico del tiempo   6c
wedding   la boda   11c, 29a
Wednesday   el miércoles   5a
week   la semana   4c
weekend   el fin de semana   5a
weekly   semanal, por semana   4c
weigh   pesar   3b, 11a, 24o
weight   el peso   3a, 11a, 31
welfare   la asistencia pública   43
well-mannered   cortés, bien   11e
west   el oeste   3d
western   occidental   3d, 11d
whale   la ballena   15c
What?   ¿Cómo?   9
what   qué *(adj, pron)*   9
wheat   el trigo   14a, 24i
wheel   la rueda   32c, 33e
wheelchair   la silla de ruedas   40a
When?   ¿Cuándo?   9
when   cuande *(conj)*   4e
Where?   ¿Dónde?   9

where donde 3d
whether si 8o
Which (one)? ¿Cuál? 9
while mientras 4e, 8o
whiskey el whiski 24k
whisper cuchichear, susurrar 17a
white blanco 7a
Who? ¿Quién? 9
who que, quien 8m
wholesale la venta al por mayor 26
whose cuyo 8l
Why? ¿Por qué? 9
wide ancho 3b
widow viuda 11c, 38b
widower viudo 11c, 38b
width la anchura 3b
wife la esposa 10a, 11c
will (document) el testamento 41
willing dispuesto 11e
win ganar (v); la victoria (n) 27b
wind el viento 6a
wind dar* cuerda a (v) 4d, 25i
window la ventana 23a, 32c
windshield el parabrisas 33
windshield wiper el limpiaparabrisas 33e
wine el vino 24k
wine cellar la bodega 23b
wine list la lista de vinos 24m
wing el ala (f) 15b, 32c
winter el invierno 5c
wire el alambre 25b
wisdom la sabiduría 11e, 22a
wise sabio 11e
with con 8g
withdraw retirar 26
withdrawal el retiro 26
within dentro de 4e
without sin 8g, 8o
witness el testigo 41
wolf el lobo 15a
woman la mujer 11a
woods el bosque 13c
wool la lana 13c, 25l
word la palabra, el vocablo 17a, 19c
word processor el procesador

de texto 19d, 38c, 42b
work el trabajo (n); trabajar (v) 11f, 38d
work (literature, art) la obra 28d
world el mundo 13a, 30a
worm el gusano 15d
wound herir* (v); la herida (n) 39b, 39c
wrench la llave inglesa 25b
wrestling la lucha libre 27b
wrist la muñeca 12a
wristwatch el reloj (de pulsera) 4d
write escribir 19e, 20a, 37f
writer el (la) escritor(a) 28d, 38a
wrong incorrecto 37f

X, Y, Z

x-rays rayos X 40b
yawn bostezar (v); el bostezo (n) 17a
year el año 4c, 37a
yearly anual, anualmente 4c
yellow amarillo 7a
yellow pages las páginas amarillas 18a
yes sí 16c
yesterday ayer 4a
yet todavía 4e
yield ceder el paso 33d
yogurt el yogur 24h
you tú, usted, nosotros, ustedes 8h; te, lo, la, os, los, las 8i
young joven 11b
young lady la señorita, la joven 11a
young man el joven 11a
your tu, tus, su, sus, vuestro, vuestra, vuestros, vuestras 8e
yourself te, se 8k
yourselves os 8k
youth hostel el albergue juvenil 35a
zebra la cebra 15a
zero cero 1a, 6c
zipper la cremallera 25g
Zodiac el Zodíaco 5d
zone la zona 13e
zoo el parque zoológico 15a
zoological zoológico 15a
zoology la zoología 15a, 37e
zoom el zoom 25d
zucchini el calabacín 14e, 24e